# ALFRED HITCHCOCK

## INTERVIEWS

CONVERSATIONS WITH FILMMAKERS SERIES
PETER BRUNETTE, GENERAL EDITOR

Photo credit: Photofest

# ALFRED HITCHCOCK

## INTERVIEWS

EDITED BY SIDNEY GOTTLIEB

UNIVERSITY PRESS OF MISSISSIPPI / JACKSON

www.upress.state.ms.us

Copyright © 2003 by University Press of Mississippi
All rights reserved
Manufactured in the United States of America

11  10  09  08  07  06  05  04  03    4  3  2  1
♾
Library of Congress Cataloging-in-Publication Data

Alfred Hitchcock : interviews / edited by Sidney Gottlieb.
    p. cm.—(Conversations with filmmakers series)
    Includes index.
    ISBN 1-57806-561-5 (cloth : alk. paper)—ISBN 1-57806-562-3
(pbk. : alk. paper)
    1. Hitchcock, Alfred, 1899– —Interviews.  2. Motion picture
producers and directors—Great Britain—Interviews.  I. Gottlieb,
Sidney.  II. Series.
PN1998.3.H58 A5  2003
791.43′0233′092—dc21                              2002013641

British Library Cataloging-in-Publication Data available

# CONTENTS

# INTRODUCTION

PERHAPS MORE THAN any other filmmaker, Alfred Hitchcock has earned the right to be introduced with a bit of night club or after-dinner speech *schtickerie* as the man who needs no introduction. Even twenty years after his death, and nearly fifty or more years after his creative peak, he is still arguably the most instantly recognizable director in name, appearance, vision, and voice. Long ago, through a combination of timing, talent, genius, energy, and publicity, he made the key transition from proper noun to adjective that confirms celebrity and true stature, and it is a rare filmwatcher indeed who could not define "Hitchcockian," or resonate to the particular world and cinematic experience this term connotes.

Familiarity, though, can breed content—a particularly unHitchcockian quality!—and a reintroduction to Hitchcock via a collection of interviews spanning nearly his entire career as a filmmaker, even while they inevitably reconfirm much that we already know about him, alerts us to the limitations of trying to fix him in a formulated phrase. At his center and horizon Hitchcock is perennially "strange," and the best of his interviews both penetrate and reiterate this strangeness: sometimes answering questions, other times conveying an experience of uncanny unanswerability, borne of the attempt (Hitchcock's as well as the interviewers') to know the unknowable about the creative process, the world, or the human predicament. Claude Chabrol continually pressed Hitchcock to find "the figure in your carpet," and seemed satisfied that he was able to discover such a thing. But the composite, multi-perspectival picture that emerges from the interviews herein presents a

Hitchcock who remains elusive, and a body of work that displays many figures, many carpets.

It is a mixed blessing that there is no lack of material to choose from. Janet Maslin notes that Hitchcock "is one of the most over-interviewed people imaginable." Just to give some indication of the scale we are talking about, relatively early in his promotional tour for *Topaz* in 1969, Hitchcock casually remarked to Martha Deane on WOR radio that this was the 121st interview of his current campaign. Even if he did not always operate at such a high level of activity, there is no doubt that through his extremely long career he gave thousands of interviews. Many of these were, to be sure, perfunctory, superficial, repetitive, and forgettable, but perhaps only in the full context of a lifelong grind of publicity events and more than occasional soul-searching confrontations with reporters and critics can one adequately glimpse Hitchcock publicizing and repeating but also inventing and reinventing himself. In the limited selection herein, I have tried to include interviews that highlight the latter qualities, catching Hitchcock at key moments of transition (from silent to sound pictures, from England to America, from thrillers to complex romances, from director to producer-director, and so on), and dramatizing his shifting attitudes on a variety of cinematic matters that engaged and challenged him (the role of stars, the importance of story, the attraction and perils of realism, and so on).

Maslin's term "over-interviewed" calls attention to the fact that interviews have for a long time played a very prominent role in our understanding of Hitchcock, and betrays a bit of impatience shared by many who have delved into them at any length: perhaps we have reached a stage where enough is enough. In particular, some feel that the well-known and easily available book-length compilations of interviews by François Truffaut and Peter Bogdanovich may contain most of what we know and need to know about Hitchcock—or at least what Hitchcock can tell us about Hitchcock.[1]

One may rightly approach a new collection of Hitchcock interviews not only with a touch of impatience but also with a certain amount of apprehension. Hitchcock's reputations precede him: as one of the most important and influential filmmakers to date, he attracts and invites us to hear what he has to say, but as an interviewee he makes us wary. He told Maslin that when facing interview after interview, "the trick is to always be able to give a different answer," a fit motto for a fascinating but, at least in conventional terms, unreliable subject (and also a reminder that, no matter what some claim,

Hitchcock did far more than simply repeat himself in his interviews). Bogdanovich noted that especially when confronted by serious questions, Hitchcock would adopt "a quietly bemused attitude" and "tell his interrogators
exactly what they wanted to hear."[2] And André Bazin, Chabrol, and Truffaut
(the latter two of whom yield to no one in their appreciation of and enthusiasm for Hitchcock) were all at various points outraged and exasperated by
their discovery that in his interviews Hitchcock was a gleeful manipulator
and sometimes, as they saw it, a downright and irresponsible liar.

The more we want our information straight, the more likely we are to
bristle at Hitchcock's repetitions, manipulations, evasions, and fabrications.
But our feelings change if we make a slight adjustment in our expectations
and understanding of the broader purposes and dynamics of an interview. In
his fascinating study of the interview as an emerging artistic genre that in
many ways helps define the modern and now the postmodern age, John
Rodden stresses that interviews are not solely and in many cases not even
primarily conduits for "hard" information but often rather opportunities for
creative and provocative performance. What results is not a secondary reference source but a primary "text" that, like other forms of art, is composed of
(among other elements) a blend of self-disclosure, playful and serious self-
expression, and complex self-formation.[3] Hitchcock is a master of the art
that Rodden describes. Without discounting the informational value of the
interviews that follow, we should be alert to another dimension, in which
Hitchcock's films make, as it were, cameo appearances as he pursues other
goals beyond mere explanation and commentary. We should not be so preoccupied with matters of literal and factual truth—the main interest of those
whom Hitchcock somewhat condescendingly and ruefully labeled the "plau-
sibles"—that we miss the subtle drama of a complicated artist not only talking about himself and his art but acting out in the fullest sense of the term,
revealing (although not always directly) and creating himself before our eyes.

For the purposes of this volume I have defined "interview" broadly as a
published transcription of Hitchcock responding to one or more interlocu-
tors. Most often this involves a conventional conversation or question and
answer session with one interviewer, but I also include examples with multiple interviewers, exchanges with both professional and non-professional
audiences, and recollections and reports of what Hitchcock said, prompted
by a question but without the full record of back and forth dialogue and real-
time flow that we often associate with a traditional interview. We should

bear in mind that in nearly all cases transcriptions of interviews are edited, often drastically: shaped by the interviewer (although sometimes with after-the-fact input by the person interviewed), cut, compressed, revised to eliminate infelicities and repetitions, and rearranged for continuity and drama. This is not to say that we lose Hitchcock's "voice" and idiom completely or irrecoverably in the process of translation into print, but we perhaps do need to be reminded that when a published piece puts quotation marks around Hitchcock's words, there is reason to believe that this may represent in varying ways an approximation, not always an exact copy, of what he said.

In making the selections for this volume, I have tried to cover Hitchcock's entire career. This involved searching out early pieces, and indeed I think that the selections from the 1920s and 1930s, however brief, nicely complement those already gathered in *Hitchcock on Hitchcock: Selected Writings and Interviews.*[4] But also important are his retrospective looks at his years as a "cub" director, as he once described himself, and lacking full-length interviews from the 1920s we can at least be grateful for his later recollections in his seventies in such interviews as "The German Years." I have tended to avoid easily available interviews in favor of important ones more difficult to get and not often cited, like the conversation with Arthur Knight. I have restricted myself to English language interviews, with the exception of two in French, by Chabrol and by Rui Nogueira and Nicoletta Zalaffi, translated into English for the first time by James M. Vest.

My hope is that this collection will appeal to the less as well as the more experienced *cineaste*, and as a result I have purposely included some broadly comprehensive pieces that round up what for many may seem to be the usual subjects—important subjects, I should add, such as Hitchcock's definition of pure cinema and suspense, explanation of the MacGuffin, discussions of violence, attractive villains, and avoiding the cliché, and famous and familiar anecdotes about bombs, knives, trains, actors, and blondes. At the same time, I have also sought out interviews that go beyond the territory we have come to expect and contain many fresh anecdotes, reminiscences, behind-the-scenes stories, and impressions (both by and of Hitchcock), as well as detailed examinations of infrequently highlighted but often surprisingly important topics, such as his relationship to the medium of television, the "musicality" of his films, his verbal as well as visual and situational humor, the many technical challenges he faced in "ordinary" circumstances as well as in his experimental moments and films, and the tensions inherent in attempting to construct a cinema based on clashing, if not contradictory, elements: pleasure and pain, directorial self-effacement and indulgence, audience immersion and detachment, realism and fantasy, commerce and art.

Finally, I have tried to include examples of the full range of "types" of Hitchcock interviews, catching Hitchcock not only at different times in his career but in different moods and operating in different modes. Rodden usefully distinguishes three types of interviewee: the traditionalist, who gives straightforward information and takes pains to be accurate, clear, factual, and sincere; the raconteur, who delights in telling stories, placing personal drama at the center of the interview; and the advertiser, who is concerned primarily with the interview as a mode of publicity, self-display, and often outrageous performance. One of the great joys of reading the interviews collected herein comes from watching Hitchcock slip in and out of all these roles, sometimes within the space of a single interview, and observing him not only act but interact with interviewers and audiences who are often fascinating characters themselves, and who, as Rodden notes, add to the dynamic of the occasion by playing roles that range from a recording documentarist to a supportive dialogist to a challenging, even intrusive provocateur.

The range and variety in these interviews is evident even in a quick summary. The word "talkie" figures prominently in the first three selections here, which report Hitchcock's thoughtful comments on the ripple effect of the new sound technology and the redefinition of cinema underway at that time. Characteristically, when "The Talkie King Talks" about talkies in 1929, he discusses the advantages of synchronized sound in the broader context of cinema's capacity for realism, visual as well as auditory, that makes it an immeasurably more powerful medium than the theater. For Hitchcock, "pure cinema" will always be essentially a visual medium, but from the beginning he was intrigued by certain advantages offered by talkies: for example, he told the interviewer from *Close Up* that sound rescues filmmakers from the "clumsiness" of silent films, which attempt to represent thoughts by such artificial devices as superimposed images on a character's head. He was also attracted to the creative possibilities of using "vocal tricks" and counterpointed sound (where what is heard does not necessarily emanate from but rather comments on what is shown), as he did in *Murder!* Creative use of sound—including music—is an integral part of the Hitchcock "touch" throughout his career, and deserves far more attention than it has received to date. Hitchcock himself calls attention to this aspect of his film-making in "Half the World in a Talkie," where he uses his recently finished *The Skin Game* as an example of how counterpointed dialogue emphasizing the reaction of the listener rather than the face of the person speaking can help one avoid the trap he repeatedly warned against: turning films into mere pictures of people talking. This brief interview also contains many substantive comments on other subjects as well, including the importance of story, a warning against excessive "Continental" stylization (a warning he did not always heed), and the need to broaden the range of cinematic subjects and settings.

The "Pen Portrait of Alfred Hitchcock" by Norah Baring, one of the featured actresses in *Murder!*, is particularly valuable for what it reveals about Hitchcock's working method and "the mystery of his almost magnetic power over his cast." Much of this power derives from his relentless devotion to cinema, complemented by his ability to help actresses like herself and Madeleine Carroll relax and be natural. Baring's description of "Hitch's 'gift'" of making jokes and keeping things "off the 'intense level,' so difficult to avoid in film circles" is an early version of what Hitchcock later cultivated as his professed belief that "It's only a movie"—a witty statement, to be sure, but one that should not be taken as a full and final statement of his artistic credo. Further comments on his treatment of actors and actresses appear in "Britain's Leading Film Director Gives Some Hints to the Film Stars of the Future," also interesting because of its discussion of the techniques of lighting and shooting stars as well as directing the nuances of and using color to enhance their expressions.

Frank S. Nugent's comments about "Hitch's early indifference to romance" miss the extent to which Hitchcock's British period films focus repeatedly on male-female relations, the pursuit of love, and the terrors as well as comforts of various forms of the couple. "Mr. Hitchcock Discovers Love" could have been a headline far earlier in his career, but in any event the release of *Notorious* and the turn to *The Paradine Case* as his next project afford Nugent the opportunity to assert the centrality of romance to Hitchcock, and Hitchcock the opportunity to describe his particular kind of "backhanded romantic technique." Especially interesting are Hitchcock's comments on his preference for psychological films—"a particular way of telling a story, by trying to get at the characters and at the action through the characters"—rather than more circumscribed psychoanalytical films, a genre he dipped into both before and long after this interview, but here labels "a passing phase."

"Production Methods Compared" is one of the real "finds" contained in the volume, and I am grateful to Charles Barr for calling my attention to it and sending me a copy. The first section, the text of a paper by Hitchcock read at a meeting of cinema technicians, has been reprinted several times and is therefore not included herein, but it is followed by a transcription of a lengthy question and answer session during which the technically-trained audience members pushed Hitchcock to elaborate on his ideas about such topics as shooting in sequence, the long take and moving camera, and his particular approach to scriptwriting and preproduction work. What comes through strikingly here—ironically, at a time when he is often accused of losing himself in narrowly conceived stylistic exercises such as *Rope* and *Under Capricorn*—is Hitchcock's flexibility, his deep concern to develop an integrative style that allows him to use the full range of cinematic resources (for example, cuts as well as long takes, close-ups as well as long shots, moving actors as well as moving cameras). Equally important, his responses to questions from these highly-skilled professionals illustrate that even at his most "technical," he rarely forgets the real end in sight: the effect on the film audience of the styles and techniques he so carefully plans and executes.

All the interviews in one way or another assay "Hitchcock's Working Credo," but the one with that specific title moves beyond a survey of Hitchcock's characteristic subjects and working habits to broach the topic of his conception of the medium he worked in. Hitchcock's repeated comments here on "conscience" and "responsibility" pulling him in two directions add an edginess to his long-standing awareness of the unstable mix of commerce and art inherent in his approach to filmmaking, and his image of his activity as "in the end . . . really a kind of constant tight-rope walking" comes more and more to haunt him in the later part of his career.

Claude Chabrol's "Story of an Interview" preserves many self-consciously witty and outrageous comments by Hitchcock, including several stunning and ultimately inscrutable dismissals of his American films—inscrutable because it is difficult to know for sure where the joke ends and a nervous confession begins—but he is acutely aware of the wheels turning as Hitchcock maneuvers through the reporters' questions, and he is primarily interested in penetrating the director's obvious disingenuousness and dissembling. Chabrol memorably captures the complex choreography of a

Hitchcock interview, a process of mutual manipulation and misunderstanding that the French inquisitor both witnesses and participates in. The result is a "story" confirming, however equivocally, the relevance of the *Cahiers* critics' insistence that beneath Hitchcock's thrillers and romances lies a bedrock of moral, metaphysical, and spiritual inquiry.

Ian Cameron and V. F. Perkins shrewdly keep Hitchcock focused on his films from *Rear Window* through *The Birds*, and their interview contributes to the increasing critical awareness that these films form a distinct American period in Hitchcock's career worth close attention. New emphases emerge: for example, in contrast with earlier interviews, where Hitchcock talked a great deal about story and audience involvement with characters, here he dismisses plot as "a necessary evil," and in the process of criticizing "dull logic" and insisting that "film should be stronger than reason," he stresses the emotional power of music and cinematic style.

The interview with Oriana Fallaci is especially memorable because of the fireworks between her and Hitchcock. This is one of the few interviews of Hitchcock conducted by someone not captivated by his talent and charm and prepared to challenge him from the very first word. Fallaci begins by describing how deeply disappointed she was in her first meeting with a man she expected to be interesting, witty, and imaginative. She found him to be none of these, and in fact seems to enjoy calling attention to what she takes to be his physical grossness, morbidity, self-absorption, and unimaginative disinterest in anything outside his own little world. She must take part of the blame for the repetitiousness and familiarity of some of his comments here: as much as she complains about his habit of responding as if "reciting a lesson learned by heart," she virtually sets him up to do this by raising questions about tried-and-true topics: suspense vs. surprise, the MacGuffin, some of his personal habits, and so on. Still, the interview is very lively, punctuated by Fallaci's interruptions and teasing responses, some of which seem to encourage Hitchcock to disclose more about his feelings, fears, and opinions than usual. They are worthy combatants, and their exchanges provide useful insight into not only Hitchcock's films, career, and persona, but also his playful and agonistic art of being interviewed.

Huw Wheldon is far more cordial in his talk with Hitchcock, and while this approach does not produce fireworks, it helps generate pithy and elegant expressions to describe some of the essential components of his art. Particularly important are his succinct description of "the satisfaction of temporary pain" that underlies the effect he aims for, his simple reminder that talk should be "part of the atmosphere," not the focal point, in order to realize the vast "power of cinema in its purest form," and his summary of one of his key artistic dilemmas—whether he should please himself or his audiences and producers—as "the question of ethics with other people's money." And even without being badgered by a philosophically-minded French critic, he casually admits to Wheldon that his art hovers near an abyss: "It must look real, but it must never be real, because reality is something none of us can stand, at any time."

Not surprisingly, the interviews of the 1970s take on an increasingly retrospective tone. Hitchcock was still an active filmmaker, and the interviews from this period contain important comments on his current projects and latest thoughts on the art of filmmaking, contemporary trends and developments, and so on. But they tend to range widely through his career, and perhaps by mutual agreement of interviewer and interviewee often take on the task of summing up what he has achieved. There is also a heightened sense of Hitchcock as a personality and a performer, repeated glimpses of him playing with—and sometimes against—his persona, and scene-setting acknowledgments by the interviewer that he or she is entering into a Hitchcock world.

Emerson Batdorf's appreciative "Let's Hear It for Hitchcock" allows Hitchcock to reminisce about his early years in cinema and comment particularly on such films as *The Lodger, North by Northwest,* and *Psycho,* but it is also one of the most extensive interviews focusing on Hitchcock's humor, a subject that merits more critical attention. As the interview proceeds, familiar anecdotes about his practical jokes and, at least as far as he was concerned, amiably rude comments give way to more revealing examples of the kind of pictorial wit that was an important part of his visual imagination and the verbal wit—especially the awful (a word with particular relevance when used in connection with Hitchcock) puns and Cockney rhyming slang—so integral to the way he spoke, the language of his films, and the style and "attitude" of many of his key characters.

The interviews with Janet Maslin and Nogueira and Zalaffi concentrate on Hitchcock's final films (with the exception of *Family Plot*), and the combination of production details (always a favorite topic for Hitchcock in interviews) and the director's assessment of what he was trying to do in these films and how they figure in his career adds interest to lesser works that perhaps otherwise might be skipped over quickly. In speaking with Maslin, Hitchcock calls attention to some of the subtleties and complexities of *Frenzy*, for example, analyzing the strangulation scene as, like the shower murder sequence in *Psycho*, a *tour de force* of montage that moves the audience by suggesting rather than showing violence. But in general he talks not so much about the film's horror as its humor, finely nuanced and detailed realism, and overall concern with the spectacle of human nature "put to the test." In the interview with Noguiera and Zalaffi, Hitchcock discusses the attractive villain and slowly developing, grudging sympathy for the "innocent" man in *Frenzy*, difficulties with star actresses and Method actors in *Torn Curtain*, and the compromised ending of *Topaz*. But perhaps the most intriguing comments come at the very beginning when Hitchcock reflects on the "auteur theory," and both accepts the notion of an identifiable stylistic "stamp" marking a serious artist's work and also complains about the limitations of such recognizability and the way it may be not only a product of free artistic growth but also commercial pigeonholing. Interestingly, painting is Hitchcock's key reference point in defining himself as an artist here. His anecdotes are amusing and revealing, and the three painters he names as examples of auteurs take us to the heart of his work: Rousseau, Van Gogh, and Klee, masters respectively of stylized realism, expressive agony, and comic and philosophical abstraction.

Part of what makes Charles Thomas Samuel's interview with Hitchcock so unusual and valuable is his determination to make Hitchcock follow the rule that was so important in his filmmaking practice: the avoidance of cliché. During their five-hour conversation, Samuels admits, Hitchcock simply repeated much of what he told Truffaut, but this is edited out from Samuels' published text. What remains is a remarkably fresh and far-ranging series of reflections by a director, in Samuels' words, "wholly confident of his credo," pushed to new depth and detail in describing this credo and saved from self-plagiarism by a gifted interviewer. With Samuels' help, Hitchcock skips nimbly from Ingmar Bergman to Fellini, from *Murder!* to *Frenzy*, from the importance of cinematic speed to the need for firmly established concrete milieu. Few interviewers capture—or call forth—Hitchcock's thoughtfulness and intellectual agility as well as Samuels.

The remaining interviews in the volume emphasize one last time several key tones and themes that have been woven in and out of everything that has come before: the nostalgic (and, I should add, seriously self-analytical), the technical, and the mischievous. A late publicity trip throughout Europe prompted Hitchcock to reminisce to Bob Thomas about his early filmmaking experiences in Germany and the result is a brief but very direct statement of the pivotal influence of early German directors, production practices, and cinematic styles on his entire career. Hitchcock reminisced in far more detail in his long "Conversation" with Arthur Knight, and the result is a remarkably comprehensive survey of his films, working method, and definition of cinema that could be read either first or last, since it so effectively introduces as well as sums up his career. This interview is especially valuable because of its extensive references to his own films (*Foreign Correspondent*, *Under Capricorn*, and *The Wrong Man*, along with the more familiar *North by Northwest*, *Psycho*, and *The Birds*), and its concise and often witty descriptions of what is "essentially cinematic"—and Hitchcockian. For example, no short phrase better captures his penchant for outrageous humor, audience manipulation, and blend of romantic melodrama and thriller than his remark that in his films he aims to "leave not a dry seat in the house."

He downplays the witticisms in his American Film Institute "Dialogue on Film," but his consistent focus remains on how he attempts to move those watching his films. This dialogue with film technicians, writers, and critics represents perhaps Hitchcock's most concentrated and sustained discussion of the technical aspects of his filmmaking, and it is particularly—and in some ways surprisingly—evident that what he calls "cinematics" here is a rhetoric as well as an aesthetic of film. There is much in this interview and elsewhere that supports a definition of Hitchcock as a formalist, especially his overall description of the basic task of a filmmaker as filling "that square, white rectangle . . . with a succession of images" and his meticulous concern for image size, placement, and the orchestration of shots. But his ultimate reference point in discussing technical details is audience response, and anyone who takes completely seriously Hitchcock's frequent claim that he wished he didn't have to shoot his pictures, presumably because the truly creative work is completed once a film is envisioned, needs to pay more attention to Hitchcock's repeated insistence that the audience—real, not just imagined—is an essential component, never far from his mind as he conceptualized, visualized, shot, and assembled his films.

Finally, the mischievous Hitchcock emerges full-blown in the concluding piece in the volume, a transcription of the wacky encounter between a representative of 50 + years of hard-won and deserved celebrity with the ultra-hip spokesperson for 15 minutes of fame, Andy Warhol. Reversing the common pattern of an interviewer entering into a Hitchcock world, this one chronicles Hitchcock stepping into a Warhol film, presented not as a slice of cake, as Hitchcock preferred, but as a slice of life: disorienting, rambling, rough, protean, and hyper-real. The interview weaves back and forth from discursive to telegraphic style, presenting Hitchcock as not only a gossip and storyteller but also a kind of beat poet and master of ellipsis. (Allen Ginsberg coming from a retrospective at the Thalia indeed might have written something like what we find here: "Grace Kelly / Janet Leigh / Vera Miles / Eva Marie Saint / these cool blondes.") The informational value of this encounter is refracted by the playfulness of both Hitchcock and Warhol, but there is enough substance as well as performance and ambiance, centripetal as well as centrifugal energy, in this postmodern profile to make it a fitting conclusion to a volume that began by asserting that Hitchcock cannot—and should not—be wrapped up into too tidy a package.

The interviews are reprinted as they originally appeared and have not been substantively edited any further (e.g., to eliminate repetition in the volume or to compress the material). Small mistakes and misspellings have been silently corrected, format has been regularized (e.g., the use of italics for film titles), and section headings, call-outs, blurbs, introductory scene setting, explanatory notes, and photographs in the originals have been eliminated.

I am very grateful to Patricia Hitchcock O'Connell for granting the permission of the Hitchcock Estate to reprint the material herein. Other rights holders are acknowledged on the opening page of each interview, in notes that do not adequately convey my deep appreciation of the cooperation of the many people I corresponded and negotiated with to secure permissions to reprint. Amy Stoller in particular was a lifesaver—or at least a book-saver—helping me through what had come to seem like an endless permissions labyrinth.

Charles Barr, Joseph Garncarz, Bob Kapsis, Alain Kerzoncuf, Pat McGilligan, Ken Mogg, and Eric Monder were valuable correspondents, sharing their ideas with me and often turning me toward out-of-the-way Hitchcock material. At the Museum of Modern Art Film Study Center, Charles Silver was gracious and helpful, as always. Will Gould patiently and authoritatively explained what to me was a mystifying reference in "Production Methods Compared" to the Independent Frame process, which links Hitchcock to the efforts of producers and directors like J. Arthur Rank and Michael Powell to establish innovative, efficient, and flexible preproduction and production techniques. John Rodden sent me a pre-publication copy of his invaluable book, *Performing the Literary Interview*. Jim Vest translated two French interviews especially for this volume, and sent me translations of other interviews as well as several chapters from his forthcoming book on the critical reception of Hitchcock in France. At Sacred Heart University, my chairperson, David Curtis, and dean, Claire Paolini, arranged for much-needed (and appreciated) release time for research, and at the University Press of Mississippi, Anne Stascavage has helped greatly by being a patient and forgiving as well as skilful editor and taskmaster.

David Sterritt gave me enormous support, advice, and encouragement throughout the unexpectedly long time I was working on the book, as did Mark Estrin, who also checked sources and copied material for me while he was in London working on his volume on Orson Welles for the Conversations with Filmmakers series. My good friend Chris Sharrett and much more than good friend Suzanne Golub rode my usual roller coaster with me for the duration, for which I owe them in the very least many dinners at Miya's.

I had long hoped to end these acknowledgments and my work on this project on a note of thoroughly joyful celebration, but instead must be satisfied with a more somber but no less deeply felt dedication of the book to my incomparably wonderful niece Sonia Erlich and, sadly, now the memory of Jeff Rosen, who have taught me much about love and loss.

## Notes

1. François Truffaut, with Helen G. Scott. *Hitchcock*, rev. ed. (New York: Simon and Schuster, 1984); Peter Bogdanovich, "Alfred Hitchcock," in *Who the Devil Made It* (New York: Knopf, 1997), pp. 471–557.

2. Bogdanovich, *Who the Devil Made It*, p. 480.

3. John Rodden, *Performing the Literary Interview: How Writers Craft Their Public Selves* (Lincoln: University of Nebraska Press, 2001).

4. Sidney Gottlieb, ed. *Hitchcock on Hitchcock: Selected Writings and Interviews* (Berkeley and Los Angeles: University of California Press, 1995).

# CHRONOLOGY

1899    Born Alfred Joseph Hitchcock in the Leytonstoke section of London, England on August 13, the third child of William and Emma Hitchcock.

1910–13    Attends Saint Ignatius College, London, a Jesuit-run secondary school, which leaves him with lasting memories of mental and physical discipline.

1915    Begins work at Henley Telegraph and Cable Company, studies art and drawing, and practices the latter when he moves to the advertising department of Henley's.

1920    Takes a job at the Famous Players–Lasky Corporation studio at Islington, first writing and illustrating title cards for silent pictures but soon branching out to become scenario writer, set designer, assistant director, production manager, and occasionally camera operator.

1924    Works in Germany on *The Blackguard*, for which he wrote the script and supervised the production. He is deeply influenced by his direct experience of German films and filmmaking theories and practice.

1925    First major directing assignments, *The Pleasure Garden* and *Mountain Eagle* (the latter now lost), shot in Germany and Italy.

1926    Directs *The Lodger*, often described as the first true Hitchcock film.

On December 2, marries Alma Reville, an experienced film editor and scriptwriter with whom he had been working. For the rest of their life together, Alma was a valuable contributor and consultant for Hitchcock, in both credited and uncredited ways. Their one child, Patricia Alma, is born on July 7, 1928.

1929　After nine silent films, Hitchcock makes *Blackmail*, released as a silent feature but also as what is advertised as the first all-talking British film, widely commented on for its imaginative use of sound.

1934–38　Becomes increasingly identified as a maker of popular but also cinematically imaginative spy-thrillers, including such works as *The Man Who Knew Too Much* (1934), *The 39 Steps* (1935), and *The Lady Vanishes* (1938).

1939　His so-called "British" period ends as he and his family move to Hollywood. Signs agreement to make films for David Selznick, beginning with *Rebecca* (1940).

1940–46　Alternates films with wartime settings (*Foreign Correspondent* [1940], *Saboteur* [1942], *Lifeboat* [1944], *Notorious* [1946]) with more domestic suspense thrillers, including *Suspicion* (1941), his first film with Cary Grant, and *Shadow of a Doubt* (1943), which he often singled out as one of his favorite films.

1946　Forms his own production company with Sidney Bernstein, Transatlantic Pictures. Directs *Rope* (1948), his first color film, first film with James Stewart, and a radical experiment in making a film out of uninterrupted long takes, and *Under Capricorn* (1949).

1949　Transatlantic Pictures disbanded, and Hitchcock signs with Warner Brothers. He often describes the films he made during this period as "running for cover," but they include *Strangers on a Train* (1951), now commonly considered one of his important films.

1954　Sandwiched between two diverting "entertainments," *Dial M for Murder* (1954), made in 3-D, and *To Catch a Thief* (1955), starring Cary Grant and Grace Kelly and establishing a model for the "caper" film, Hitchcock makes *Rear Window* (1954), with James Stewart and Grace Kelly.

1955    Debut of *Alfred Hitchcock Presents*, a 30-minute television series, on October 2. This enormously popular series runs until 1962, and is followed by a successful three-year run of the *Alfred Hitchcock Hour*. Hitchcock's appearances at the beginning and end of each episode make his image and droll, macabre sense of humor instantly recognizable. Hitchcock directed eighteen episodes for his television series (and two for similar series).

1958    *Vertigo*, starring James Stewart and Kim Novak.

1959    *North by Northwest*, starring Cary Grant and Eva Marie Saint.

1959    *Psycho*, starring Janet Leigh and Anthony Perkins. Shot on a low budget by the crew from his television series, this film returns an enormous profit on its investment and becomes a prototype for the modern psychological horror film.

1963    *The Birds*, starring Tippi Hedren and Rod Taylor. The special effects of this film and Hitchcock's shrewd and tireless publicity campaign help make the film an immediate success.

1966    Meets with François Truffaut for a week-long series of extensive interviews covering his entire career to that point. These become the basis of a book published in French in 1966 and in English in 1967. This book, subsequently expanded and updated with material from further interviews, is an important part of the critical acceptance of Hitchcock as a serious and important filmmaker and thoughtful and self-conscious artist as well as a popular entertainer.

1964    *Marnie*, starring Tippi Hedren and Sean Connery, is released to disappointing critical and commercial response.

1972    *Frenzy*, starring Jon Finch and Barry Foster, is hailed as a return to form for Hitchcock, after the critical and commercial failure of *Torn Curtain* (1966) and *Topaz* (1969), but its disturbing brutality also gains much attention.

1976    *Family Plot*, starring Karen Black, Bruce Dern, Barbara Harris, and William Devane, Hitchcock's last completed film. He works on various projects, but is unable to continue the strenuous job of directing.

1979    Honored by the American Film Institute in March with a Life
        Achievement Award. Named a Knight Commander of the British
        Empire by Queen Elizabeth II in December.

1980    Dies on April 29.

# FILMOGRAPHY

1927
THE PLEASURE GARDEN (silent)
Producer: Michael Balcon
Production company: Gainsborough-Emelka
Director: **Alfred Hitchcock**
Assistant director: Alma Reville
Screenplay: Eliot Stannard, based on the novel by Oliver Sandys
Director of photography: Baron Ventimiglia
Cast: Virginia Valli (Patsy), Carmelita Geraghty (Jill), Miles Mander (Levett), John Stuart (Hugh), George Snell (Hamilton), C. Falkenburg (Prince Ivan), Frederick Martini (Mr. Sidey), Florence Helminger (Mrs. Sidey). [Uncredited but sometimes claimed: Nita Naldi (Native girl)]
Running time: 7,508 feet; 68 minutes

THE MOUNTAIN EAGLE (U.S. release title: *Fear o' God*) (silent) [lost film: no known prints]
Producer: Michael Balcon
Production company: Gainsborough-Emelka
Director: **Alfred Hitchcock**
Screenplay: Eliot Stannard
Director of photography: Baron Ventimiglia
Cast: Bernard Goetzke (Pettigrew), Nita Naldi (Beatrice), Malcolm Keen (Fear o' God), John Hamilton (Edward)
Running time: 7,503 feet; 89 minutes

THE LODGER: A STORY OF THE LONDON FOG (U.S. release title: *The Case of Jonathan Drew*) (silent)
Producer: Michael Balcon
Production company: Gainsborough
Director: **Alfred Hitchcock**
Assistant director: Alma Reville
Screenplay: Eliot Stannard, based on the novel *The Lodger*, by Marie Belloc Lowndes
Director of photography: Baron Ventimiglia
Editor: Ivor Montagu
Art directors: C. Wilfrid Arnold and Bertram Evans
Title designs: E. McKnight Kauffer
Cast: Marie Ault (Mrs. Bunting), Arthur Chesney (Mr. Bunting), June (Daisy), Malcolm Keen (Joe), Ivor Novello (the Lodger). **Hitchcock** cameo as newspaper editor (and, some claim, as part of the crowd at the end, when the Lodger is captured).
Running time: 7,685 feet; 93 minutes

DOWNHILL (U.S. release title: *When Boys Leave Home*) (silent)
Producer: Michael Balcon
Production company: Gainsborough
Director: **Alfred Hitchcock**
Assistant director: Frank Mills
Screenplay: Eliot Stannard, based on the play by David LeStrange (pseud. Ivor Novello and Constance Collier)
Director of photography: Claude McDonnell
Editor: Lionel Rich
Art director: Bert Evans
Cast: Ivor Novello (Roddy), Robin Irvine (Tim), Lillian Braithwaite (Lady Berwick), Isabel Jeans (Julia), Ian Hunter (Archie), Ben Webster (headmaster)
Running time: 6,500 feet; 83 minutes

EASY VIRTUE (silent)
Producer: Michael Balcon
Production company: Gainsborough
Director: **Alfred Hitchcock**
Assistant director: Frank Mills

Screenplay: Eliot Stannard, based on the play by Noël Coward
Director of photography: Claude McDonnell
Editor: Ivor Montagu
Art director: Clifford Pember
Cast: Isabel Jeans (Larita), Franklyn Dyall (her husband), Eric Bransby Williams (the artist), Ian Hunter (lawyer for plaintiff), Robin Irvine (John), Dacia Deane (his older sister), Dorothy Boyd (his younger sister), Enid Stamp Taylor (Sarah), Violet Farebrother (Mrs. Whittaker), Benita Hume (telephone operator). **Hitchcock** cameo walking by tennis court.
Running time: 6,500 feet; 61 minutes

THE RING (silent)
Producer: John Maxwell
Production company: British International
Director: **Alfred Hitchcock**
Assistant director: Frank Mills
Screenplay: **Alfred Hitchcock**
Director of photography: John J. Cox
Art Director: C. W. Arnold
Cast: Carl Brisson (Jack), Lillian Hall Davis (Nellie), Ian Hunter (Bob), Harry Terry (the showman), Gordon Harker (Jack's trainer), Clare Greet (fortune teller)
Running time: 8,454 feet; 109 minutes

1928
THE FARMER'S WIFE (silent)
Producer: John Maxwell
Production company: British International
Director: **Alfred Hitchcock**
Assistant director: Frank Mills
Screenplay: **Alfred Hitchcock**, based on the play by Eden Phillpotts
Director of photography: John J. Cox
Art director: C. Wilfrid Arnold
Editor: Alfred Booth
Cast: Jameson Thomas (Farmer Sweetland), Lillian Hall Davis (Araminta), Gordon Harker (Churdles), Maud Gill (Thirza), Louise Pounds (Widow Windeat), Olga Slade (Mary), Antonia Brough (Susan)
Running time: 100 minutes

CHAMPAGNE (silent)
Producer: John Maxwell
Production company: British International
Director: **Alfred Hitchcock**
Assistant director: Frank Mills
Screenplay: Eliot Stannard
Adaptation: **Alfred Hitchcock**, based on a story by Walter C. Mycroft
Director of photography: John J. Cox
Art director: C. Wilfrid Arnold
Cast: Betty Balfour (the Girl), Jean Bradin (the Boy), Theo Von Alten (the Man), Gordon Harker (the Father), Clifford Heatherley (impresario), Hannah Jones (servant at club), Claude Hulbert (guest at club)
Running time: 8,038 feet; 89 minutes

1929
THE MANXMAN (silent)
Producer: John Maxwell
Production company: British International
Director: **Alfred Hitchcock**
Assistant director: Frank Mills
Screenplay: Eliot Stannard, based on the novel by Hall Caine
Director of photography: John J. Cox
Editor: Emile de Ruelle
Art director: C. Wilfrid Arnold
Cast: Carl Brisson (Pete), Malcolm Keen (Philip), Anny Ondra (Kate), Randle Ayrton (her father)
Running time: 8,163 feet; 82 minutes

BLACKMAIL (sound and silent)
Producer: John Maxwell
Production company: British International
Director: **Alfred Hitchcock**
Assistant director: Frank Mills
Screenplay: **Alfred Hitchcock**, based on the play by Charles Bennett
Dialogue: Benn Levy (sound version)
Director of photography: John J. Cox
Editor: Emile de Ruelle

Art director: C. Wilfrid Arnold
Sound: R. R. Jeffrey
Music: Campbell and Connelly
Cast: Anny Ondra (Alice; voice by Joan Barry), Sara Allgood (Mrs. White),
Charles Paton (Mr. White), John Longden (Frank), Donald Calthrop (Tracy),
Cyril Ritchard (the artist), Hannah Jones (landlady), Sam Livesey (chief
inspector in sound version), Harvey Braban (chief inspector in silent ver-
sion), Phyllis Monkman (gossiping neighbor in sound version), Phyllis Kons-
tam (gossiping neighbor in silent version). **Hitchcock** cameo as passenger
on underground train.
Running time: 85 minutes

1930 (all sound films hereafter)
JUNO AND THE PAYCOCK
Producer: John Maxwell
Production company: British International
Director: **Alfred Hitchcock**
Assistant director: Frank Mills
Screenplay: Alma Reville, based on the play by Sean O'Casey
Director of photography: John J. Cox
Editor: Emile de Ruelle
Art director: J. Marchant
Sound: C. Thornton
Cast: Sara Allgood (Juno), Edward Chapman (Captain Boyle), Maire O'Neill
(Mrs. Madigan), Sidney Morgan (Joxer)
Running time: 85 minutes

ELSTREE CALLING
Production company: British International Pictures
Director: Adrian Brunel, with **Alfred Hitchcock** directing sketches and inter-
polated scenes
Ensemble numbers staged by André Chariot, Jack Hulbert, and Paul Murray
Screenplay: Val Valentine
Director of photography: Claude Freise-Greene
Editor: A. C. Hammond
Sound: Alec Murray
Music: Reg Casson, Vivian Ellis, Chick Endor, Ivor Novello, and Jack Strachey

Cast: Will Fyffe, Cicely Courtneidge, Jack Hulbert, Tommy Handley, Lily Morris, Helen Burnell, the Berkoffs, Anna May Wong, Jameson Thomas, John Longden, Donal Calthrop, Gordon Harker, Hannah Jones
Running time: 86 minutes

MURDER! (German version shot by **Alfred Hitchcock** with a different cast, titled *Mary*)
Producer: John Maxwell
Production company: British International
Director: **Alfred Hitchcock**
Assistant director: Frank Mills
Adaptation: **Alfred Hitchcock** and Walter Mycroft, based on the novel *Enter Sir John* by Clemence Dane and Helen Simpson
Screenplay: Alma Reville
Director of photography: John J. Cox
Editor: Rene Marrison
Art director: J. F. Mead
Sound: Cecil V. Thornton
Music: John Reynders
Cast: Norah Baring (Diana), Herbert Marshall (Sir John), Miles Mander (Druce), Esme Percy (Handel Fane), Edward Chapman (Mr. Markham), Phyllis Konstam (Mrs. Markham), Donald Calthrop (Ion Stewart), Hannah Jones (Mrs. Didsome), Una O'Connor (Mrs. Grogram). (The German version featured Walter Abel as Sir John.) **Hitchcock** cameo walking by in street as Sir John talks to the Markhams.
Running time: 100 minutes

1931
THE SKIN GAME
Producer: John Maxwell
Production company: British International
Director: **Alfred Hitchcock**
Assistant director: Frank Mills
Screenplay: Alma Reville, based on the play by John Galsworthy
Adaptation: **Alfred Hitchcock**
Director of photography: John J. Cox
Editors: A. Cobbett and Rene Marrison

Art director: J. B. Maxwell
Sound: Alec Murray
Cast: C. V. France (Mr. Hillcrist), Helen Haye (Mrs. Hillcrist), Jill Esmond (Jill), Edmund Gwenn (Mr. Hornblower), John Longden (Charles), Phyllis Konstam (Chloe)
Running time: 89 minutes

RICH AND STRANGE (U.S. release title: *East of Shanghai*)
Producer: John Maxwell
Production company: British International
Director: **Alfred Hitchcock**
Assistant director: Frank Mills
Screenplay: Alma Reville and Val Valentine, based on the novel by Dale Collins
Adaptation: **Alfred Hitchcock**
Directors of photography: John J. Cox and Charles Martin
Editor: Rene Marrison
Art director: C. Wilfrid Arnold
Sound: Alec Murray
Music: Hal Dolphe
Cast: Henry Kendall (Fred), Joan Barry (Emily), Percy Marmont (Commander Gordon), Betty Amann (the princess), Elsie Randolph (the old maid), Hannah Jones (Mrs. Porter)
Running time: 87 minutes

1932
NUMBER SEVENTEEN
Producer: John Maxwell
Production company: British International
Director: **Alfred Hitchcock**
Assistant director: Frank Mills
Screenplay: Alma Reville, **Alfred Hitchcock**, and Rodney Ackland, based on the play by J. Jefferson Farjeon
Directors of photography: John J. Cox and Bryan Langley
Editor: A. C. Hammond
Sound: A. D. Valentine
Music: A. Hallis

Cast: Leon M. Lion (Ben), Anne Grey (Nora), John Stuart (Fordyce/Barton), Donald Calthrop (Brant), Barry Jones (Doyle), Ann Casson (Rose), Henry Caine (Mr. Ackroyd), Garry Marsh (Sheldrake).
Running time: 65 minutes

1934
WALTZES FROM VIENNA (U.S. release title: *Strauss's Great Waltz*)
Producer: Tom Arnold
Production company: Tom Arnold Productions
Director: **Alfred Hitchcock**
Assistant director: Richard Beville
Screenplay: Guy Bolton and Alma Reville, based on the play by Heinz Reichert, A. M. Willner, and Ernest Marischka
Director of Photography: Glen McWilliams
Editor: Charles Frend
Sound: Alfred Birch
Art director: Oscar Werndorff
Music: by Johann Strauss (father and son), adapted by Hubert Bath, directed by Louis Levy
Cast: Jessie Matthews (Rasi), Esmond Knight (Strauss the younger), Edmund Gwenn (Strauss the elder), Frank Vosper (the prince), Fay Compton (the countess)
Running time: 80 minutes

THE MAN WHO KNEW TOO MUCH
Producer: Michael Balcon
Production company: Gaumont-British
Director: **Alfred Hitchcock**
Screenplay: Edwin Greenwood and A. R. Rawlinson, based on a story by Charles Bennett and D. B. Wyndham Lewis
Director of photography: Curt Courant
Editor: Hugh Stewart
Sound: F. McNally
Music: Arthur Benjamin
Cast: Leslie Banks (Bob Lawrence), Edna Best (Jill Lawrence), Nova Pilbeam (Betty Lawrence), Peter Lorre (Abbott), Frank Vosper (Ramon), Hugh Wakefield (Clive), Pierre Fresnay (Louis Bernard), Cicely Oates (nurse), D. A. Clarke

Smith (police inspector). **Hitchcock** cameo, according to some critics, as passerby in raincoat after scene at Tabernacle of the Sun.
Running time: 76 minutes

1935
THE 39 STEPS
Producer: Michael Balcon
Production company: Gaumont-British
Director: **Alfred Hitchcock**
Screenplay: Charles Bennett, based on the novel by John Buchan
Dialogue: Ian Hay
Director of photography: Bernard Knowles
Editor: D. N. Twist
Art director: Oscar Werndorff
Wardrobe: Marianne
Sound: A. Birch
Music: Louis Levy
Cast: Robert Donat (Hannay), Madeleine Carroll (Pamela), Lucie Mannheim (Annabella Smith), Godfrey Tearle (Prof. Jordan), John Laurie (the crofter), Peggy Ashcroft (his wife), Helen Haye (Mrs. Jordan), Frank Cellier (sheriff), Wylie Watson (Mr. Memory). **Hitchcock** cameo walking outside the Music Hall.
Running time: 87 minutes

1936
SECRET AGENT
Producer: Michael Balcon
Production company: Gaumont-British
Director: **Alfred Hitchcock**
Screenplay: Charles Bennett, after the play by Campbell Dixon, based on stories by W. Somerset Maugham
Dialogue: Ian Hay
Director of photography: Bernard Knowles
Editor: Charles Frend
Art director: Oscar Werndorff
Dresses: J. Strassner
Sound: Philip Dorté

Music: Louis Levy

Cast: John Gielgud (Ashenden), Madeleine Carroll (Elsa), Peter Lorre (the General), Robert Young (Marvin), Percy Marmont (Caypor), Florence Kahn (Mrs. Caypor), Charles Carson ("R"), Lilli Palmer (Lilli), Michel Saint-Denis (coachman)

Running time: 86 minutes

SABOTAGE (U.S. release title: *A Woman Alone*)

Producer: Michael Balcon

Production company: Gaumont-British

Director: **Alfred Hitchcock**

Screenplay: Charles Bennett, based on the novel *The Secret Agent* by Joseph Conrad

Dialogue: Ian Hay

Director of photography: Bernard Knowles

Editor: Charles Frend

Art director: Oscar Werndorff

Wardrobe: Marianne

Sound: R. Cameron

Music: Louis Levy

Cast: Sylvia Sidney (Mrs. Verloc), Oscar Homolka (her husband), Desmond Tester (Stevie), John Loder (Ted), Joyce Barbour (Renee), William Dewhurst (the Professor). **Hitchcock** cameo, some say, as passerby outside cinema when lights go on.

Running time: 76 minutes

1937

YOUNG AND INNOCENT (U.S. release title: *The Girl Was Young*)

Producer: Edward Black

Production company: Gaumont-British

Director: **Alfred Hitchcock**

Screenplay: Charles Bennett, Edwin Greenwood, and Anthony Armstrong, based on the novel *A Shilling for Candies* by Josephine Tey

Director of photography: Bernard Knowles

Editor: Charles Frend

Art director: Alfred Junge

Wardrobe: Marianne

Sound: A. O'Donoghue
Music: Louis Levy
Cast: Nova Pilbeam (Erica), Derrick de Marney (Robert), Percy Marmont (Col. Burgoyne), Edward Rigby (Old Will), Mary Clare (Erica's aunt), John Longden (Detective Kent), George Curzon (Guy), Basil Radford (Erica's uncle), Pamela Carme (Christine). **Hitchcock** cameo as photographer standing outside courthouse.
Running time: 82 minutes

1938
THE LADY VANISHES
Producer: Edward Black
Production company: Gaumont-British
Director: **Alfred Hitchcock**
Screenplay: Sidney Gilliat and Frank Lauder, based on the novel *The Wheel Spins* by Ethel Lina White
Director of photography: John J. Cox
Editor: R. E. Dearing
Sound: S. Wiles
Music: Louis Levy
Cast: Margaret Lockwood (Iris), Michael Redgrave (Gilbert), Dame May Whitty (Miss Froy), Paul Lukas (Dr. Hartz), Cecil Parker (Mr. Todhunter), Linden Travers (his mistress), Naunton Wayne (Caldicott), Basil Radford (Charters), Mary Clare (baroness), Catherine Lacey (the nun). **Hitchcock** cameo walking in the railway station at the end of the film.
Running time: 97 minutes

1939
JAMAICA INN
Producer: Erich Pommer
Production company: Mayflower
Director: **Alfred Hitchcock**
Screenplay: Sidney Gilliat and Joan Harrison, based on the novel by Daphne du Maurier
Dialogue: Sidney Gilliat
Directors of photography: Harry Stradling and Bernard Knowles
Editor: Robert Hamer

Special Effects: Harry Watt
Costumes: Molly McArthur
Sound: Jack Rogerson
Music: Eric Fenby
Cast: Charles Laughton (Pengallen), Leslie Banks (Joss), Marie Ney (Patience), Maureen O'Hara (Mary), Emlyn Williams (Harry), Wylie Watson (Salvation), Mervyn Johns (Thomas)
Running time: 100 minutes

1940
REBECCA
Producer: David O. Selznick
Production company: Selznick Studios
Director: **Alfred Hitchcock**
Screenplay: Robert E. Sherwood and Joan Harrison, based on the novel by Daphne du Maurier
Adaptation: Philip MacDonald, Michael Hogan
Director of photography: George Barnes
Editors: James Newcom and Hal Kern
Art director: Lyle Wheeler
Special Effects: Jack Cosgrove
Sound: Jack Noyes
Music: Franz Waxman
Cast: Laurence Olivier (Maxim), Joan Fontaine (his wife), Judith Anderson (Mrs. Danvers), George Sanders (Favell), Florence Bates (Mrs. Van Hopper), Nigel Bruce (Giles Lacey), Gladys Cooper (Mrs. Lacey), Leo G. Carroll (the doctor). **Hitchcock** cameo standing outside phone booth.
Running time: 130 minutes

FOREIGN CORRESPONDENT
Producer: Walter Wanger
Production company: Wanger Productions
Director: **Alfred Hitchcock**
Screenplay: Charles Bennett and Joan Harrison, based on *Personal History*, memoirs of Vincent Sheean
Director of photography: Rudolph Maté
Editors: Otto Lovering and Dorothy Spencer

Art director: Alexander Golitzen
Special effects: Paul Eagler and William Cameron Menzies
Costumes: I. Magnin & Co.
Sound: Frank Maher
Music: Alfred Newman
Cast: Joel McCrea (Johnny Jones/Huntley Haverstock), Laraine Day (Carol Fisher), Herbert Marshall (Stephen Fisher), George Sanders (ffolliott), Albert Basserman (Van Meer), Robert Benchley (Stebbins), Edmund Gwenn (Rowley), Harry Davenport (Mr. Powers), Eduardo Ciannelli (Krug). **Hitchcock** cameo as man reading newspaper.
Running time: 120 minutes

1941
MR. AND MRS. SMITH
Producer: Harry E. Edington
Production company: RKO
Director: **Alfred Hitchcock**
Story and screenplay: Norman Krasna
Director of photography: Harry Stradling
Editor: William Hamilton
Art director: Van Nest Polglase
Special effects: Vernon Walker
Costumes: Irene
Sound: John E. Tribby
Music: Edward Wand
Cast: Carole Lombard (Ann Smith), Robert Montgomery (David Smith), Gene Raymond (Jeff), Philip Merivale (his father), Lucile Watson (his mother), Jack Carson (Chuck). **Hitchcock** cameo walking by the Smith's apartment house.
Running time: 95 minutes

SUSPICION
Producer: Harry E. Edington
Production company: RKO
Director: **Alfred Hitchcock**
Screenplay: Samson Raphaelson, Joan Harrison, and Alma Reville, based on the novel *Before the Fact* by Frances Iles

Director of photography: Harry Stradling
Editor: William Hamilton
Art director: Van Nest Polglase
Special effects: Vernon Walker
Costumes: Edward Stevenson
Sound: John E. Tribby
Music: Franz Waxman
Cast: Joan Fontaine (Lina), Cary Grant (Johnny), Sir Cedric Hardwicke (General McLaidlaw), Dame May Whitty (Mrs. McLaidlaw), Nigel Bruce (Beaky), Isabel Jeans (Mrs. Newsham), Heather Angel (Ethel), Leo G. Carroll (Captain Melbeck). **Hitchcock** cameo at a mailbox at the beginning of the film.
Running time: 100 minutes

1942
SABOTEUR
Producer: Frank Lloyd
Production company: Universal
Director: **Alfred Hitchcock**
Screenplay: Peter Viertel, Joan Harrison, and Dorothy Parker
Director of photography: Joseph Valentine
Editor: Otto Ludwig
Art directors: Jack Otterson and Robert Boyle
Sound: Bernard B. Brown
Music: Frank Skinner
Cast: Robert Cummings (Barry), Priscilla Lane (Pat), Otto Kruger (Tobin), Alma Kruger (Mrs. Van Sutton), Norman Lloyd (Fry). **Hitchcock** cameo, according to some critics, as man at newsstand at drug store.
Running time: 109 minutes

1943
SHADOW OF A DOUBT
Producer: Jack H. Skirball
Production company: Universal
Director: **Alfred Hitchcock**
Screenplay: Thornton Wilder, Sally Benson, and Alma Reville, based on a story by Gordon McDonnell
Director of photography: Joseph Valentine

Editor: Milton Carruth
Art director: John B. Goodman
Costumes: Adrian, Vera West
Sound: Bernard B. Brown
Music: Dimitri Tiomkin
Cast: Joseph Cotten (Uncle Charlie), Teresa Wright (Charlie Newton), Mac-Donald Carey (Graham), Patricia Collinge (Emma Newton), Henry Travers (Joe Newton), Hume Cronyn (Herb), Edna May Wonacott (Ann Newton), Charles Bates (Roger Newton), Wallace Ford (Fred Saunders). **Hitchcock** cameo playing cards on train.
Running time: 108 minutes

1944
LIFEBOAT
Producer: Kenneth Macgowan
Production company: 20th Century-Fox
Director: **Alfred Hitchcock**
Screenplay: Jo Swerling, based on the story by John Steinbeck
Director of photography: Glenn MacWilliams
Editor: Dorothy Spencer
Art directors: James Basevi and Maurice Ransford
Special effects: Fred Sersen
Costumes: Rene Hubert
Sound: Bernard Freericks and Roger Heman
Music: Hugo W. Friedhofer
Cast: Tallulah Bankhead (Constance), John Hodiak (Kovac), William Bendix (Gus), Walter Slezak (Willie), Mary Anderson (Alice), Hume Cronyn (Stanley), Henry Hull (Rittenhouse), Heather Angel (Mrs. Higgins), Canada Lee (Joe). **Hitchcock** cameo in newspaper ad for "Reduco."
Running time: 96 minutes

BON VOYAGE
Producer: Sidney Bernstein
Production company: Phoenix Films, for the British Ministry of Information
Director: **Alfred Hitchcock**
Screenplay: J. O. C. Orton and Angus MacPhail, based on a subject by Arthur Calder-Marshall

Director of photography: Gunther Krampf
Cast: John Blythe (Sergeant Dougall), The Molière Players
Running time: 26 minutes

AVENTURE MALGACHE
Producer: Sidney Bernstein
Production company: Phoenix Films, for the British Ministry of Information
Director: **Alfred Hitchcock**
Director of photography: Gunther Krampf
Cast: The Molière Players
Running time: 31 minutes

1945
SPELLBOUND
Producer: David O. Selznick
Production company: Selznick Studios
Director: **Alfred Hitchcock**
Screenplay: Ben Hecht, based on the novel *The House of Dr. Edwardes* by Francis Beeding
Adaptation: Angus MacPhail
Director of photography: George Barnes
Editor: Hal Kern
Art director: James Basevi
Special effects: Jack Cosgrove
Dream sequence designs: Salvador Dali
Sound: Richard DeWeese
Music: Miklos Rozsa
Cast: Ingrid Bergman (Constance), Gregory Peck (John), Leo G. Carroll (Dr. Murchison), Norman Lloyd (Garmes), Rhonda Fleming (Mary), Michael Chekhov (Dr. Brulov). **Hitchcock** cameo walking out of elevator.
Running time: 111 minutes

1946
NOTORIOUS
Producer: **Alfred Hitchcock**
Production company: RKO
Director: **Alfred Hitchcock**

Screenplay: Ben Hecht, based on the story "The Song of the Dragon," by John Taintor Foote
Director of photography: Ted Tetzlaff
Editor: Theron Warth
Art directors: Carroll Clark and Albert S. D'Agostino
Special effects: Vernon L. Walker and Paul Eagler
Costumes: Edith Head
Sound: John E. Tribby and Terry Kellum
Music: Roy Webb
Cast: Ingrid Bergman (Alicia), Cary Grant (Devlin), Claude Rains (Sebastian), Leopoldine Konstantin (Madame Sebastian), Louis Calhern (Prescott), Reinhold Schuenzel (Dr. Anderson), Ivan Triesault (Mathis), Alex Minotis (Joseph), Eberhard Krumschmidt (Hupka), Sir Charles Mendl (Commodore), Moroni Olsen (Beardsley), Ricardo Costa (Dr. Barbosa). **Hitchcock** cameo at party drinking champagne.
Running time: 101 minutes


1947
THE PARADINE CASE
Producer: David O. Selznick
Production company: Selznick International-Vanguard Films
Director: **Alfred Hitchcock**
Screenplay: David O. Selznick, based on the novel by Robert Hichens
Director of photography: Lee Garmes
Editors: Hal Kern and John Faure
Art director: Thomas Morahan
Special effects: Clarence Slifer
Costumes: Travis Banton
Sound: James G. Stewart
Music: Franz Waxman
Cast: Alida Valli (Mrs. Paradine), Gregory Peck (Anthony Keane), Ann Todd (Gay Keane), Charles Laughton (Lord Horfield), Ethel Barrymore (Lady Horfield), Charles Coburn (Sir Simon), Joan Tetzel (his daughter), Louis Jourdan (Andre Latour), Leo G. Carroll (Sir Joseph). **Hitchcock** cameo at railroad station with cello case.
Running time: 114 minutes

1948
ROPE
Producer: **Alfred Hitchcock** and Sidney Bernstein
Production company: Transatlantic Pictures
Director: **Alfred Hitchcock**
Screenplay: Arthur Laurents
Adaptation: Hume Cronyn, based on the play by Patrick Hamilton
Director of photography: Joseph Valentine
Editor: William H. Ziegler
Art director: Perry Ferguson
Costumes: Adrian
Sound: Al Riggs
Music: Leo F. Forbstein
Cast: James Stewart (Cadell), John Dall (Brandon), Farley Granger (Philip), Sir Cedric Hardwicke (Mr. Kentley), Constance Collier (Mrs. Atwater), Douglas Dick (Kenneth), Edith Evanson (Mrs. Wilson), Joan Chandler (Janet), Dick Hogan (David). **Hitchcock** cameo crossing street at beginning of film. His profile is also seen in a neon sign visible outside the apartment window.
Running time: 80 minutes

1949
UNDER CAPRICORN
Producer: **Alfred Hitchcock** and Sidney Bernstein
Production company: Transatlantic Pictures
Director: **Alfred Hitchcock**
Screenplay: James Bridie, after the play by John Colton and Margaret Linden, based on the novel by Helen Simpson
Adaptation: Hume Cronyn
Director of photography: Jack Cardiff
Editor: A. S. Bates
Costumes: Roger Furse
Sound: Peter Handford
Music: Richard Addinsell and Louis Levy
Cast: Joseph Cotten (Flusky), Ingrid Bergman (Lady Flusky), Michael Wilding (Adare), Margaret Leighton (Milly), Cecil Parker (Governor), Denis O'Dea (Corrigan). Some critics note a **Hitchcock** cameo appearance outside the Government House.
Running time: 117 minutes

1950
STAGE FRIGHT
Producer: **Alfred Hitchcock**
Production company: Warner Bros.–First National
Director: **Alfred Hitchcock**
Screenplay: Whitfield Cook, based on the novel *Man Running* by Selwyn Jepson
Adaptation: Alma Reville
Director of photography: Wilkie Cooper
Editor: E. B. Jarvis
Sound: Harold King
Music: Leighton Lucas and Louis Levy
Cast: Marlene Dietrich (Charlotte), Jane Wyman (Eve), Michael Wilding (Wilfrid), Richard Todd (Jonathan), Alastair Sim (Commodore Gill), Sybil Thorndike (Mrs. Gill), Kay Walsh (Nellie), Patricia Hitchcock (Chubby). **Hitchcock** cameo walking by Eve on the street.
Running time: 110 minutes

1951
STRANGERS ON A TRAIN
Producer: **Alfred Hitchcock**
Production company: Warner Bros.–First National
Director: **Alfred Hitchcock**
Screenplay: Raymond Chandler and Czenzi Ormonde, based on the novel by Patricia Highsmith
Adaptation: Whitfield Cook
Director of photography: Robert Burks
Editor: William Ziegler
Art director: Edward S. Haworth
Special effects: H. F. Koenekamp
Costumes: Leah Rhodes
Sound: Dolph Thomas
Music: Dimitri Tiomkin
Cast: Robert Walker (Bruno), Farley Granger (Guy), Laura Elliott (Miriam), Ruth Roman (Ann), Patricia Hitchcock (Barbara), Leo G. Carroll (Senator Morton), Marion Lorne (Mrs. Anthony). **Hitchcock** cameo boarding train with double-bass case.
Running time: 101 minutes

1953
I CONFESS
Producer: **Alfred Hitchcock**
Production company: Warner–First National
Director: **Alfred Hitchcock**
Screenplay: George Tabori and William Archibald, based on the play *Nos Deux consciences* by Paul Anthelme
Director of photography: Robert Burks
Editor: Rudi Fehr
Art direction: Edward S. Haworth
Sound: Oliver S. Garretson
Costumes: Orry-Kelly
Music: Dimitri Tiomkin
Cast: Montgomery Clift (Father Logan), Anne Baxter (Ruth), Karl Malden (Inspector Larrue), Roger Dann (Grandfort), O. E. Hasse (Keller), Dolly Haas (his wife), Brian Aherne (Willy Robertson). **Hitchcock** cameo walking across steps at the beginning of the film.
Running time: 95 minutes


1954
DIAL M FOR MURDER
Producer: **Alfred Hitchcock**
Production company: Warner Bros.–First National
Director: **Alfred Hitchcock**
Screenplay: Frederick Knott, based on his play
Director of photography: Robert Burks (shot in 3-D)
Editor: Rudi Fehr
Art director: Edward Carrere
Sound: Oliver S. Garretson
Costumes: Moss Mabry
Music: Dimitri Tiomkin
Cast: Ray Milland (Tony), Grace Kelly (Margot), Robert Cummings (Mark), Anthony Dawson (Lesgate/Swann), John Williams (Inspector Hubbard). **Hitchcock** cameo in photograph of class reunion.
Running time: 105 minutes

REAR WINDOW
Producer: **Alfred Hitchcock**
Production company: Paramount
Director: **Alfred Hitchcock**
Screenplay: John Michael Hayes, based on the story by Cornell Woolrich
Director of photography: Robert Burks
Editor: George Tomasini
Art directors: Hal Pereira and Joseph MacMillan Johnson
Special effects: John P. Fulton
Costumes: Edith Head
Sound: Harry Lindgren and John Cape
Music: Franz Waxman
Cast: James Stewart (Jefferies), Grace Kelly (Lisa), Thelma Ritter (Stella), Wendell Corey (Doyle), Raymond Burr (Lars Thorwald), Irene Winston (Mrs. Thorwald), Judith Evelyn (Miss Lonelyhearts), Ross Bagdasarian (composer), Georgine Darcy (Miss Torso), Jesslyn Fax (scluptress). **Hitchcock** cameo winding clock in musician's apartment.
Running time: 112 minutes


1955
TO CATCH A THIEF
Producer: **Alfred Hitchcock**
Production company: Paramount
Director: **Alfred Hitchcock**
Screenplay: John Michael Hayes, based on the novel by David Dodge
Director of photography: Robert Burks
Editor: George Tomasini
Art directors: Hal Pereira and Joseph MacMillan Johnson
Costumes: Edith Head
Sound: Harold Lewis and Arthur Crams
Music: Lyn Murray
Cast: Cary Grant (John Robie), Grace Kelly (Frances Stevens), Jessie Royce Landis (Mrs. Stevens), John Williams (H. H. Hughson), Brigitte Auber (Danielle), Charles Vanel (Bertani). **Hitchcock** cameo sitting at back of bus.
Running time: 97 minutes

THE TROUBLE WITH HARRY
Producer: **Alfred Hitchcock**
Production company: Paramount
Director: **Alfred Hitchcock**
Screenplay: John Michael Hayes, based on the novel by J. Trevor Story
Director of photography: Robert Burks
Editor: Alma Macrorie
Art directors: John Goodman and Hal Pereira
Special effects: John P. Fulton
Sound: Harold Lewis and Winston Leverett
Music: Bernard Herrmann
Cast: Edmund Gwenn (Capt. Wiles), John Forsythe (Sam), Shirley MacLaine
(Jennifer), Mildred Natwick (Miss Graveley), Mildred Dunnock (Mrs. Wiggs),
Jerry Mathers (Arnie), Royal Dano (Calvin Wiggs), Parker Fennelly (million-
aire), Philip Truex (Harry). **Hitchcock** cameo, some say, walking past road-
side stand.
Running time: 100 minutes

1956
THE MAN WHO KNEW TOO MUCH
Producer: **Alfred Hitchcock**
Production company: Paramount
Director: **Alfred Hitchcock**
Screenplay: John Michael Hayes, based on the story by Charles Bennett and
D. B. Wyndham Lewis
Director of photography: Robert Burks
Editor: George Tomasini
Art directors: Hal Pereira and Henry Bumstead
Special effects: John P. Fulton and Gene Garvin
Costumes: Edith Head
Music: Bernard Herrmann
Cast: James Stewart (Ben McKenna), Doris Day (Jo McKenna), Christopher
Olsen (Hank McKenna), Bernard Miles (Drayton), Brenda de Banzie (Mrs.
Drayton), Reggie Nalder (Rien), Daniel Gélin (Louis Bernard). **Hitchcock**
cameo in crowd watching acrobats.
Running time: 120 minutes

THE WRONG MAN
Producer: **Alfred Hitchcock**
Production company: Warner Bros.–First National
Director: **Alfred Hitchcock**
Screenplay: Maxwell Anderson and Angus MacPhail, based on a story by Anderson
Director of photography: Robert Burks
Editor: George Tomasini
Sound: Earl Crain, Sr.
Music: Bernard Herrmann
Cast: Henry Fonda (Balestrero), Vera Miles (Rose Balestrero), Anthony Quayle (O'Connor), Esther Minciotti (Balestrero's mother), Harold J. Stone (Lt. Bowers), John Heldabrand (Tomasini), Doreen Lang (Mrs. James), Laurinda Barrett (Constance), Norma Connolly (Betsy), Lola D'Annunzio (Olga Conforti), Nehemiah Persoff (Gene Conforti), Robert Essen (Gregory Balestrero), Kippy Campbell (Robert Balestrero), Dayton Lummia (judge), Charles Cooper (detective). **Hitchcock** voiceover, narrating prologue.
Running time: 105 minutes

1958
VERTIGO
Producer: **Alfred Hitchcock**
Production company: Paramount
Director: **Alfred Hitchcock**
Screenplay: Alec Coppel and Samuel Taylor, based on the novel *D'Entre les morts* by Pierre Boileau and Thomas Narcejac
Director of photography: Robert Burks
Editor: George Tomasini
Art directors: Hal Pereira and Henry Bumstead
Special effects: John Ferren
Costumes: Edith Head
Sound: Harold Lewis and Winston Leverett
Music: Bernard Herrmann
Cast: James Stewart (Scottie), Kim Novak (Madeleine/Judy), Barbara Bel Geddes (Midge), Tom Helmore (Elster), Konstantin Shayne (Pop Liebl), Henry Jones (coroner), Ellen Corby (hotel manager). **Hitchcock** cameo walking on sidewalk carrying a case when Scottie visits Gavin Elster.
Running time: 128 minutes

1959
NORTH BY NORTHWEST
Producer: **Alfred Hitchcock**
Production company: MGM
Director: **Alfred Hitchcock**
Screenplay: Ernest Lehman
Director of photography: Robert Burks
Editor: George Tomasini
Titles: Saul Bass
Art directors: William A. Horning and Merrill Pye
Special effects: Arnold Gillespie and Lee LeBlanc
Sound: Frank Milton
Music: Bernard Herrmann
Cast: Cary Grant (Thornhill), Eva Marie Saint (Eve), James Mason (Vandamm), Jessie Royce Landis (Thornhill's mother), Leo G. Carroll (The Professor), Philip Ober (Townsend), Martin Landau (Leonard). **Hitchcock** cameo as man missing bus.
Running time: 136 minutes

1960
PSYCHO
Producer: **Alfred Hitchcock**
Production company: Paramount
Director: **Alfred Hitchcock**
Screenplay: Joseph Stefano, based on the story by Robert Bloch
Director of photography: John L. Russell
Editor: George Tomasini
Titles: Saul Bass
Art direction: George Tomasini
Special effects: Clarence Champagne
Costumes: Helen Colvig
Sound: George Milo
Music: Bernard Herrmann
Cast: Anthony Perkins (Norman), Janet Leigh (Marion), Vera Miles (Lila), John Gavin (Sam), Martin Balsam (Arbogast), John McIntire (Al Chambers), Lurene Tuttle (Mrs. Chambers), Simon Oakland (psychiatrist), Frank Albertson (Cassidy), Patricia Hitchcock (Caroline), Vaughn Taylor (Lowery), Mort

Mills (highway patrolman), John Anderson (car saleman). **Hitchcock** cameo standing outside realtor's office.
Running time: 109 minutes

1963
THE BIRDS
Producer: **Alfred Hitchcock**
Production company: Universal
Director: **Alfred Hitchcock**
Screenplay: Evan Hunter, based on the story by Daphne du Maurier
Director of photography: Robert Burks
Editor: George Tomasini
Titles: James S. Pollak
Art director: Robert Boyle
Special effects: Lawrence A. Hampton, Ub Iwerks, and Albert Whitlock
Costumes: Edith Head
Electronic sound production: Remi Gassmann and Oskar Sala
Consultant on sound: Bernard Herrmann
Cast: Tippi Hedren (Melanie), Rod Taylor (Mitch), Jessica Tandy (Mrs. Brenner), Suzanne Pleshette (Annie), Veronica Cartwright (Cathy), Ethel Griffies (Mrs. Bundy), Charles McGraw (Sebastian), Doreen Lang (mother in café).
**Hitchcock** cameo walking two dogs into pet store.
Running time: 120 minutes

1964
MARNIE
Producer: **Alfred Hitchcock**
Production company: Universal
Director: **Alfred Hitchcock**
Screenplay: Jay Presson Allen, based on the novel by Winston Graham
Director of photography: Robert Burks
Editor: George Tomasini
Art directors: Robert Boyle and George Milo
Special effects: Albert Whitlock
Costumes: Edith Head, Vincent Dee, Rita Riggs, and James Linn
Sound: Waldon O. Watson and William Russell
Music: Bernard Herrmann

Cast: Tippi Hedren (Marnie), Sean Connery (Mark), Diane Baker (Lil), Louise Latham (Bernice), Martin Gabel (Strutt), Bob Sweeney (Bob), Alan Napier (Mr. Rutland), Mariette Hartley (Susan), Bruce Dern (sailor). **Hitchcock** cameo in hotel corridor.
Running time: 131 minutes

1966
TORN CURTAIN
Producer: **Alfred Hitchcock**
Production company: Universal
Director: **Alfred Hitchcock**
Screenplay: Brian Moore
Director of photography: John F. Warren
Editor: Bud Hoffman
Art director: Frank Arrigo
Special effects: Albert Whitlock
Costumes: Edith Head and Grady Hunt
Sound: Waldon O. Watson and William Russell
Music: John Addison
Cast: Paul Newman (Armstrong), Julie Andrews (Sarah), Lila Kedrova (Countess), Wolfgang Kieling (Gromek), Tamara Toumanova (ballerina), Ludwig Donath (Professor Lindt), David Opatoshu (Jacobi). **Hitchcock** cameo holding baby in hotel lobby.
Running time: 128 minutes

1969
TOPAZ
Producer: **Alfred Hitchcock**
Production company: Universal
Director: **Alfred Hitchcock**
Screenplay: Samuel Taylor, based on the novel by Leon Uris
Director of photography: Jack Hildyard
Editor: William Ziegler
Special effects: Albert Whitlock
Costumes: Edith Head
Sound: Waldon O. Watson and Robert R. Bertrano
Music: Maurice Jarre

Cast: Frederick Stafford (Devereaux), John Forsythe (Nordstrom), Dany Robin (Nicole), John Vernon (Rico), Karin Dor (Juanita), Michel Piccoli (Jacques), Philippe Noiret (Henri), Claude Jade (Michele), Roscoe Lee Browne (Philippe), Per-Axel Arosenius (Kusenov), Michel Subor (Picard). **Hitchcock** cameo in wheelchair at airport.
Running time: 127 minutes

1972
FRENZY
Producer: **Alfred Hitchcock**
Production company: Universal
Director: **Alfred Hitchcock**
Screenplay: Anthony Shaffer, based on the novel *Goodbye Picadilly, Farewell Leicester Square* by Arthur La Bern
Director of photography: Gil Taylor
Editor: John Jympson
Art director: Bob Laing
Special effects: Albert Whitlock
Sound: Gordon K. McCallum
Music: Ron Goodwin
Cast: Jon Finch (Blaney), Barry Foster (Rusk), Barbara Leigh-Hunt (Brenda), Anna Massey (Babs), Alex McCowen (Inspector Oxford), Vivien Merchant (his wife), Billie Whitelaw (Hetty), Clive Swift (her husband), Bernard Cribbins (Forsythe), Elsie Randolph (Gladys). **Hitchcock** cameo in crowd at beginning of the film.
Running time: 116 minutes

1976
FAMILY PLOT
Producer: **Alfred Hitchcock**
Production company: Universal
Director: **Alfred Hitchcock**
Screenplay: Ernest Lehman, based on the novel *The Rainbird Pattern* by Victor Canning
Director of photography: Leonard South
Editor: J. Terry Williams
Art director: Henry Bumstead

Special effects: Albert Whitlock
Costumes: Edith Head
Sound: James W. Payne, James Alexander, and Robert L. Hoyt
Music: John Williams
Cast: Karen Black (Fran), Bruce Dern (Lumley), Barbara Harris (Blanche), William Devane (Adamson), Ed Lauter (Maloney), Cathleen Nesbitt (Julia Rainbird), Katherine Helmond (Mrs. Maloney), Warren J. Kernmerling (Grandison), Edith Atwater (Mrs. Clay), William Prince (bishop), Nicolas Colasanto (Constantine). **Hitchcock** cameo as shadow-figure behind office window.
Running time: 120 minutes

*Films made for TV*

REVENGE
Screenplay by Francis Cockrell and A. I. Bezzerides, based on a story by Samuel Blas. Broadcast on *Alfred Hitchcock Presents*, October 2, 1955. 25 minutes.

BREAKDOWN
Screenplay by Francis Cockrell and Louis Pollock, based on a story by Pollock. Broadcast on *Alfred Hitchcock Presents*, November 13, 1955. 25 minutes.

THE CASE OF MR. PELHAM
Screenplay by Francis Cockrell, based on a story by Anthony Armstrong. Broadcast on *Alfred Hitchcock Presents*, December 4, 1955. 25 minutes.

BACK FOR CHRISTMAS
Screenplay by Francis Cockrell, based on a story by John Collier. Broadcast on *Alfred Hitchcock Presents*, March 4, 1956. 25 minutes.

WET SATURDAY
Screenplay by Marian Cockrell, based on a story by John Collier. Broadcast on *Alfred Hitchcock Presents*, September 30, 1956. 25 minutes.

MR. BLANCHARD'S SECRET
Screenplay by Sarett Rudley, based on a story by Emily Neff. Broadcast on *Alfred Hitchcock Presents*, December 23, 1956. 25 minutes.

ONE MORE MILE TO GO
Screeenplay by James P. Cavanagh, based on a story by F. J. Smith. Broadcast on *Alfred Hitchcock Presents*, April 7, 1957. 25 minutes.

FOUR O'CLOCK
Screenplay by Francis Cockrell, based on a story by Cornell Woolrich. Broadcast on *Suspicion*, September 30, 1957. 50 minutes.

THE PERFECT CRIME
Screenplay by Stirling Silliphant, based on a story by Ben Ray Redman. Broadcast on *Alfred Hitchcock Presents*, October 20, 1957. 25 minutes.

LAMB TO THE SLAUGHTER
Screenplay by Roald Dahl, based on a story by Dahl. Broadcast on *Alfred Hitchcock Presents*, April 13, 1958. 25 minutes.

DIP IN THE POOL
Screenplay by Robert C. Dennis and Francis Cockrell, based on a story by Roald Dahl. Broadcast on *Alfred Hitchcock Presents*, September 14, 1958. 25 minutes. **Hitchcock** cameo in photo on the cover of *Alfred Hitchcock Mystery Magazine*, read by Mr. Renshaw.

POISON
Screenplay by Casey Robinson, based on a story by Roald Dahl. Broadcast on *Alfred Hitchcock Presents*, October 5, 1958. 25 minutes.

BANQUO'S CHAIR
Screenplay by Francis Cockrell, based on a story by Rupert Croft-Cooke. Broadcast on *Alfred Hitchcock Presents*, May 3, 1959. 25 minutes.

ARTHUR
Screenplay by James Cavanagh, based on a story by Arthur Williams. Broadcast on *Alfred Hitchcock Presents*, September 27, 1959. 25 minutes.

THE CRYSTAL TRENCH
Screenplay by Stirling Silliphant, based on a story by A. E. W. Mason. Broadcast on *Alfred Hitchcock Presents*, October 4, 1959. 25 minutes.

INCIDENT AT A CORNER
Screenplay by Charlotte Armstrong, based on a story by Armstrong. Broadcast on *Ford Startime*, April 5, 1960. 50 minutes.

MRS. BIXBY AND THE COLONEL'S COAT
Screenplay by Halsted Welles, based on a story by Roald Dahl. Broadcast on *Alfred Hitchcock Presents*, September 27, 1960. 25 minutes.

THE HORSEPLAYER
Screenplay by Henry Slesar, based on a story by Slesar. Broadcast on *Alfred Hitchcock Presents*, March 14, 1961. 25 minutes.

BANG! YOU'RE DEAD
Screenplay by Harold Swanton, based on a story by Margery Vesper. Broadcast on *Alfred Hitchcock Presents*, October 17, 1961. 25 minutes.

I SAW THE WHOLE THING
Screenplay by Henry Slesar, based on a story by Henry Cecil. Broadcast on *The Alfred Hitchcock Hour*, October 11, 1962. 50 minutes.

ALFRED HITCHCOCK

**INTERVIEWS**

# The Talkie King Talks

*EVENING NEWS*/1929

WE ARE ONLY JUST at the beginning of the talkie, he told me.

It will change the whole character of the films as known to the cinema-going public.

The big stars will for the most part, I believe, disappear, or appeal by their names and personality in a much lesser degree.

The really good play on the legitimate theatre will not be affected by the advent of the talkie, but the poor stuff naturally will.

The theatre has certain advantages over the talkie, such as the actual physical presence of the actors and actresses, but very little more.

And the advantages of the mechanical processes are infinitely greater than those of the theatre.

I can put Piccadilly Circus on the films.

I can have my hero and heroine actually talking audibly in the middle of Piccadilly Circus, with the noise of the traffic—as strong or weak as I want it—going on around them.

The theatre version of Piccadilly would be funny as compared to mine.

But then we are working on a bigger canvas than the theatre producers.

Remember that the silent picture has done an immense amount to prepare the way of the talking picture.

It has created a demand for realism that is not demanded in the ordinary theatre.

---

From *Evening News* (London), June 25, 1929; in scrapbook for *Blackmail* in Hitchcock Collection, Herrick Library.

Think what cinema-goers would say if they saw a film version of a door that flapped when opened or shut, like the canvas stage door always does.

No, the public demands real doors, real scenes, real animals, real everything.

And I think we will be able to hold our own with America now that the talkie has arrived.

We have as good equipment, better authors, and, I think, better actors.

No, I can see no reason why they should leave us behind this time.

# Advance Monologue

## OSWELL BLAKESTON/1930

''THE TALKIES,'' Alfred Hitchcock said to me, "have given most of us a past about which we need to be ashamed. Why, we used to bore a hole in an actor's head and superimpose tiny images representing his thoughts! Sound has done away with such clumsiness. I am thinking of a sequence from *Enter Sir John* [*Murder!*]. A murder has been committed. There is a shot of the curious outside the villa in which the body was found; a picture with a Fleet Street look. Then, a cut to the notice-board in the green-room of the local theatre; attention being focussed on the fact that an under-study is playing. After that, a glimpse of the curtain rising: immediately followed by a close up of the grille opening into the cell of the condemned actress. The camera holds her face, but the voices in the theatre talk about the understudy. The woman's eyes just respond to the comments and her thoughts are pretty plain. Such touches, of course, can only be added to a good story; those who lose the significance of the finer points being satisfied with the drama alone."

"*Potemkin*," he continued with a twinkle in his eye, "is the only Russian film I have seen. Personally, I place a good deal of trust in my feeling for musical formulas. *Blackmail*, AS I PLANNED IT, began with the arrest of the felon and ended with the arrest of the girl. Two unknown detectives, in the very last shot, were to be shown talking about the girls they were going to take out to Lyons. Coda. Also, according to the disciples of the happy end, uncommercial."

From *Close Up*, 7, no. 2 (August 1930), 146–47.

"And then this quick cutting. Each cut means a new set up. Supposing I have the simple notion of following my characters with the camera on a trolley. It means taking away the ceiling (of the kind of sets I principally used in *Enter Sir John*) and putting down a new floor. Time is money, as you know, or, rather, as the supervisors know. Again, naturalism! My audiences would go crazy looking at the kind of wall-paper the Russians would put in the rooms of my last film."

"I have tried to make worthwhile compromises with *Enter Sir John*. The plot hinges on vocal tricks exploited by the actor hero; the voice of conscience is materialised; and the villain is exposed by being given a play to read."

"And it was amusing," Alfred finished, "to direct the German and English artistes. For example, the English hardly like to come into the room where a murder has been committed, and the Germans are most curious about it."

It *would* be amusing to have all the ideas of a Hitchcock, but it would, at the same time, be something of a strain to see that they were properly carried out.

# Half the World in a Talkie

*EVENING NEWS*/1931

A GENERAL COMPLAINT against British films is that the stories happen too much and too long in one room or one house.

Elstree appears to have taken the hint as far as Alfred Hitchcock's next film is concerned. The subject which he is now adapting for the screen starts in London and embraces scenes in Paris, Monte Carlo, Marseilles, Port Said, Colombo, Singapore, and Hong Kong! It is going to be the most ambitious and expensive film Mr. Hitchcock has yet made.

Film photographers are already at work in the Far East obtaining exterior scenes for the picture. It does not follow that the artists concerned will visit these places. Such an enterprise would tax the financial resources of even an American company. But some of the places may be visited.

I expect the scenic constructors of British International Pictures are going to be put on their mettle. They have already shown that they can build streets and houses of all kinds in the fields of Elstree which rival Hollywood's best. And in our variable climate the task is no enviable one.

I spent some time with Mr. Hitchcock yesterday while he told me about his ideas for this new film. As yet it is untitled, but it is to be an adaptation of Dale Collins's novel, *Rich and Strange*.

"Our hero and heroine," said Mr. Hitchcock, "are an ordinary London suburban couple, typical of thousands of cinema-goers. I think their adventure will appeal to every London worker and his wife.

"Our City clerk is fed up with London and life generally. In view of this

From *Evening News* (London), March 5, 1931.

discontent a rich relative decided to let him have a large legacy in advance. The clerk and his wife proceed to employ their new freedom and riches in taking a world tour.

"Arrived in Paris, like good Londoners, they visit the *Folies Bergères*. They go to Monte Carlo and see the gamblers.

"Then they join the boat at Marseilles for Port Said. Here the fun begins, for our hero, although not a particularly fine fellow, is certainly handsome, and while bathing he meets and is intrigued by a beautiful foreign princess. At the same time his wife, a little woman of the kind who can look after any man, becomes interested in an English planter who is returning to the East.

"A rift occurs and widens until one day, rather tactlessly, the planter suggests that the clerk is a poor sort of fellow who should be left to go his own way.

His remark has an unexpected effect, for the wife realises that her husband needs her. This realization grows when the vessel is wrecked and the clerk and his wife are rescued by a Chinese junk.

"They come to the decision that life with riches can be just as uncomfortable and dissatisfying as life in Suburbia. And the film closes with them very happily established at home again.

"That is only a very sketchy idea of the story. I hope to get a lot of fun into it and as I see it at present it is going to be a real film, with plenty of movement and change of scene and a very sparing use of talk. I am looking forward to some amusing scenes showing how typically fed up with his typical routine is the London clerk of the story."

One little joke that Mr. Hitchcock is looking forward to comes towards the end of the film. At Hong Kong the couple meet a film director and they try to persuade him that their adventure would make a good picture. "It isn't like life," he says, and dismisses the idea.

Alfred Hitchcock is going to play the part of the film director!

The problem of casting the picture is causing the director not a little worry at present. It may be surprising, but as we talked over the story we could not hit on two perfect and available stars to take the leading parts. Who could satisfactorily portray the unassuming but strong-minded, motherly little wife? And who is a handsome young man and a first-class actor at the same time? There is an English male actor in view, and the casting of the planter is practically decided on. But the two women are a problem. It may be that an American girl will be chosen. The question of expense and present contracts enters here.

Production of the film begins in about a month's time. Meanwhile, Mr. Hitchcock is working it out on paper. Following his usual custom in adapting a book or play for the screen, he has memorized the story and put the novel away. He reconstructs anew in terms of picture and action. Only when he is held up for an idea or for dialogue does he see if the book can help him.

Mr. Hitchcock, who, it is generally agreed, is the leading film director in this country, is now satisfied that talk is a definite asset to the screen.

"The film," he said, "must still be primarily a medium for telling a story in pictures. The advent of talkies has given the screen every advantage of the stage, but we must not be content because of that to tell our stories in words.

"The extra mobility of the film and its larger canvas enable us to make much more use of dialogue than the stage can. We should not, for example, be content to show a close-up of a man talking. By changing to the face of the person who is addressed we can emphasise the words by showing his reaction to what is said.

"In *The Skin Game*, for instance, which I have just finished, I think we were able to get much more excitement into the auction scene than the stage could do because we were able to flash from bidder to bidder, while the auctioneer's voice was heard, showing how the drama of the mounting sum affected each person.

"It seems to me that with this double advantage the screen will become *the* medium of the future for entertainment. The future of the stage does not appear to be half as bright as that of the screen.

"That does not mean that I whole-heartedly support the advanced technique of the Continental producers. The story is always the most important part of a film, and I find that the better the plot the less opportunity there is for extreme 'treatment.' Only a poor story lends itself to treatment."

# The Man Who Made *The 39 Steps:* Pen Portrait of Alfred Hitchcock

## NORAH BARING / 1935

F EW BRITISH FILMS have created such outstanding interest during the past twelve months as *The 39 Steps*. It brought together two stars for the first time in a British film—Robert Donat, riding on the crest of popularity after his big American success *The Count of Monte Cristo,* and Madeleine Carroll. It gave Madeleine a "different" role, with a distinct comedy angle to it, instead of the "serene highness" to which we had grown accustomed. More than all this, it has proved itself a record-breaking film in London *and* New York.

Applaud Robert Donat and Madeleine Carroll as you will—but save full measure of praise for the man who directed the film—Alfred Hitchcock. It is of "Hitch," as he is called, that I am going to write this week.

In more ways than one he is an outstanding figure in British films. A big man, his height is dwarfed by his huge girth; and a glance at his big head tells you that here is a man with "personality" as well as genius.

Directors vary very much in their methods of dealing with artistes. Some are very concise and obvious in their explanations; other men are more subtle and, though they get what they want, the actor never discovers how they do it.

Alfred Hitchcock belongs to the latter category, and I tried recently to unravel the mystery of his almost magnetic power over his cast.

I lunched with him and we talked naturally about his new picture *Secret Agent.*

From *Film Pictorial*, November 23, 1935, pp. 14–15.

"Of course," he told me, "Scrubby Carroll is in it again."

I looked puzzled and he smiled, as though at some private joke.

"*Madeleine* Carroll," he explained.

I felt horrified that this statuesque, dignified beauty should be referred to so disrespectfully. Then I remembered how, in *The 39 Steps*, "Hitch" had put her through her paces, casting her dignity to the four winds and giving her a new, vivid vitality. We spoke for a moment about *The 39 Steps*.

"It is strange," "Hitch" told me, "how very well Madeleine fitted into the part. I had heard a lot about her as a tall, cold, blonde beauty, dignified and all that. Not exactly," he went on, with a twinkle in his eye, "the real type for a boisterous role or where intense activity would give little chance for draping herself round the furniture and what not. You see, I had seldom seen her on the screen, because I very rarely take a busman's holiday. I knew only her photographs. Calm and serene barely describes them! They were certainly beautiful, but so very cold. My word, they would almost chill a refrigerator!"

He soon changed his opinion, for after their first meeting he decided she was perfectly natural and had a great sense of humour.

"Why is it," he said, "that actors and actresses are almost invariably cast exactly to type? In her case her obvious good looks had nearly been her downfall. It is very hard with merely the material of good looks to create a character, especially when they are completely devitalized by absence of action."

"Hitch" paused for a moment and I recognized that special look of concentration he wears when he is determined to put himself over.

"After meeting her," he went on a moment later, "I made up my mind to present her to the public as her *natural* self. You see what I mean? In *The 39 Steps* the public is seeing a Madeleine Carroll who has no time to be calm and serene. She is far too busy racing over moors, rushing up and down embankments, and scrambling over rocks."

In a little while, our conversation switched from work to pleasure. "Hitch" told me something of his travels this summer. He soaks himself so entirely in his film work that a real holiday is a rare occurrence in his life. "We did manage a few weekends at our summer cottage," said "Hitch," "and we went some time ago to Rome. We had a grand time, my wife and I and our daughter, Pat, too. She was so keen to go all over the place and see everything, that

I had quite a difficulty to tear myself away from her long enough to have an audience with the Pope."

There must have been a surprised look in my eyes, for he went on.

"Oh yes, I had an audience with His Holiness."

Then, I broke in: "I suppose you noticed every little detail to use in a film one day soon."

"Who knows?" said "Hitch," a faraway look in his eyes, and I realized that it might really be true.

Apart from his delightful home in Surrey, and his wife and daughter, he has few other interests. His wife is Alma Reville, the scenario writer.

He is fortunate enough to have a wife who, far from resenting the intrusion of business into every hour of his life, encourages and sympathizes with his enthusiasm. With true feminine intuition she can pick out the sheep from the goats in the crowd which inevitably surrounds him, thus saving his precious energy. It is all done so unobtrusively that one is never conscious of this "selective scrutiny."

It is a subtle characteristic she shares with her husband and reminded me of the occasion when I first met him just before the production of *Murder!*, with Herbert Marshall. I referred to this and I asked him if he always picked out his stars with as little ado as he did me.

"Do you really think of it like that," "Hitch" began. "Shows how little you know about it. You see, there you were. You had the type of face and the personality I had in mind, but you were all tied up with nerves and so tense that at first I hadn't a ghost of an idea whether you would be any use to me at all. I didn't know if you would photograph or record well enough. There was only one thing to do—give you a chance and see.

"It was nothing new to me to see an actress jittering with nerves. When a girl is in that state there's only one thing to do—to make her relax. And the easiest way is to play the fool for her benefit. You see the idea? You felt I was no end of an ass when I stood there spouting nonsense at you, didn't you?"

"Well," I admitted, "frankly I was a bit scared at first. I thought you were crazy. Then I thought you were pulling my leg. And at last I began to see the point of the silly jokes you were making, and to enjoy them. That's what put me right for my camera test. I remember that at the last moment I did have an uneasy feeling that you were having a good laugh to yourself at my expense."

"So I was," said "Hitch," "but only because you had swallowed my prescription and it was working out according to plan."

"Have you the same sort of theories about getting people to act?" I asked innocently.

"What do you think?" he countered.

"I think perhaps you have," I acknowledged after a moment's pause.

"Hitch," however, no longer has the power to embarrass me, as he used to when he made gentle fun of me in the studio. It is the power to keep things off the "intense level," so difficult to avoid in film circles, that is "Hitch's" gift. Having this power, he is able to get exactly what he wants from his players in the most uncanny fashion. Even when I resented with all my youthful conceit the fact that he seemed to be poking fun at me, I had to do as he wanted me to in a picture *simply because he did not allow me to get so strung-up that I could not express the emotions the part required.* As I have said, he has a magnetic power.

At the time I was working with "Hitch," he had a passion for acting in his own pictures. He did not star himself, nor look out [for] plums for his own glorification. Far from it! He liked to be an extra. Whenever there was a crowd scene, he made for it.

"Why don't you go to the cinema and watch other people's work?" I asked.

"For several reasons," "Hitch" replied. "First, because I have my own methods; but I am human, and every time I see someone else's films I may be tempted to try their methods instead of my own. Theirs seem so logical. I do it, and I fail. Their methods may be good, but not for me. The second reason is that I may unconsciously crib their stuff. An idea, a lighting effect, a way of doing something that is characteristic of some other director may attract me, and I might unconsciously employ it in my next picture. There it would look ridiculous because it is not characteristic of me. Therefore I consider it best to leave other people's films alone."

# Britain's Leading Film Director Gives Some Hints to the Film Stars of the Future

MARY BENEDETTA/1938

ALFRED HITCHCOCK, though still under 40, is Britain's foremost film director. Responsible in the silent film days for such pictures as *The Lodger* and *The Ring*, he won high praise for *Blackmail*, the first British all-talking film, and since then he has directed *The Man Who Knew Too Much*, *The 39 Steps*, and *Young and Innocent*, as well as a number of other films, all bearing the well-known "Hitchcock touch."

Mr. Hitchcock will direct Charles Laughton in the film version of Daphne du Maurier's novel, *Jamaica Inn*, but has first gone to Hollywood to make a film for David Selznick.

People who go to see films will always want to be entertained by them—forgetting all their own worries and sorrows. They are most entertained by fairy stories, for tradition holds good and everybody has been brought up on Cinderella.

They will still want their spies and villains to go through hair-raising adventures, and their heroines to take the town by storm.

This was the view of Alfred Hitchcock, who has done so much to advance the quality of British films.

"There is a general idea," he said, "that people now want much more original, highly sophisticated stories. But that is only one generation. The majority of the public want the same old stories told in a new way."

But in the making of pictures he foresaw some interesting changes and I followed that vivid practical imagination of his into a studio of the future.

From *Star* [London], July 14, 1938.

"I would like to make pictures using just the ordinary lighting you would find in a room. We should have the camera and the microphone set up where we wanted them, but there would be no other apparatus necessary.

"Before we started, I might have to have a standard lamp changed to another position, or the armchair altered to a different angle. But we could go straight ahead then and shoot the whole scene without interrupting its emotional sequence.

"Lighting is the biggest drawback in present-day filming. Nowadays we have to use very bright lights, which take a lot of time to adjust. We have to spend perhaps an hour and a half lighting one single shot. During that time I have to be there to see they get the intended effect.

"The star has to be kept waiting and she has to have a 'stand-in' to take her positions while they are preparing the lighting. And all the actress has to do perhaps is to take the telephone and say, 'I'm sorry I can't come to dinner with you to-night after all.'

"But for that one line and that single action a number of people have to hang about for an hour and a half until the lighting is fixed, and it is all that time before I can begin the actual directing.

"Supposing I wanted the actress to stand near the fireplace, with her arms resting on the mantelpiece, and then stoop down and poke the fire. For lighting purposes I would have to think of that action as three separate still photographs.

"First when she was standing up against the mantelpiece—I would have to see that her profile was outlined becomingly, that lighting caught the back of her hair prettily and that there was firelight on her skirt.

"Then as she stooped down I would have to be careful to light her so that during the movement she was not plunged into darkness. Again, when she reached her stooping position, I would have to get the effect of the firelight full on her face. And for each of those still pictures it would take quite a while to set up the lighting.

"All this lighting difficulty is what spreads the making of a picture over such a length of time, and, since time costs money in filming, it is the chief cause of the expense. When we can make our pictures with the ordinary lighting you would have in a room we should not only save money on apparatus, but on the stars and directors as well by saving of their time."

I asked him how this step could be reached, and he suggested that it might be reached by improved camera lenses.

"Not so much through new lenses as there isn't very much scope left for improving them now," he said, "but by using 'faster,' that is, more sensitive film."

This he felt would be possible. He told me that there was plenty of experimenting going on with film "stock" (the unused film) to make it reach a greater degree of sensitiveness.

"When talkies came in," he said, "they had been accustomed to using arc lights. But then they had to stop using them because they made a noise, so they took to using lights that were not half so strong. These did not do, and they had to find other means. This led to the discovery of more sensitive film."

Mr. Hitchcock said that acting in the films would tend to grow more and more controlled.

"It is all the little nuances of expression that tell you what that character is feeling, without reminding you that he is just an actor playing a part. They must be ever so slight, but all in varying degrees according to the kind of character and the amount of upbringing and training they have had.

"For instance, if someone came into this room now, and said, 'Mr. Hitchcock, there's a policeman waiting for you outside,' my expression would change very slightly and become almost dead for a second."

He showed me, in a perfect example of controlled acting with his own face, how it would happen. "But if I were somebody who presumably would not be so trained to hide my feelings, then I would show more of my thoughts." And he showed me how the change of expression would be more marked and give him away more.

Most interesting of all were Hitchcock's ideas on the future possibilities of colour films, of which he is a keen advocate.

"To my mind," he said, "colour should be used not just to give pictorial effect, but as a means of expression. I would like to film London in a fog—London in the rain. A girl who is unhappy—her face is drab and colourless, in contrast to the people round her. Or a man who is pale, and starved—to see him have his first meal and a flush gradually mount into his cheeks."

What a wonderful way to add to those delicate touches which he already portrays so cleverly in black and white.

# Mr. Hitchcock Discovers Love

FRANK S. NUGENT/1946

ALFRED HITCHCOCK HAS CONCLUDED that the war is over.
He regrets it—in a purely professional way, of course—for, as Hollywood's
deftest hand at melodrama, Hitch has been reveling for years in dirty work
at international crossroads. But with his current *Notorious* he is putting away
his polished foreign agents, his sinister saboteurs, and his diplomatic intrigu-
ers. The cycle of great spy films, begun with *The 39 Steps*, has come at last to
an end. Fortunately, Hitch has found a new subject. It is a war which has few
truces and never an armistice, which drips with intrigue and double-dealing
and not infrequently with human gore. Hitch has discovered the Battle of
the Sexes.

"Love Conquers All," whooped Bosley Crowther a few Sundays ago in his
column on *Spellbound* and *Notorious*, Hitch's most recent bulletins from the
romantic front, and recalled that the Hitch of the old days wouldn't give
love house room. This is undeniable. Hitch's early indifference to romance
was almost comic. Although he was a family man, his pictures would have
been no help to a man wondering how to become one. And on those infre-
quent occasions when the tender emotion insisted on forcing its way into a
scene, Hitch would hurry by with all the embarrassment of a Clarence Day
Sr. terminating his man-to-man talk with Junior—"There are some things
gentlemen do not discuss!"

"We wouldn't be able to tell you exactly what came over Mr. H.," wrote

From *New York Times*, November 3, 1946, Sunday Magazine section, pp. 12–13, 63–64.

Mr. C., winking at his typewriter. "Nothing personal, we'd imagine. He isn't precisely the type."

Now that was a dirty dig, for Mrs. Hitchcock and their daughter, Pat, obviously find nothing wrong with Hitch's type at all. Maybe he is not the latest model and has been described—this was before his diet reduced him to a shadowy 195—as looking a bit like two balloons tied one above the other. Yet he is durable, humorous and a splendid provider. Hitch doubtless would have challenged Mr. Crowther to a duel had he not read the rest of the review, which was fairly ecstatic.

His reply to Mr. Crowther, then, should be read aloud and in tones of dignified reproof—slightly belied by the twinkle in Mr. Hitchcock's eye.

"I hope," he says, "that it won't be considered due to a kind of middle-aged spread."

The primary fact behind Mr. Hitchcock's conversion is, as Mr. Crowther should have suspected, commercial necessity. If love does not make the world go round, certainly it spins the box office turnstiles. Alva Johnson once reported that Orson Welles saw *The Lady Vanishes* eleven times, while James Thurber went to it thirteen. Hitch and his producers probably were flattered by this upper-bracket patronage, but received no bouquets from exhibitors in Paterson, N.J., Harrisburg, Pa., or Beaufort, S.C. *Spellbound,* on the other hand, which was made for $1,700,000, will gross $8,000,000, and *Notorious,* which cost $2,000,000, is expected to bring back $9,000,000—to the vast delight of David O. Selznick, who sold script, stars (Bergman and Grant) and director to RKO for $800,000 cash and 50 per cent of the profits.

Mr. Hitchcock, who still dislikes love stories, wishes it were possible to ignore such statistics, but Hollywood will not permit him to. "Beyond that," he says, with a half-note of apology in his voice, "there's the constant pressure. You know: people asking, 'Do you want to reach only the audiences at the Little Carnegie or to have your pictures play the Music Hall?' So you compromise. You can't avoid it. You do the commercial thing, but you try to do it without lowering your standards.

"It isn't easy. Actually the commercial thing is much harder to do than the other. There are more taboos, more restrictions. Sometimes I feel that is why the pictures made in England are, in the main, so good. Over there you work without reference to the commercial thing. In Hollywood's eyes, this proves that the English film industry isn't educated sufficiently. It doesn't understand about the box office. It doesn't know everything about love."

And now that Hitch has become a self-accredited war correspondent, we presumed that he did know everything about love?

"I wouldn't exactly say that," he replied, "but I do know that many of the screen's conventions about love are completely ridiculous. For example, a man kisses a woman. Everyone in the audience expects him to follow it up with 'I love you' or 'I think you're wonderful.' Or to say something which shows that he has his mind on his, shall we say, work. In real life it is far more likely that his mind is elsewhere. He might be noting the time, or wondering what's cooking for dinner. And if he speaks at all it might be to utter some vagrant thought not connected with the kissing. In other words, I believe that people can behave physically in a certain way while talking about seemingly unrelated things."

Hitch's current illustration of this back-handed romantic technique is the scene fairly early in *Notorious* when Mr. Grant and Miss Bergman discover they are made for each other and celebrate the discovery with such nuzzlings and butterfly kisses as to waft a sorority house away on a sigh. And what was Mr. Grant engaged in most of the while? A telephone conversation with his FBI boss. And Miss Bergman? She was planning a roast chicken dinner. It was Hitch, by the way, not his literary collaborator, Ben Hecht, who planned and wrote the scene. Mr. Hecht's baffled remark was, "I don't get all this talk about a chicken."

In other aspects of love Mr. Hitchcock—the Dorothy Dix of the cinema—preferred not to be quoted, but admitted balefully that it is his intention to make life as miserable as possible for all future screen lovers coming within range of his cameras. His record to date is not bad. He bedeviled Joan Fontaine in *Rebecca* and *Suspicion* and Miss Bergman in *Spellbound* and *Notorious*. His Romeos have been homicidal maniacs, actual or potential, and he has done much to spread the notion that Dan Cupid is actually an Igorot in disguise carrying a blowgun and a quiver full of poisoned darts.

"I sometimes wonder," he will say blandly, "whether I am not—as all my friends insist—a sadist." Whereupon he will whistle for his two dogs—spoiled but loveable urchins—and make them beg while he feeds them a fistful of salted cashews.

Hitch's next assignment will be *The Paradine Case*, based on the Robert Hichens novel about a London attorney—a married man—who falls in love with his client, a woman on trial for the murder of her blind war-hero husband. Metro had owned the story originally, had wanted Garbo to play Mrs.

Paradine. Garbo resisted—the story being that she was annoyed by a certain resemblance between Mrs. Paradine's past and her own: Mrs. Paradine once had been a barber's assistant in Copenhagen, while Garbo had been apprenticed in Stockholm. Now the part will be played by Alida Valli, an Italian actress.

Hitch's interest in the story is less in its romantic potentials—although they will be exploited—than in the opportunity to realize two of his cinematic dreams. He long has wanted to show a trial at the Old Bailey—"supremely dispassionate conversation about the most passionate things"—and he also has been curious to know how the police would arrest a soignée society woman. James Bridie, the English playwright-physician, found out for him and Hitch promptly chucked the novel's first four chapters out the window so that he could open his picture with the arrest.

"It's a wonderful springboard," he says immodestly. "A woman at the piano, a butler, a drawing room. The butler says dinner will be in fifteen minutes. The front bell. Butler says, 'Inspector So-and-So is here.' 'Show him in.' 'Good evening, Inspector.' He introduces Sergeant So-and-So. She says, 'There's really very little more that I can tell you.' He says, 'I have a warrant for your arrest.' She murmurs something about getting some clothes. Very quickly he says, 'I'll go with you.'

"Here's a woman being arrested for murder in the politest terms possible. To me it's more dramatic than shouting to high heaven."

When Hitch tells a story, he sits very quietly. He makes few gestures. But his face is mobile and his eyes are electric. He never raises his voice above a conversational tone. A lifted finger is enough to hold a room at attention and people it with imaginary players awaiting his cue to move again. He never prates of art or tries to pretend that his technique is beyond mere human analysis.

"It all comes to this," he says bluntly. "How do you apply glue to the seat of the audience? That is the problem one always faces. In a play it is different. Your first act delineates characters and poses their problem. The audience flies outside for a smoke and to talk about the characters and analyze them. The second act begins the story. In the movies one has no time for this leisurely character development. The audience has no opportunity to pause and reflect. It wants to see something happening. Moviegoers are rather like the little boy of five who, on being told a story by his mother, breaks in every now and then to ask, 'And then what happens?'

"I prefer an oblique opening. You think of all the obvious ways to begin the film and then you discard them. It's what you leave out that makes a picture. You have to tell character and story simultaneously. And you have to use a springboard."

It's just as simple as that.

Hitch declines to get excited over the current vogue for so-called psychological films. "You would have to make a distinction," he says, "between psychological films and psychoanalytical films. The latter, I think, can be dismissed as a passing phase. It probably is true that the war and the world's general emotional upset have made the public more receptive to these explorations of the subconscious. But the run on films of this sort is due most likely to good old commercial Hollywood. Our business always moves in waves and the psychoanalytical film seems capital at the moment.

"The psychological film is quite a different thing. Of course, we really haven't touched that yet. But if, by psychological film, you mean a particular way of telling a story, by trying to get at the characters and at the action through the characters, why there's nothing new there. It is true the screen has not done as much as it should. It has depended too much on stereotypes. I think it is inevitable that the psychological approach to story will be employed more and more frequently as the screen comes of age. But that is something quite apart from films about split personality, amnesia and the like."

Mr. Hitchcock, despite his eight years in Hollywood, appears to be preserving his own personality unsplit and even unchipped. When he arrived from England, he met the idolatrous New York critics wearing a double-breasted blue suit and a puzzled smile. He had the air of a man who feels that the welcoming committee has met the wrong train but hates to tell them they have made a mistake. Today, with an unbroken record of box office and (largely) critical successes, Hitch still wears an untypical (for Hollywood) blue suit and carries his laurels in his hip pocket.

He and his family live in a pleasant home in Bel-Air overlooking a golf course—Hitch doesn't play—and few things give him more satisfaction than watching the country club's groundskeepers mowing what he calls "my lawn." He still refuses to drive a car because of his dread of policemen, still loathes the sight of eggs and still won't have a sauce bottle on his table. And he still insists on sneaking into every picture he makes but has learned now not to reveal his plans too far in advance.

In *Notorious*, he wanted to play a deaf-mute walking inconspicuously through a street scene "talking" in sign language to his woman companion. Just as they passed the camera, she was to slap his face. Word of this project got out and Hitch received scores of letters from deaf-mutes protesting they never said things like that and asking him not to hold them up to contempt, ridicule and so on. So Hitch, in deference to their wishes, contented himself by drinking a glass of champagne at Miss Bergman's party. Practically no one saw him. Being slimmer, he doesn't stand out the way he used to except as a director of melodramas—and love stories, dammit.

# Production Methods Compared

## THE CINE-TECHNICIAN/1948

ALFRED HITCHCOCK THEN APPEARED and was greeted with loud applause before the meeting opened for questions.

MR. HARRY WATT. *We would very much like to hear the comparative analysis of production in America and this country.*

THE AUTHOR. It is almost the same. There is a great deal left in the hands of the Production Department in America. 20th Century Fox have an administrative building which contains all the producers' and writers' resources and the creative side of picture making. The production building, which is the physical side, is definitely separated.

When the script is finished in its early draft it is sent into the production department and they go to work on it for budget. The property department work entirely on a script and in three days the property master has all the props laid out on a table with selections for what he wants.

The stages are presumably the same in two countries. Americans anticipate as many defects as they can. You are served by the various departments but the floor work is presumably the same as anywhere else.

MR. FRANK ELLIS. *In view of your present ideas of serial takes what is your present opinion of the old ideas of cutting that one reads about? Aren't you losing too much time tracking in and out?*

---

From *The Cine-Technician*, November-December 1948, pp. 174–76, 178. The first part of this article, the text of a talk by Hitchcock, has been republished in *Hitchcock on Hitchcock*. The concluding question and answer session is reprinted here for the first time.

THE AUTHOR. Quick cutting is useful still. I am still doing it. With the continual technique you are constantly filling in your pattern of scene stories. You cannot track in and out on dead footage. In the old system it was not kept going but now you must, and keep the dialogue alive.

In a scene from *Notorious* the camera had to follow the characters from a vestibule to a telephone and out into a hallway. The story and dialogue continue all through that. You get back from a distance and see people move. If you maintain close interest and keep the audience close to the people, even though they are moving, you can maintain the concentration on the scene regardless of its geographical movement.

MR. CHARLES FREND. *How much of the dialogue was generally post-synced in the two reels we have seen?*
THE AUTHOR. Not more than about 20 per cent. Only when there was movement through a door from one room to another was post-syncing necessary. In that picture we had one and a half hours dubbing. After each take a full sound was done. Due to the fact that artistes had long rehearsals beforehand it was like a stage performance. We did it through again and when you had got it that was it. Only 15 or 20 lines had to be post-synced.

MR. RIDLEY. *What are the reactions of the actors to this new technique and is there more rehearsal?*
THE AUTHOR. The actors run through the whole movement with rough lines and once the scene was laid out and the light-men were at work I would go off to another stage where there was a dummy set and rehearse the cast completely. Every movement had to be perfect. First we went through the lines and then went over to the physical side and did that. Then we would go back to the real set, but I was always ready long before the lighting.

MR. RIDLEY. *Don't stage actors prefer this type of take?*
THE AUTHOR. The only complaints are from the temperamental ones who call the camera coming nearer "like a devouring dragon." When they see the result on the screen it is a case of "I see it all now."

The system is more exacting on the actor. Coming back in the car Joseph Cotten was completely exhausted. He told me that he felt very tired after every long scene because of the amount of action required on his part.

MR. KENNETH ANNAKIN. *The camera should be unobtrusive and should not be felt consciously by the audience. Isn't there a danger in the continuous swinging around that it is annoying to the audience?*

THE AUTHOR. It depends how near you are to the individual. Naturally nothing is perfect and there are imperfections. The main object is to move the actor and not the camera.

MR. FRANCIS RODKER. *On long scenes taking nine and a half minutes would you not find that the actors had felt great strain after a time? Is it your intention to film, as far as possible, scenes of that length?*
THE AUTHOR. It depends entirely on the scene. In the present picture Ingrid Bergman has a monologue lasting nine minutes and 20 seconds. Most scenes last not more than three and a half minutes. I made no effort to get a long scene for its own sake. It just happens if it fits in.

MR. THOROLD DICKINSON. *After playing a reel for seven or eight minutes, how do you decide what to cut and when to cut?*
THE AUTHOR. It is not an arbitrary cut, it is a dramatic cut.

A VISITOR. *In the last two reels of the film* Rope *why did we see so little of the third character, and why was the camera always kept on the speakers' faces?*
THE AUTHOR. It depends whether the third character has anything of interest to say or do. In this case he could not add anything of dramatic importance to the scene. If you wanted to look at the third character you must have been bored and that meant that the other two were not good enough.

There has been a habit of chopping the camera over from one person who is speaking to another just listening. I think there is nothing duller than just looking at a blank face.

MR. WALTER LASSALLY. *When making a film by this new technique do you find yourself bound to stick to the long take technique all through or do you find yourself free to inter-cut short scenes?*
THE AUTHOR. No. In my present picture I mix techniques.

MR. GORDON HALES. *In the last two scenes of* Rope *how were the dialogue and effects done? Was it built up of several pieces of dialogue track?*
THE AUTHOR. I had the street scene written as a dialogue scene. We went out on the back lot and put a mike up about six storeys high and played the scene on the back lot. The recording of the car siren was started one and a

half miles away. I refused the many sirens that the stock department offered. Sound tracks were made on the actual location of this eleventh storey apartment in New York in the hours during the actual time it was being played.

MISS KAY MANDER.  *In these long scenes the camera is presumably not on tracks but on a free dolly.*
THE AUTHOR.  That's right.

MISS MANDER.  *How are the camera crew cued, and do the actors have to pay attention to the camera?*
THE AUTHOR.  When the first rehearsal takes place the camera crew have their rehearsal period. In *Rope* there was a 10 day period of camera rehearsal only. We had a spotlight underneath the lens hitting the floor and when the camera hit the position, that spot was marked on the floor with a number for position. Also there was a backmark for the dolly itself. So there were two sets of marks, one of the dolly position and one for the front lens because of the swing of the arm. All the shots were marked out on a plan in squares and this made re-takes easy. We re-took five reels because of colour problems.

MISS MANDER.  *How were the cues given?*
THE AUTHOR.  The continuity girl on the back of the dolly did the dolly cueing by tapping the operator on the shoulder when he was in position. A man with a pointer pointed to the next spot so that the man swinging the arm would know where to go.

MR. TANNER.  *What is the work of the editor?*
THE AUTHOR.  The editor works on the script ahead of shooting. My present picture was laid out in the rough and the editor made his comments after the cameraman. He now works on paper, not on the film.

MR. A. FARMER.  *You say your shooting script was a visual script with sketches.*
THE AUTHOR.  Yes.

MR. STANLEY IRVING.  *With everything pre-planned where is the director situated during the actual shooting?*

THE AUTHOR. I don't look. I am just praying the shot gets through and looking the other way.

MR. PETER HOYLE. *Has the boom operator plenty of opportunity for rehearsal?*

THE AUTHOR. He gets more opportunities for rehearsal this way than the other way. Nothing is improvised.

MR. RIDLEY. *You described among other things the correct way of preparing your detailed script. It reminded me very much of the Independent Frame process. What are your reactions to Independent Frame?*

THE AUTHOR. I don't know anything about it. I gather that it is as though you had made a picture and took all the cuts apart and set them up individually. It feels to me as though there is a restriction of movement.

MR. J. ADKINS. *If you can have attached to your camera a television system showing the picture all the time, do you think, in spite of your tendency to look the other way, that it would be advantageous?*

THE AUTHOR. Definitely. This *is* television. There is a great similarity in technique.

MR. T. MARSHALL. *As the technicians take over while the actual scene is being shot who, in that case, decides whether there should be another take of that particular shot?*

THE AUTHOR. It is a committee decision.

MR. RIDLEY. *You mentioned the similarity to television but television sometimes uses two or three cameras.*

THE AUTHOR. Television is using the technique that we used on the first sound pictures in 1929.

MR. LAWSON. *I have to disagree with that. It depends a lot on the producer. Some producers use the old fashioned technique. Others use a similar technique to what you are now using.*

MR. CHARLES FREND. *What is the time saved on the over-all schedule?*

THE AUTHOR. The time saved is about 25 per cent. *Rope* ran for 7,200 feet and was shot in 36 days, including 10 days rehearsal and five reels of re-take. It was a short picture but the present picture I am doing will end up about 55 days.

MR. FREND. *What about comparative budget costs?*
THE AUTHOR. When you shoot ahead of schedule you have merely a saving of time. In *Spellbound* the schedule was 57 days and the picture was completed in 48 days. Although 20 per cent of the time was saved there was only a saving of 10 per cent of the cost. The costs of the story and salaries of the stars, and director, were the same.

A VISITOR. *Is there no saving in set construction?*
THE AUTHOR. About 20 per cent.

MR. M. HARVEY. *Do you feel you will be limited in the type of story you can handle by this method?*
THE AUTHOR. No. If you have a story with a number of sequences you can take each sequence and treat it in this way. You can also mix your technique. Certain sequences you can shoot in continuous takes and others you can cut.

MR. IRVING. *Have you felt that the old method of shooting has been wrong and was that why you went over to long takes?*
THE AUTHOR. I have been doing the new system for a long time. In *Rope* I think it was automatic because the subject of the story played in its own time. This story plays in one hour, twenty minutes. It plays in its own set. I felt it was an opportunity to develop the thing to give the audience a feeling of not being interrupted by anyone.

The system does not restrict you to any story because you can do whole sequences in a story by the same method. But very few stories play in the same time that you see them on the screen, which is one of the ideal things about motion pictures. The nearest thing you get is the short story where you take a single idea and go through it.

MR. KENNETH ANNAKIN. *Is it possible to get to the stage where you can prepare entirely on paper and the results you get are exactly as you expected? When the thing becomes film and you get your first rough out it does take on a slightly different life of its own from that of the paper. Do you feel that it is impossible to* get a complete conception on paper so that in the film you don't want to take any-thing away?

THE AUTHOR. I have a complete conception of the film in the mind and not on paper. It has to be built. Add something to it on the stage. If you are bothered about a rough script then you are storytelling when you should have already done so.

MR. ANNAKIN. *Do you find that after getting an idea for a sequence that when you come to rehearse the actor his personality, or the way he is reacting under your direction, causes you to alter the plan?*

THE AUTHOR. Sometimes. I don't think that you should restrict the actor to the marks on the floor. You have to give him a certain amount of stage and you must be prepared to make adjustments.

MR. MAX SANDERS. *Do you feel that to some extent the continual technique restricts the audience? With it one can never go to the viewpoint of one of the characters.*

THE AUTHOR. That depends on whether you are using a subjective treat-ment. In *Rope* we were not using a subjective treatment. The audience is not a technical audience. The movie-going public will not necessarily say "I missed a close-up there." The physical eye is constantly moving.

MR. LINDGREN. *I could not help being conscious of the dominance of the dia-logue in* Rope.

THE AUTHOR. It is in the nature of the subject and not the technique. Pat-rick Hamilton's play is stuck to pretty closely.

A VISITOR. *The opening of the lid of the chest broke my continuity. Was there some purpose in doing so?*

THE AUTHOR. That was the end of a set-up. We were limited to the amount of film in the camera.

MR. A. LEWIS. *If you don't watch the scene when it is being shot and don't go to the rushes, when do you see the film and do you like it?*

THE AUTHOR. I avoid it like the plague and I am not a movie-goer.

MR. PEARCE. *As you are largely limited to two shots, very much in profile, do your actors have to give a little more than in normal technique?*
THE AUTHOR. That is not strictly so. The actors are making their own close-ups when they move. Acting technique should be nearer the stage. In movies we have been awfully lazy and we have just staged the scene around to pick up the actor's face wherever it may be. By letting the actor move around he tends to help us more.

MR. J. MILLS. *Can the system be adapted to a smaller studio? It seems rather necessary to be able to rehearse outside the stage in which you are shooting.*
THE AUTHOR. You want a large stage to get outside the confines of the set, but I have rehearsed in a scene dock. You don't have to have another stage to rehearse.

MR. RIDLEY. *Have you ever filmed large crowd scenes by this method?*
THE AUTHOR. Yes, but the scene was not longer than about two minutes because there was a dramatic reason for breaking it up. You rehearse the crowd independently of camera movement.

A VISITOR. *Do the long takes necessitate better equipment than we have in this country?*
THE AUTHOR. It needs an electric dolly because it is more mobile and more sensitive.

A VISITOR. *Wasn't the old method of shooting a habit rather than a necessity? A mixture of the two techniques to an audience conditioned to the older technique will tend to break into relief this newer technique.*
THE AUTHOR. You can only mix the two in relation to the dramatic content of the scene. If you have a film where the dramatic content is more coloured you can use the cutting technique for the purpose of excitement.

A VISITOR. *There must be a certain amount of wasted frame at some point in the long take which is not as good as you would like it to be. That tends to increase audience consciousness of camera technique.*
THE AUTHOR. That depends on whether the content of the film is interesting to the audience.

A  V I S I T O R .  *How does the longer take effect the stills cameraman?*
T H E  A U T H O R .  The still man has a take all for himself. We are now doing stills in action. We play the film just the same and the still man goes through and takes instantaneous pictures and the result is quite astounding.

A  V I S I T O R .  *Does the dolly run on the normal studio floor?*
T H E  A U T H O R .  In each case we have had to lay a special floor because we found that the average studio floor was not at all good for a camera without tracks. Floors wave and warp. At present we have an asphalt floor covering the whole studio. In *Rope* a wooden floor was placed on top of the one in the studio.

M R .  T H O R O L D  D I C K I N S O N .  *Did the dialogue of the play have to be altered much?*
T H E  A U T H O R .  We had to make cuts in Hamilton's play of *Rope* but I felt he had one glaring omission. He invited the parents of the dead boy to a party but made no mention of the boy while they were there as guests of their son's friends. We changed the device of a theatre ticket in the play and used a piece of rope as the main clue. We also emphasised the attitude of the younger boy as a clue. One of the main items of the film is that the father of the dead boy is given some books, and these books are tied with the piece of rope that strangled the boy. They are the main changes and the dialogue was developed a bit.

M R .  A .  F A R M E R .  *Most of your past films have used original scripts written for the screen. Now you have gone to plays do you intend to continue to do so?*
T H E  A U T H O R .  I used the play because the story was very suitable for the technique, but I still feel that film scripts should be written as film scripts.

A  V I S I T O R .  *In the early part of* Rope, *which we have not seen, do we ever see the fourth wall of the room?*
T H E  A U T H O R .  Yes. The camera goes right round and shows one corner of the fourth wall.

M R .  T A N N E R .  *Was there any special reason for using Technicolor in* Rope?
T H E  A U T H O R .  It is used to make the set more elegant and add mood to the picture. It is played in bright light. No devices, like darkened corners, are

used and colour was included to give it even more brightness and light. I know no other colour system than Technicolor.

A VISITOR. *Has the lighting cameraman restrictions which don't give him such good results as under normal conditions?*
THE AUTHOR. With all the restrictions we are getting excellent results on our present picture.

A VISITOR. *Do you think the new technique will be applied to all your future films?*
THE AUTHOR. Where it is useful, and within a given sequence, this technique will be applied to my other films. If you have a sequence that is an objective one you obviously must cross-cut.

A VISITOR. *Did you ever feel that you had sacrificed one part of a shot because the whole shot had gone through?*
THE AUTHOR. Sometimes, yes.

MR. RIDLEY. *Does it take time to train technicians in the new technique?*
THE AUTHOR. It adds to the cost of the first week. After that it's O.K.

A VISITOR. *Can you show on the script your camera movements?*
THE AUTHOR. You show your main positions and you indicate the movement from that particular set-up to the next one—a series of punctuations.

A VISITOR. *Is your visual script in the form of perspective drawings, or of plans?*
THE AUTHOR. Both; a plan of the sequence with drawings of all key movements. They are very rough.

A VISITOR. *How much longer does this method take to plan out?*
THE AUTHOR. As long as you can give it. Two or three months if necessary. Once you have your script ready the editor, cameramen and art director will spend two or three weeks of concentrated work. By the older method once they have a script, if they have a script, they go right into the studio and work it out on the stage while all the electricians are hanging around.

MR. THOROLD DICKINSON. *We must now close the discussion, which was intensely interesting, and own that this new method has a certain austerity in it. It comes off with a director with the visual sense of "Hitch," but a director who has not that visual sense may provide you with a duller picture than the old method in the hands of the expert.*

# Alfred Hitchcock's Working Credo

## GERALD PRATLEY/1950

''HITCH,'' AS ALFRED HITCHCOCK is called by everybody who works with him, arrived in Quebec to make *I Confess* with Anne Baxter and Montgomery Clift, 50 technicians, and Robert Burks, his cameraman, who also photographed *Strangers on a Train*. He was followed by three trucks laden with everything necessary for location shooting. It had taken 11 days to come from California.

Hitchcock had mulled *I Confess* over for three years. It is based on a French play of 1902 by Louis Verneuil [actually Paul Anthelme (Bourde), although Verneuil brought it to Hitchcock—ed.] and involves a murder and the sanctity of the Confessional. He had given his personal attention to the script, as it was being written by George Tabori and William Archibald, for everything in Hitchcock pictures is thought out in advance. They are never edited, and the sequences he shoots are merely assembled.

Because Alfred Hitchcock is an affable man and is never worried while shooting—he discusses the set-ups the night before and leaves the issuing of almost all the orders to Cameraman Burks—I did not hesitate to ask him to take a little time out so that I might interview him for the Canadian Broadcasting Company's network.

He began answering my questions by saying he regarded *Shadow of a Doubt* as the best picture he has made in America, and *Blackmail* and *The Lady Vanishes* as the best pictures of his preceding British period.

From *Films in Review*, 3, no. 10 (December 1952), 500–03.

He then remarked that he rarely went to see the work of other directors lest he unconsciously plagiarize their ideas.

To my observation that *I Confess* was a rather odd film for him to make, he replied:

"Well, I like to make different kinds of melodramas. Some are more or less exciting action pictures. Others are more psychological. *Shadow of a Doubt* has psychological overtones and is set in a small American town. *I Confess* is somewhat similar, except it's laid in the city of Quebec. First, because the original story had a French setting, but chiefly because our treatment of the script calls for the murderer, who works in a rectory, to put on a cassock as a kind of disguise. He is seen leaving the house by two little girls and the whole plot starts from this "springboard situation" as we call it. Now there's no other town on the North American continent, at least to my knowledge, where priests walk around wearing their cassocks, so Quebec is the only suitable city in which to start the plot this way."

I asked him if he liked shooting on location.

"Yes. The film that met most of the conditions I enjoy working under was *Shadow of a Doubt*, which was a location job. Thornton Wilder and I went to a town and—what is the American word—we cased it. Then we went back and wrote the script and later shot the film in that town. It was quite strongly characterized and I found it very satisfying shooting the whole thing in a real town, just as we are doing now in Quebec. After all, motion pictures were driven into the studios by sound. Until sound they had always been made in the open. I prefer shooting on location because it enables you to utilize atmosphere. The only drawback is, when you get down to intimate scenes, it's very difficult to concentrate."

Which I took to be an allusion to the fact that more than 8,000 people had watched him shoot a scene with Baxter and Clift on the promenade overlooking the St. Lawrence river.

I asked him if he devised his "touches" before filming begins.

"Oh yes," he answered quickly. "You must. The preparation required is quite considerable. If you think of it on the spur of the moment it might take a whole day to rearrange things so you could include it. The films I make are usually edited prior to shooting. In other words, I don't guess at what we are going to put on the screen and shoot a lot of material and then see how it works out in the cutting room. I like to have a completely preconceived idea as to how the film is to be cut, and I shoot it accordingly. With regard to sound, it depends on what I have written in the script. Like cuts, sound effects should be in one's mind before one starts the picture so they can be incorporated into the script and included as we go along."

I said that an effective Hitchcock touch in *Strangers on a Train* had been his photographing the strangulation reflected in the lenses of the victim's glasses as they lay on the ground.

"That involved a double printing job," he said. "We took a large concave mirror and photographed the murder scene in it. Next, we photographed the glasses as they lay on the grass. Then the image filmed in the concave mirror was diminished and printed into the frames of the glasses."

Thereupon I ventured the remark that unlike some directors, who want to make films their way, and run into opposition from studio executives, he seemed to get along without much trouble.

"One is always compromising about almost everything," he answered soberly. "You compromise on casting when you put a star in a role. The novelist always has ideal casting in mind in his novel because he creates a character and has complete freedom in shaping it. If one were making a film purely for artistic purposes or shall we say—I really hate the word artistic—a film that is fully integrated as far as characters are concerned, you would certainly cast it with unknown people, just as the novelist casts his novel with unknown people. But with stars we bend a little bit and don't quite get the character we had in mind. So there is where compromise starts.

"On the other hand, from the audience's point of view, the star helps, because he or she increases the potency of the story, so far as the audience is concerned. To take a crude example: if the heroine is tied to a railroad track and the train is bearing down on her, and the audience doesn't know who she is, it will say, how awful, the poor woman is going to be killed. But if it's a star like Claudette Colbert or Greer Garson, then they are going to scream because it's like a relative being run over. The effectiveness is increased a hundred fold.

"I had to compromise in *The Paradine Case*. Selznick wanted Gregory Peck to play an English lawyer. Well, the public knew that he was Gregory Peck and that he was an American so they naturally weren't so affected storywise as if he had been an English actor indigenous to the scene like Ralph Richardson, Laurence Olivier, or Ronald Colman, even though Colman has been in America a long time."

I asked Hitchcock if he agreed with John Huston about directing actors. He replied that he did up to a point and added:

"However, if you are shooting a naturally pre-cut picture you can't just turn the actor loose. He may not react visually to conform with the cut effects you may require.

"We must not forget that the basis of cinema is the way two pieces of film are joined together to make a common effect. It is the essence of the subjective element of film making. An actor looks at an object and you cut to that object, which makes another piece of film. When you join it to the actor's look it makes a complete scene."

I asked him if he was satisfied with the kind of films he makes.

"When you say satisfied, it depends on what kind of satisfaction," he answered forthrightly. "If you mean the satisfaction of serving your employer to the best of your ability, I would say yes. As for one's own satisfaction, well, frankly, I have too much conscience to take a million dollars and make a film that would please only me and the critics. I don't think that's really what one should do.

"I might like to make a film that would satisfy me completely but a lot of people probably wouldn't like it. One often hears of films that play art theatres and are seen by very few people. But our medium happens to have a universal appeal, and it would seem to me that making a film to show to one's friends and to critics who are rarely satisfied, is a different thing from making films to appeal to the vast public.

"I would say it is harder to make a film that has both integrity and wide audience appeal than it is to make one that merely satisfies one's own artistic conscience. It is difficult to say what the director's responsibility is. It can be either commercial or artistic—only in rare cases can it be both. I think a director's responsibilities are to his employers to a great extent.

"After all, they have invested a large amount of money in the picture. But the director also has a responsibility to his conscience not to compromise too much. So, in the end, it is really a kind of constant tight-rope walking."

# Story of an Interview

## CLAUDE CHABROL/1954

IT ALL BEGINS WITH a phone call from my friend François Truffaut. Mme. Ferry from Paramount has invited representatives of *Cahiers* to a press conference given by Alfred Hitchcock in his rooms at the Hotel George V.

We prepare carefully for it: the soon-to-be indispensable tape recorder in one hand and paper in the other, and in our hearts more fear than hope—because we have in mind reports from André Bazin, in his role as special correspondent to Cannes, reports that are not very encouraging from our point of view.

Mme. Ferry receives us at the door of suite 104–105 and introduces us. The gathering is rather eclectic: France Roche, Robert Chazal, Didier Daix, for *Le Figaro*, and several charming ladies. Hitch, who is not so overweight as he used to be, gets us chairs. Everyone is clustered around him, ready to drink in his words. He invites us to ask questions. The first ones concern *To Catch a Thief*. He is very content; he has experienced no difficulty filming in France, except for the sun that too often refused to shine. At Monte Carlo he's had a sumptuous restaurant constructed, which in his opinion deserves three stars in the Michelin guide, with a tree in front and the casino in the background, and the whole in VistaVision. Georgette Anys is also in VistaVision. Someone

"Histoire d'une Interview," *Cahiers du cinéma*, no. 39 (Oct. 1954): 39–44. Translated from the French by James M. Vest. (Portions of this translation are included in his book, *Hitchcock and France: The Forging of an Auteur*, forthcoming from Praeger.) Words between asterisks are in English in the original French text, a feature worth preserving since part of the story of this interview hinges on wordplay and misinterpretations.

finds her dimensions perfectly suited for such a process; Hitchcock jokes. Somebody asks how he chose his French actors. He looks surprised and replies, "By looking at the films they've made." There follows an amused critique of the annoying craze of using passers-by for important roles.

Then he attempts to solicit other, more serious questions. I look at Truffaut, who looks at me. We don't know where to begin with this crafty dissembler. We try to hook up the tape recorder and it refuses to start (a point against the Hotel George V, whose electrical outlets don't work). Meanwhile the conversation has moved to *Rear Window*, about which the auteur speaks at great length, all the while making fun of us: "We built thirty-two apartments, of which twelve were completely furnished, with bathrooms and all." Then he adds, magisterially, "We'll see everything from the apartment of James Stewart. What goes on in that apartment will be enacted normally and all the rest in pantomime. So there are two techniques. Two different techniques in the film."

If this continues, we'll go away empty-handed. So I decided to ask him a question calculated to get him to say something interesting. I reflect a little while before asking it: "What would you say is your worst American film?" I have the satisfaction of watching him ruminate, smelling a trap—and the disappointment of hearing him put me in checkmate, with a big laugh: "All of them." We all protest, mentioning titles, lots of titles. For each one, he admits certain good qualities. So none of this is serious; he's just taking us for a ride.

I throw out *Under Capricorn*. He claims to have personal reasons for not liking it (his falling out with Bergman) and says that film has not been successful in America because people consider him—Hitchcock—as a maker of "thrillers" just as C. B. De Mille is considered a maker of epics, and people are disappointed not to have cold shivers when they see *Under Capricorn*. With perfect disingenuousness, he proceeds to add: "This is a film for Bergman, not a Hitchcock film." It would be easy to respond that he was already preparing this film when he was making *The Paradine Case*, but I refrain from putting him on the spot in front of everyone. He gives the appearance of wanting to uphold the legend of Hitchcock, master of anxiety, of Hitchcock the commercial filmmaker, the money-maker. All the same I ask him point blank whether Transatlantic Pictures is really him. He reassures me: it is. And the Transatlantic films would be *Rope* and *Under Capricorn*? Yes, that's *Rope* and *Under Capricorn*. I refrain from mentioning a small contradiction with his answers to Bazin: since *Under Capricorn* did not make money he was not such a good businessman after all.

He returns to *Rear Window* and *Dial M for Murder* and notes their use of color for dramatic rather than pictorial ends. He talks about his appearances in his films. He comes close to talking about his diet. He repeats anecdotes that apparently have ceased to make him laugh some time ago. Then he speaks of his next project, "a story about a corpse that a little boy discovers," that will also be in VistaVision. France Roche, who seems bored (that's bad, because all this is very amusing, if not very productive!), attempts to advance the debate in her own way: "Are thrillers a commercial vehicle for you or a matter of inner necessity?" "I have always been afraid of the police. I was raised by Jesuits and I've always feared policemen." The ladies laugh. Hitch repositions himself smugly. Then a brief silence. I take advantage of it to uncloak my assault weapons.

"Do you believe in the devil?"

Something happens. With a slightly astonished air, he fixes me with his eyes. He blurts out:

"But the devil is in each of us."

He tells stories about *Rear Window*. I ask whether he liked *I Confess*. He answers, "So-so. It lacks humor." He turns toward the ladies: "I like the macabre in a sunbeam." The ladies burst into laughter and look at the ceiling as if inspired.

Thinking this an excellent concluding point, he asks if we have any other questions, but is clearly disposed to dismiss us. I ask him whether he participates in the preparation of his scripts. "Very closely," is the answer, "from the beginning to the end, and I have the final word on the shooting script." It would be easy to reply that in that case he can make the films he wants, but he would hide behind those well-known commercial restrictions that he brandishes like a shield.

Wanting to show him that I'll not be taken in, I hazard a final question that strikes Robert Chazal as daft (he's wrong):

"In *I Confess*, the water glass balanced on the Prosecutor's forehead . . . is that idea yours?"

At first he doesn't understand, or pretends not to. I act out the scene. He smiles, then says, "Yes, that idea is mine."

Trying to establish a rapport between us, I affirm that it's an excellent idea. The ladies agree.

This time, it's over. Everyone stands up to leave. He shakes hands with each one in turn, as at a funeral. He has indeed done us in. We thank him; he thanks us. Truffaut and I leave last, dejectedly. In the hallway France Roche vents her disappointment: "Even somebody like Mervyn LeRoy will eventually say something interesting."

We return to the *Cahiers* office, our heads lowered. Then Truffaut has an inspiration. He suggests I call back to the George V. I get Hitchcock on the line and request a few more minutes to ask four or five questions. He tells me he will be leaving the hotel in twenty minutes. I express my disappointment but don't insist for fear of intruding. An initial kindness: he invites me to ask these questions over the phone. I make an attempt: "What is the figure in your carpet?"

"The what?"

"The figure in your carpet?"

Oh. Yes. *Well. Come up. Five minutes.*"

I don't wait to be asked twice.

He's standing at a table filling out a form. A small graying woman—Alma Reville, I suppose—is packing the bags. She shows me in. Hitch is all smiles, all kindness. He invites me to sit and looks me in the eye.

"*Well!*"

I've carefully prepared my question. I am only half-satisfied with it, since it expresses something false or at least inexact; however it has, I think, the advantage of immediately situating the debate on a higher level and of not wasting time getting him to say what I'd like him to say. So I set it forth:

"Some of my colleagues and I (forgive me, please, Schérer, Rivette, Truffaut, for this breach of trust) have discovered in your works a carefully hidden theme, and that is the search for God. What do you think of that?

In my somewhat flawed English I said "*Search of God.*" He understands somewhat imperfectly and what he says is revealing.

"*Search of good?* Oh yes, yes; there is a search of good."

His look is full of sympathy. France Roche would be happy: he seems much more intelligent than earlier. But I set things straight.

"Not good: God himself."

He looks somewhat astonished, or rather surprised.

"God! A search of God? Maybe, but it is unconscious."

I attempt to justify my question, because I'm far from convinced. I want to get him to talk.

"You understand, your heroes are caught in a net of evil."

I say "*evil.*" He corrects on his own: "*Of Devil, yes they are.*"

". . . and they can escape only through avowal, through confession."

"Sincere confession, yes; contrition."

He adds with a disconcerting smile, "But I become aware of it only after the fact." These disclaimers are all the more disturbing since he makes it very clear that they are indeed dissimulations. I counter with a specific example:

"In *Strangers on a Train*, when Farley Granger phones his wife and, becoming furious, threatens her life, his words are covered by the sound of a train. The symbolism is obvious."

His smile deepens.

"There, of course, I was aware beforehand."

And in his turn he confesses.

"You see, for me the screenplay is nearly secondary. I make the film before knowing the story. It comes to me as a form, as an impression of a whole. Afterward I develop a script and make it correspond to what I have in my mind.

"But all stories don't suit you."

"No. Certainly not. I select one that I can make correspond to what I have in my head, and with the writers I adapt it to suit me. And often that no longer resembles the original story. I chose the novel on which *Stage Fright* is based because the girl falls in love with a detective and doesn't know which way is up."

"And the setting?"

"It has no importance in and of itself. The problems have always been the same. I pay attention to the setting for credibility."

"We are far from realism."

"I'm not a realist at all. I am drawn to the fantastic. I see things *larger than life.*"

"Metaphysically?"

"*Thank you.* That's why I love melodrama (not exactly melodrama in the pejorative sense, but drama with lots of ups and downs). Realism shows people on a certain level, uniform. Melodrama diminishes them to the lowest level, and I attempt to bring them up as high as possible."

He gesticulates broadly as he speaks, tracing horizontal planes, then raising his hands suddenly like a geyser.

I don't want to outstay my welcome. From the corner of my eye, I see the last bag being latched. I stand up and ask politely:

"*Really, you don't like your American films?*"

He laughs as he shakes my hand:

"*Not really.*"

# Hitchcock

## IAN CAMERON AND V. F. PERKINS/ 1963

*Can you tell us something about* The Birds?
It's taken from a well-known short story by Daphne du Maurier. It concerns the attack by domestic birds on a group of people living in a community: the film is laid in northern California, northern San Francisco. The series of attacks start very mildly and increase in seriousness as it goes on.

*What would you say was the theme of the film?*
If you like you can make it the theme of too much complacency in the world: that people are unaware that catastrophe surrounds us all.

*The people are unwilling to believe that the birds are going to take over?*
That's true, yes.

*What particularly attracted you to science fiction?*
This isn't science fiction at all, not at all. It's treated quite naturally and quite straightforwardly. Many of the incidents in the film are based on actual fact. Birds have attacked and do attack, all the time. As a matter of fact, one of the incidents we have in the film was based on an actual incident which occurred at La Jolla, California, on April 30, 1960. A thousand swifts came down a chimney into the living room of some people. These are birds that nest in masonry rather than in trees, in roofs and chimneys and so forth. And the people were completely swamped with them for half an hour.

From *Movie*, no. 6 (January 1963), pp. 4–6.

Another incident occurred in the very place we were working, in Bodega Bay in northern San Francisco, where a farmer reported to the *San Francisco Chronicle* that he was losing a lot of lambs due to crows diving and pecking at their eyes and then killing them. So there are precedents for all these things. That's what makes it more or less accurate, in terms of facts rather than science-fiction.

*There are also precedents in your films for birds, aren't there? Particularly in* Psycho.
Oh yes.

*Is this any particular fondness for birds?*
Not particularly, no.

*Do you find them threatening in some way?*
No. No, not at all. I'm personally not interested in that side of content. I'm more interested in the technique of story telling by means of film rather than in what the film contains.

*As far as telling this particular story goes, had you a lot of problems?*
Oh, I wasn't meaning technical problems. I was meaning the technique of story telling on film *per se*. Oh no, the technical problems are prodigious. I mean films like *Ben Hur* or *Cleopatra* are child's play compared with this. After all we had to train birds for every shot practically.

*You had some trouble with the American version of the R.S.P.C.A. . . . .*
Not really; that was a technicality. You're allowed to catch so many birds. I think the bird-trainer had about four over his quota, really.

*Did you restrict yourself in the bird kingdom, or did every sort of bird take over?*
Oh no. No birds of prey at all. Purely domestic birds. Seagulls. Birds you see every day. Seagulls, crows, ravens, finches, and canaries and that sort of bird.

*You're not using music?*
No music at all, no. We're using electronic sound, all the way through, a simulated sound of actual things. For example the sound of birds' wings and

birds' cries will be stylised to some extent. And that will occur all the way through the picture.

*You have used music a lot in your previous films. This is going to fulfill exactly the role of music?*
Oh, it should do, yes. After all, when you put music to film, it's really sound, it isn't music *per se*. I mean there's an abstract approach. The music serves as either a counterpoint or a comment on whatever scene is being played. I mean we don't have what you call "tunes" in it at all.

*The shrilling in* Psycho *is rather of that sort.*
Yes, you see you have the screaming violins. It was a motif that went through the murder scenes.

*You will use your strange sounds as motifs in that way?*
Yes.

*I hear* Psycho *made a lot of money.*
Yes, that was a secondary consideration. *Psycho* is probably one of the most cinematic films I've made and there you get a clear example of the use of film to cause an audience to respond emotionally.

*It was primarily an emotional response you were after from your audience?*
Entirely. That's the whole device. After all, the showing of a violent murder at the beginning was intended purely to instill into the minds of the audience a certain degree of fear of what is to come. Actually in the film, as it goes on, there's less and less violence because it has been transferred to the minds of the audience.

*The use of Janet Leigh to be killed early in the film, is to upset one's sense of security because the star is expected to survive to the end.*
Oh, no question about it. The ordinary person would have said "Janet Leigh, she's the leading lady, she must play the lead." But that was not the intention at all. The intention in the early part was to portray average people and in this particular case to deliberately divert the audience's attention into a character in trouble, you see. And you follow the adventures of a girl deliber-

ately detailed to keep you away from anything that's going to turn up later on, you see.

North by Northwest. *Near the beginning, in the mad car chase, one knows that Cary Grant can't be killed this early. So why is one excited?*
That again is purely the use of film in terms of the substitution of the language of the camera for words. That is the most important function of film. As a substitute for words. I wouldn't say substitute. I don't think that does film even sufficient justice. It's the mode of expression. And the use of the size of the image. And the juxtaposition of different pieces of film to create emotion in a person. And you can make it strong enough even to make them forget reason. You see when you say that Cary Grant can't possibly be killed so early in the film, that's the application of reason. But you're not permitted to reason. Because the film should be stronger than reason.

*Above all of your films the one that seems stronger than reason is* Vertigo.
There you get, in a sense, a remote fantasy. In *Vertigo* you have a feeling of remoteness from ordinary worldly things. You see the attitude of the man, the woman's behaviour. Of course behind it lies some kind of plot, which I think is quite secondary. I don't bother about plot, or all that kind of thing.

*You got rid of it very early in the film.*
Yes, that's, what shall I call it? That's a necessary evil. But that's why I'm always surprised at people and even critics who place so much reliance on logic and all that sort of thing. I have a little phrase to myself. I always say logic is dull.

*You seem rather to distrust the psychiatrist's explanation of Norman Bates in* Psycho. *It isn't given all that much weight.*
Possibly the details would have been too unpleasant. I think that there perhaps we're skimming over . . . You have to remember that *Psycho* is a film made with quite a sense of amusement on my part. To me it's a *fun* picture. The processes through which we take the audience, you see, it's rather like taking them through the haunted house at the fairground or the roller-coaster, you know. After all it stands to reason that if one were seriously doing the *Psycho* story, it would be a case history. You would never present it in forms of mystery or the juxtaposition of characters, as they were placed in

the film. They were all designed in a certain way to create this audience emotion. Probably the real *Psycho* story wouldn't have been emotional at all; it would've been terribly clinical.

*Psycho is, though, very honestly presented. There is a very striking shot of Norman Bates swinging his hips as he goes upstairs. When one sees the film for the second time, one realises one* could *have solved the mystery the first time.*
Well, I'm a great believer in making sure that if people see the film a second time they don't feel cheated. That is a *must*. You must be honest about it and not merely keep things away from an audience. I'd call that *cheating*. You should never do that.

*Was this shot meant deliberately as a clue?*
Well, you might as well say that the basic clue was in the feminine nature of the character altogether.

*The very complex montage of the murder of Janet Leigh was not just intended to avoid showing some things you couldn't show . . .*
Well, I did photograph a nude girl all the way through. In other words I covered in the shooting every aspect of the killing. Actually some of it was shot in slow motion. I had the camera slow and the girl moving slowly so that I could measure out the movements and the covering of awkward parts of the body, the arm movement, gesture and so forth. I was actually seven days on that little thing; it's only forty-five seconds really.

*Is there a sexual reference in the compositions? It seemed that you were consciously cutting between soft round shapes and the hard, phallic shape of the knife to suggest copulation.*
Well, I mean you would get that in any case, with any sense of intimate nudity those thoughts would emerge naturally. But the most obvious example of that is in *North by Northwest*, the last shot with the train going into the tunnel.

*One feels of your later films that you have got much less interested in the mystery thriller element, much more interested in broadening things out.*
Well, I think it's a natural tendency to be less superficial, that's Truffaut's opinion—he's been examining all these films. And he feels that the Ameri-

can period is much stronger than the English period. It's a much stronger development. For example, I think it's necessary to get a little deeper into these things as one goes along. For example *The Birds*—you see usually in these films, which I call an "event" film—you know, like *On the Beach*, or one of those things—I felt it was much more necessary to intensify the personal story so that you get, as a result, a greater identification with the people, and therefore the fire through which you put them is much stronger.

*In* Psycho *you presumably intended the audience to identify with Janet Leigh.*
I wouldn't say *Psycho* was necessarily the best example. Because I felt there that the characters in the second part were merely figures. I was concentrating much more on the effect of the murder and the menace and the background of the boy/mother situation, rather than the other people. But in the case of *The Birds*, I think three of the four characters do go through a process which ties them directly in to the bird attacks.

*In* The Birds *you have worked without stars—or without big stars. Why?*
I felt that one should have anonymous people, not too familiar, because the subject matter itself is not quite so facetious as that of other films: although the birds do attack, it is treated quite realistically. One of the most—to me—satisfying scenes in *The Birds* is where there are no birds seen at all. You have a room which is boarded up—it comes toward the end of the picture—there are four people in the room: a child, young man and woman, and a mother, mother of the young man, sitting there in silence just waiting for them. I just keep that silence going for quite a bit until the first sounds come, then you begin to hear the attack outside and you don't see the mass of birds at all. And it's that kind of thing which permitted one to have comparatively unknown people because the thing belonged as a whole. It wouldn't have looked good to have had a familiar film star sitting there waiting, you know; it's hard to describe why; but this is quite an interesting sequence; to me it's really satisfying because there I threw everything to the audience to use their imagination; to help them along a little bit, I had one shutter blow open. The young man has to pull the shutter to and then you see just the close-up attack on his hand and the seagulls biting and drawing blood.

*The atmosphere sounds similar to that of the sequence in* North by Northwest *where Cary Grant waits at the road-side for Kaplan.*

That was, I would say, an amusing approach. This thing in *The Birds* is not. We've shown the audience sufficient samples—I had one sequence where 300 crows wait outside the schoolhouse for the children, and when the kids come out they are chased down the road: montage sequence of individual crows attacking each child on the back, pecking at them and so forth.

*Little menacing bits of dialogue—do you write these yourself: "Crop-dusting where there ain't no crops" in* North by Northwest?
Oh that's my line, yes.

*How much of your scripts do you in fact write yourself?*
Oh, quite a bit. You see I used to be a writer myself years ago. The difficulty is that one is working in the visual so much—that's why I so rarely use film writers—I always use novelists or playwrights, definitely not people working in the mystery field. They're no use to me at all. In *The Birds*, I opened the film with the shot of birds in their nicest—what *we* think are their nicest— surroundings: in their cages. They're chirruping away, and they're all beauti- fully set—all very happy, ostensibly, and there's a little light-hearted sequence. I treat the film in the beginning as a light comedy and there's some byplay with the girl and the young man where a canary gets out of a cage, and the girl is a rather rich society girl, and she is not aware that the young man knows her identity—when he gets the bird from under his hat he says, "Let's put Melanie Daniels back into her gilded cage, shall we," and that's his way of telling the girl he knows who she is. The pay-off on that one line comes much later in the story when the centre of the town is attacked by seagulls and the girl seeks refuge in a phone booth—it's glass- walled—and she can't get out. I take high shots and you see birds beating all around. The gulls are the people now you see and she's the bird. So I have to write these lines in myself because I know it's going to help appreciably later on. There's no comment made about it, but it's very clear that she's in a cage but it's no longer gilded.

*You expect quite a lot of your audience.*
For those who want it I don't think films should be looked at *once*. I think they go by too fast. But the critics sit in there at their 10:30 a.m. sitting, and they see a film through once and that seems to be sufficient. But I don't really think it is. Most films should be seen through more than once.

*Why is* The Trouble with Harry *a comedy rather than a thriller?*
I think it was a nice little *pastorale*, you know. A typically English piece of
humour, though it was set in America. It was an English novel and we followed it pretty closely. I laid it in the autumnal setting to counterpoint the
macabre of the body, but I even tried to photograph that in an amusing way.

*How do you choose your subjects?*
I don't probe particularly deeply. If something appeals to me . . . I think
instinctively one would go for a subject very often that would lend itself to
one's treatment. I'm not terribly keen on just taking a stage play. As far back
as when I made *Juno and the Paycock* I felt very frustrated about it and kind
of rather ashamed when it got terrific notices. It wasn't anything to do with
me. It belonged to Sean O'Casey. My job was just to put it on the screen. I
think that's the job of any craftsman, setting the camera up and photographing people acting. That's what I call most films today: photographs of people
talking. It's no effort to me to make a film like *Dial M for Murder* because
there's nothing there to do. On the other hand, you say to me: why do you
make a film like *Dial M for Murder*? Because I run for cover when the batteries
are running dry. You know, I might be engaged in a subject which is abor-
tive—I've done that many times, I've been half way through a subject and
found it didn't work out after all—so immediately, instead of waiting, to
keep one's hand in you go for something which is fairly routine while the
batteries are recharging.

*In* North by Northwest, *Grant seems to want Eva Marie Saint dead: he's happier
when she's an enemy or in danger than when she seems to be an available wife or
lover.*
What's that old Oscar Wilde thing? "Each man kills the thing he loves . . ."
That I think is a very natural phenomenon, really.

*You don't find it somewhat perverted?*
Well, everything's perverted in a different way, isn't it?

*Was the falling body at the end of* North by Northwest *a superimposition?*
Yes, that's a double printing job. You photograph your background first and
then you get a white backing and a large arm sticking out of the backing and
you strap the middle of the torso to the arm and then with a side worm gear

men can take that body and do *that* (twisting gesture) with it—Jimmy Stewart's done it as well. Now you take the camera close and whip it back on rails and then also by making the movement slow you can undercrank it too, so that your whip back can be taken care of that way. Then it's superimposed on the background. We're working in *The Birds* on the sodium light system. We're having to double-print a lot of birds over existing birds, where we have a small quantity of birds, trained ones, moving in and out, or whatever they're doing, then you print over that scene a lot of other birds. And we're using a sodium light process, which is a background which is lit by sodium—those yellow fog lights, you know—so that the camera picks up just the images, the background goes black, you get your colour image. And in the camera is a prism and that prism also makes the silhouette matte at the same time on a regular b/w film so that it doesn't register colour. The filter in the prism turns the image black and the sodium background plain. So you make your travelling matte at the same time as you're photographing: we use an old technicolour camera for that.

*You must have been very thrilled with your* Vertigo *effect.*
I've been trying for fifteen, twenty years to get that effect. I first tried it in *Rebecca*. I wanted to get, in an inquest scene, Joan Fontaine to start to faint and see everything receding from her. I tried everything—I even thought of printing a photograph on rubber and stretching the middle.

*You obtained the stretching of the perspective by simultaneously tracking in and zooming out, didn't you?*
Yes.

*We have an argument about* Rear Window. *One of us says that a good deal of the suspense comes from one's not being sure whether James Stewart is right, whether he's making a fool of himself. The other says that you're meant to be certain that he's right and the suspense comes from whether he will prove it in time.*
I would say that it's the latter, because it's frustration you see. The audience *are* with Stewart, the identification is direct and therefore they must feel superior to the other characters with him, but the frustration is there all the same. The interesting thing I think about *Rear Window* is that there's more pure film there, even though it's static, than in many films I've made. After all you get the famous examples that Pudovkin experimented with—where

you get Stewart looking, what he sees, and his reaction to it. And there, after all, is the most powerful thing of film. You've got three pieces of film. Let's assume, for example, Stewart looks, you see a mother and child; then you go back to Stewart and he smiles. Now you see he's rather benevolent or benign, call it what you like. Take the middle piece away and put a nude girl in there and he's a dirty old man.

*Would you say that your films now are rather more thought out than instinctive, and were more instinctive in the thirties?*
I would say so, yes. Well, I think you can have a bit of both really. But I think I got that (*i.e., more intellectual*) when I was aware of the *global* implications of audiences. That's one thing that you do learn in America, because America is a polyglot country. I often tell people, there are no Americans, it's full of foreigners. You become very audience-conscious because there are so many different types of people. Axiomatically you're appealing to your Japanese audience and your Latin-American audience as well.

*The idea of* Stage Fright *intrigues us a great deal. Do you like it?*
No. It wasn't well done. You remember I said I liked to work with playwrights and novelists preferably. I went a bit overboard—I had James Bridie and he was too careless for me, structurally. He used to say, "Well, what does it matter?"

*Whose was the basic idea of the flash-back that wasn't true?*
That was mine, but that was probably an error. That was going a bit too far because I suppose people are so accustomed to flash-backs being true that it was just confusing when it was untrue. It's like the boy with the bomb in *Sabotage*. I should never have let that bomb go off. It was a cardinal error to let that bomb go off. If you work an audience up, it's obligatory to relieve them, to release them from that.

*Having built them up, the explosion didn't release them?*
No, of course not. It got them mad.

*What next?*
I'm going to do the *Marnie* picture next. The story of the compulsive thief that I was going to do with Grace Kelly.

*Who's taking the Grace Kelly part?*
I've got a girl in mind, but we're not letting on yet.

*You're going back to big stars?*
Not necessarily. Sometimes I think big stars are useful but today they don't help a picture any more. They help it if it's good, but if it's not good the public won't go.

*And* Psycho *showed you could get along without them . . .*
Yes.

# Alfred Hitchcock: Mr. Chastity

## ORIANA FALLACI/1963

ORIANA FALLACI: *I have seen your last movie, Mr. Hitchcock. Yes, the one about the birds who eat humans. Phew! . . . The spectacle of the corpses whose very eyes have been devoured by the birds! . . . The scene of the children in flight, torn to shreds by a cloud of ferocious crows! . . . And to think you seem so innocuous, so innocent, incapable of even imagining such fearful things. Tell me something, Mr. Hitchcock: Why do you always make movies based on terror and crime, full of macabre scenes and anguish? Why do you always want to horrify and terrify us?*
ALFRED HITCHCOCK: Firstly, because if I made any other kind of movies, nobody would believe them. I explained this to Ingrid Bergman, when she asked me the same question: "Obviously, my dear, I could make a film of Cinderella. I'm a professional, good at my job. But if I make Cinderella, people will immediately start looking for the corpse." In the second place, because I'm a philanthropist: I give people what they want. People love being horrified, terrified. Have you never noticed that terror and horror have the same effect on the human species as a caress? Take a three-month-old baby. His mother bends over him and says, "Boo! I'm going to eat you up." The baby cries with fright and then smiles blissfully, while his mother smiles, too. Now take a six-year-old child on a swing. He drives the swing higher and still higher. Why? Because this frightens him and is more fun. Now take an adolescent on a roller coaster. Why does he ride on the roller coaster? Because every bend, every drop, fills him with horror, and this is fun. Now

From Oriana Fallaci, *The Egotists: Sixteen Surprising Interviews*, trans. Pamela Swinglehurst (Chicago: Henry Regnery, 1963), pp. 239–56.

take a man racing in a car and risking death at any moment. Why does he race in a car? Because risking death gives him an exquisite shudder, and that is fun. People would pay, indeed they do pay—consider my movies—to have fun with fear. And lastly . . .

*And lastly because, in spite of looking like a nice, innocuous man, you have fun yourself making these movies.*
I don't deny it. I admit it. I don't get such a kick out of anything as much as out of imagining a crime. When I'm writing a story and I come to the crime, I think happily: now wouldn't it be nice to have him die like this? And then, even more happily, I think: at this point people will start yelling. It must be because I spent three years studying with the Jesuits. They used to terrify me to death, with everything, and now I'm getting my own back by terrifying other people. And then it must be because I'm English. The English use a lot of imagination with their crimes. They have the most amusing crimes in the world. I remember that adorable case against that adorable Christie, a necrophiliac who had murdered eight women. Concerning the eighth victim there occurred the following dialogue between judge and accused: "So you knocked the woman down in the kitchen, Mr. Christie." "Yes, Your Honor." "There are three steps down into the kitchen." "Yes, Your Honor." "The poor woman fell." "Yes, Your Honor." "And you killed her." "Yes, Your Honor." "And assaulted her, too?" "I believe so, Your Honor." "Before, after, or during death?" "During, Your Honor." Oh, England's fantastic for this kind of thing. Pity that they never managed to conceal the corpse. It's much easier in America. I always suggest the rubbish disposal chute, straight into the incinerator. Or else eating it, but then it has to be tender.

*Mr. Hitchcock do you realize that criminals make use of your lessons and your movies? Do you know that, years ago, in Ankara, a journalist killed a diplomat using a revolver concealed inside a camera, exactly as you did in your movie, Special Envoy [Foreign Correspondent]?*
Yes I know. And I was very flattered. Oh, I don't know what I wouldn't give to know about all the times I've been copied. The trouble is that every day someone commits the perfect crime: one that isn't discovered. As the crime isn't discovered, I don't know whether they've copied me. But three years ago, in Los Angeles, some man who had murdered three wives said he'd murdered the third after seeing *Psycho*. The journalists telephoned me: "So

now you're happy?" "No," I told them. "He didn't say after which of my films he murdered the second. Maybe he murdered the first after drinking a glass of milk." From the glass of milk to the revolver, how often that's happened.

*Of course you fire a revolver like a champion, Mr. Hitchcock, and during the war you were doubtless a very demon.*
I've never so much as held a revolver or any other kind of weapon in my hand. I don't even know what a trigger looks like, and I was never in the Army. When World War I broke out, I was too young, thank God. When the World War II broke out, I was too old, thank God. I've never done any shooting. People who go shooting . . . you don't go shooting by any chance?

*Well, actually . . . yes.*
You're a criminal, irresponsible, heartless woman. My God! I can look at a corpse chopped to bits without batting an eyelid, but I can't bear the sight of a dead bird. Too heartrending. I can't even bear to see them suffer, birds, or get tired. During the making of my movie, in which I used fifteen hundred trained crows, there was a representative of the Royal Society for the Prevention of Cruelty to Animals on the scene at all times, and whenever he said, "That's enough now, Mr. Hitchcock, I think the birds are getting tired," I would stop at once. I have the highest consideration for birds, and, quite apart from the movie, I think it very right they should take their revenge on men that way. For hundreds of centuries birds have been persecuted by men, killed, put in the pot, in the oven, on the spit, used for writing pens, feathers for hats, turned into bloodcurdling stuffed ornaments. . . . Such infamy deserves exemplary punishment.

*I see. In other words, your movie has a profound philosophic and moral significance: don't do to others what you wouldn't like done to you.*
Not in the least. If there's one thing I'll never be able to do, it's turn my collar back to front and play the part of preacher. When people ask me what I think of movies that administer philosophic and moral lessons, I say, "Don't you think it's up to philosophers to teach philosophy and priests to teach morals?" People don't go to the movies to listen to sermons. If that were the case, then instead of buying a ticket they'd put a coin in the collection plate and make the sign of the cross before taking a seat in the stalls.

People go to the movies to be amused. And they pay a lot to be amused. Morality, you know, is much less expensive than amusement.

*Yet I know you are very keen on morality, at least on a certain kind of morality. You have never been divorced, your life is untouched by scandal, and I know that one day, when you happened to go with your wife to the Folies Bergère, you left, saying, "This is a world of perdition."*
No, no. The story didn't go like that, it was much funnier. I was thirty-one at the time, I'd been married five years, and I was writing the scenario for a movie about a young couple who go on a world tour and consequently visit the Folies Bergère, where, in the interval, the girls also belly dance. Since I'd never seen this belly dancing and couldn't even imagine what it would be, I said to my wife, "Let's go to Paris." So we went to Paris, and while we were there, we went to the Folies Bergère. The interval came, and I asked a man I took to be the manager, a fellow in a tuxedo, if we could see some belly dancing. The fellow said, "Come with me," and put us into a taxi. The taxi immediately made off through winding streets, but my wife and I were an innocent pair, and we didn't understand. Then the taxi stopped outside a house that was one of those houses where . . . well . . . anyway . . . my wife and I had never been in that kind of place, you see, and so we stood there watching in horror, you see, while those girls did things that weren't exactly belly dancing, you see, until I exclaimed, "But this is a world of perdition!" I was thirty-one. And I'd never been with any woman other than my wife.

*I see. Of course, you'd judge the whole thing very differently today.*
Oh no! I'm sixty-four now, and I can swear that I've never known any woman other than my wife—neither before nor since our marriage. When I married, I was a virgin, I promise you, and sex has never interested me much. I don't understand how people can waste so much time over sex: sex is for kids, for movies, a great bore. And since I've always avoided anything boring . . . I remember the day I had to write the screenplay for the movie *Woman to Woman*: the story of a man who has a mistress in Paris who bangs his head, loses his memory, and starts going with another woman, who gives him a child. Well, I was twenty-three years old, I'd never been with a woman, and I didn't have the slightest idea what a woman did to have a child. I had even less idea what a man did when he was with his mistress in Paris or when he was with another woman who was giving him a child. And so . . .

*Now you know, Mr. Hitchcock?*
Now I know. I have a daughter of thirty-five and three little grandchildren. Between you and me, I'm a grandfather. Still, when I think that my daughter was born when I was nearly thirty, and it was only then that I realized that babies aren't found under gooseberry bushes. . . . You won't believe it—no one ever believes it, they say it's an act to make myself a character—but until I was twenty-four, I had never tasted a drop of alcohol; until I was twenty-five, I had never smoked a cigar. I was very shy, more shy than I am today. If people told dirty stories, I used to blush like a rose. So my friends would always tell them when I wasn't there, and if I arrived, they'd say, "Silence, Hitchcock's coming." As for my wife, I married her because she asked me to. We'd been traveling around and working together for years, and I'd never so much as touched her little finger.

*But why on earth? Don't you like women, Mr. Hitchcock?*
Indeed I like them, more than men. In point of fact, I feel less shy with them than with men. For example, I could never talk like this to a man. But I like them to talk to, to dine with, not for sexual reasons. When people ask me, "Mr. Hitchcock, why are the stars in your movies always blondes? Is it because you have a weakness for blondes?" I tell them I don't know, it must be coincidence or the fact that they are ladies; I've thought since I was a child that ladies are blonde, my wife is blonde. I don't have a weakness for anyone, neither for blondes nor redheads nor brunettes nor sexy women. . . . You know who are the sexiest women, I mean the most wrapped up in sex? Nordic women. Evidently the cold makes them hot. Consider Englishwomen: they all look like schoolmistresses, but heaven help the poor fellow who finds himself in a taxi with one. At best he'll get out of it minus his clothes.

*Forgive my asking, but how do you know these things, Mr. Hitchcock?*
What a question! I listen to what people say, I find out about things. Obviously the information is secondhand. Scientists know that if you mix one powder with another powder, you'll be blown up. But they don't have to be blown up in order to know it.

*Too right. Your wife must be very grateful to you, Mr. Hitchcock.*
I hope she is. Apart from the fact that in thirty-seven years I have never been unfaithful to her, not even in thought, there aren't many husbands like me.

Just think: as we only have a daily maid, my wife has to do the cooking. But when she's getting a meal ready, I help her, and after we've eaten, I wash the dishes. I wash them and dry them and put them away.

*Well done. If you get divorced, I'll marry you myself.*
Thank you, it's always nice to feel one's wanted. But if you marry me, don't be under any illusion. For me a good stew is worth more than a pretty little nose, and the first thing I expect of my wife is to be good at cooking. Are you a good cook? My wife is an excellent cook, and I could die eating. The things that make me happiest in the world are eating, drinking, and sleeping. I sleep like a newborn babe. I drink like a fish, have you seen what a red face I have? And I eat like a pig. Even if it does make me look more and more like a porker myself. Some days ago, walking along in New York, I saw myself reflected in a window, and before I recognized myself, I let out a yell of fright. Then I called to my wife, "Who's that porker on two legs?" I didn't want to believe it when she replied, "It's you dear."

*I imagine you don't often yell with fright. Practiced as you are in frightening other people, fear must be completely unknown to you.*
On the contrary. I'm the most fearful and cowardly man you'll ever meet. Every night I lock myself into my room as if there were a madman on the other side of the door, waiting to slit my throat. I'm frightened of everything: burglars, policemen, crowds, darkness, Sundays. . . . Being frightened of Sundays goes back to when I was a child and my parents used to put me to bed at six o'clock so that they could go out and eat in a restaurant. I used to wake up at eight o'clock, my parents weren't there, there was only that dim light, that silence of an empty house. Brr! It wasn't accidental, when I married, that I said to my wife, "Every Sunday I want a fine dinner with lots of light, lots of people, and lots of noise." Being frightened of policemen started when I was about eleven. I had been on a bus ride as far as the terminal, and I didn't have the money for the return fare. I made my way back on foot and reached home after nine. We used to live in the district of Soho, in London; my father was a poultry dealer. My father opened the door and didn't say a word, not a word of reproof, nothing. He just gave me a note and said, "Take it to Watson." Watson was a policeman, a family friend. He'd no sooner got the note than he shut me in a cell, shouting, "This is what happens to bad boys who get home after nine o'clock." Brr! It was fifty-three years ago, but

every time I see a policeman, I start shaking. And then I'm frightened of people having rows, of violence. I've never had a row with anyone, and I've no idea of how to come to blows. And then I'm frightened of eggs, worse than frightened; they revolt me. That white round thing without any holes, and when you break it, inside there's that yellow thing, round, without any holes. . . . Brr! Have you ever seen anything more revolting than an egg yolk breaking and spilling its yellow liquid? Blood is jolly, red. But egg yolk is yellow, revolting. I've never tasted it. And then I'm frightened of my own movies. I never go to see them. I don't know how people can bear to watch my movies.

*That's rather illogical, Mr. Hitchcock. Come to that, your movies are illogical, too. From the logical point of view, not one of them can stand inspection.*
Agreed. But what is logic? There's nothing more stupid than logic. Logic is the result of reasoning, reasoning is the result of experience, and who's to say whether our experiences are the right ones? My dog doesn't understand music, Bach bores him to death. Does that mean that my dog is illogical? It only means that his experiences are different from Bach's. I don't attach any importance to logic. None of my movies is based on logic. They are based on suspense, not on logic. Give me a bomb, and Descartes can go boil his head. There's nothing like a good bomb for creating suspense. Suspense, not surprise.

*Enlighten me and our readers, Mr. Hitchcock. Explain suspense to us.*
Right. Suppose this interview were a scene in a movie. We're sitting here talking, and we don't know that there's a bomb hidden inside your tape recorder. The public doesn't know either, and suddenly the bomb explodes: we're blown to bits. Surprise, horror of public. But how long does it last, the surprise and the horror? Five seconds, no more. With suspense, however, we're sitting there, and we don't know that there's a bomb hidden inside your tape recorder. But the public knows, and it also knows that it will explode in ten minutes. Obviously the public gets worried, anxious, says, "Why do they sit there talking, those two? Don't they realize there's a bomb hidden inside the tape recorder?" Suspense. But a second before the ten minutes are up, I bend over the tape recorder and say, "Aha! There's a bomb inside here." I pick up the tape recorder and fling it away. End of suspense. The secret is never to let the bomb explode. I had it explode, once, in the

hands of a child who had boarded a bus, three minutes after the arranged time, and it was a very grave mistake. I'll never make the same mistake again. People must suffer, sweat, but at the end they must heave a sigh of relief.

*And do you like suspense, Mr. Hitchcock?*
Far from it. I hate it. I hate it so much that I can't even bear to stay in the kitchen when my wife is making a soufflé. Will it rise? Won't it rise? I bought an oven with a glass door so I could see whether it was rising, but it hasn't helped. I can't bear to wait the necessary eighteen minutes to see if it'll rise.

*On the subject of bombs, Mr. Hitchcock. In your movie* Notorious *you talked about the atomic bomb, which, if I'm not mistaken, hadn't yet exploded on Hiroshima.*
That's an extraordinary story, I really must tell it to you. Because MacGuffin comes into it, too. Have you got enough tape left?

*Yes, there's enough tape. Mac . . . what?*
MacGuffin. You must know that when I'm making a movie, the story isn't important to me. What's important is how I tell the story. For example, in a movie about espionage what the spy is looking for isn't important, it's how he looks for it. Yet I have to say what he's looking for. It doesn't matter to me, but it matters a great deal to the public, and most of all it matters to the character of the movie. Why should the character go to so much trouble? Why does the government pay him to go to so much trouble? Is he looking for a bomb, a secret? This secret, this bomb, is for me the MacGuffin, a word that comes from an old Scottish story. Should I tell it to you? Is there enough tape?

*Yes, yes. There's enough tape.*
Well, two men are traveling in a train, and one says to the other, "What's that parcel on the luggage rack?" "That? It's the MacGuffin," says the other. "And what's the MacGuffin?" asks the first man. "The MacGuffin is a device for catching lions in Scotland," the other replies. "But there aren't any lions in Scotland," says the first man. "Then it isn't the MacGuffin," answers the other. Clear? Logical?

*Very clear, very logical.*
Well, in 1944, then, I'm making this movie *Notorious*, with Ingrid Bergman.

She's going to South America, where some Germans are working on something. Ingrid Bergman is going there because she's a spy and has to find out for the American government what the Nazis are working on. As well as Ingrid Bergman there's Cary Grant, who has to find out the same thing because he's working for the FBI. Naturally Ingrid Bergman and Cary Grant fall in love, and when Ingrid Bergman has to go to bed with a Nazi to find out what it is, Cary Grant is very unhappy. Well, this thing they had to find out, the MacGuffin, I had no idea what it might be, and in the end I decided in favor of the atom bomb. Ingrid Bergman would have gone to South America to find out if the Nazis were preparing the atom bomb there. Naturally I didn't even know what the atom bomb might be. But I knew that uranium existed, that since 1929 the atom had been split, and I had read a book by H. G. Wells called *The Mighty Atom*. So I imagined that sooner or later someone would make the atom bomb. Clear? Logical?

*Very clear. Very logical.*
Well, I'm making the film with Selznick, and Selznick asks me, "What's Ingrid Bergman looking for in South America?" "She's looking for uranium," I reply. "What's uranium?" he asks me. "It's the thing they use to make the atom bomb," I reply. "What's the atom bomb?" he asks. "A bomb," I say. "It's about Ingrid Bergman, who falls in love with Cary Grant, and since Ingrid Bergman has to go to bed with a Nazi in order to find out if the Nazi has the atom bomb, Cary Grant is very unhappy. The atom bomb is of no importance: it's the MacGuffin." "I still don't like it," he says. And he sells me, Ingrid Bergman, Cary Grant, and the unfinished scenario to R.K.O. for eight hundred thousand dollars and 50 per cent of the profits. But I have to finish the scenario, and as I'm not sure about this uranium and how big an atom bomb is, I put my hat on and go to the California Institute of Technology, where the most important scientist of all is working: Doctor Milliken, director of the Manhattan project. Naturally I don't know he's directing the Manhattan project, I don't even know the Manhattan project exists; I only know that in New Mexico there exists a secret place where everyone goes in and no one comes out—a journalist told me about it. So I go in, "Good day, doctor. How are you?" I shake hands with the doctor, who has a bust of Einstein in a corner of the room, and I ask him, "Doctor, how big would an atom bomb be?" The scene that follows! He jumps up, yelling, "Do you want to be arrested? Do you want to get me arrested, too?" Then he spends an

hour explaining to me that it was impossible to make the atom bomb, that the atom bomb never would be made, and that consequently I should not make the atom bomb my MacGuffin. I said all right. But I still had that bottle of uranium in the scenario, a dramatic sequence. I didn't want to give up the uranium, and so I made my MacGuffin the atom bomb anyway, and two years later the bomb exploded on Hiroshima. And the movie made eight million dollars.

*Admirable, Mr. Hitchcock. But the main ingredients of your movies don't consist only of suspense and MacGuffin. I'd say your movies also consist of humor, humor mixed with the macabre.*

I can't take any credit for that. For the English it's normal to mix humor with the macabre. You know the story about the two ladies at the fair watching a man eat the heads of live rats? Well, in horror one of them says, "Doesn't he ever eat bread with them?" And the one about the famous actor who's been killed by a bomb, do you know it? Well, there's the funeral of this famous actor, and all the actors go to it. As the coffin is being lowered into the grave, a young actor leans over to a very old actor called Charlie and asks, "Charlie, how old are you?" "Eighty-nine," says Charlie. "Then there's no point in your going home," says the young actor. And it goes without saying that, if it was up to me, I wouldn't send any of them home, actors.

*I know, you aren't very fond of actors. You've boasted more than once that you have no friends among actors and cinema folk. "Actors," according to you, "are cows."*

When they aren't cows, they're children: that's something else I've often said. And everyone knows that there are good children, bad children, and stupid children. The majority of actors, though, are stupid children. They're always quarreling, and they give themselves a lot of airs. The less I see of them, the happier I am. I had much less trouble directing fifteen hundred crows than one single actor. I've always said that Walt Disney has the right idea. His actors are made of paper; when he doesn't like them, he can tear them up. If I went around with actors, how could I possibly live a quiet life in Hollywood, in an old house without a swimming pool? Think of Kim Novak. Not that she isn't an artist, of course; she paints quite nicely and in the second part of *Vertigo*, when she's dark-haired and looks less like Kim Novak, I even managed to get her to act. But the only reason I took Kim Novak was because Vera Miles was pregnant.

*That's not much of a compliment to Kim Novak.*

Nor for Vera Miles. I ask you! I was offering her a big part, the chance to become a beautiful sophisticated blonde, a real actress. We'd have spent a heap of dollars on it, and she has the bad taste to get pregnant. I hate pregnant women, because then they have children.

*And Grace Kelly? Sorry, Her Most Serene Highness Princess Grace? What do you say about her?*

Grace is better. She's sensitive, disciplined, and very sexy. People think she's cold. Rubbish! She's a volcano covered with snow. I was sorry I couldn't make *Marnie* with her, almost as sorry as she was. She was very keen to do it, you know. In point of fact I wasn't the one to go after her. It was she who came after me: "Hitch, haven't you got a part for me?" "Yes, Grace. The part of a lady robber." "Ah, splendid!" Unfortunately we broke the news at the wrong moment, when Rainier was having trouble with De Gaulle, and so they said she wanted to leave her husband just when he was having trouble with De Gaulle. Who could have expected it? Too bad. I'll use another blonde.

*But it's strange, Mr. Hitchcock, that you should be so disparaging about actors. To judge by the systematic way you appear in your own movies, one might think you have a smothered regret that you weren't an actor.*

That's a custom that I started when I didn't have enough money to pay my actors, and I had to economize by doing walkons myself. As a result it became a superstition, and I decided always to put myself in my films: I even put myself in *Lifeboat*, a film that from beginning to end takes place in an open boat in the middle of the sea. It was a bit difficult to justify my appearance on the boat; I resolved the problem like this: one of the actors, William Bendix, finds an old newspaper in the boat. He opens it, and in the middle there's an advertisement for a slimming treatment, with the photograph of a fellow like a porker. The porker is me. Of course, it's clear that I also put myself in because I know people look for me, but I do it at the beginning of the film so that people aren't distracted by looking for me, and I appear briefly because nothing embarrasses me as much as a camera. I wouldn't have liked to be an actor for anything in the world. A criminal lawyer, that's the job I'd have liked. I'd have seen so many dramas and . . .

*But, Mr. Hitchcock, aren't you able every now and then to view life as a drama? Haven't you ever by chance been involved in a dramatic situation?*

No. Never. Only in movies. I never get involved in dramatic situations. You're the one who's in a dramatic situation.

*Why, Mr. Hitchcock?*
Because you have to write an article about me. And you don't know anything about me.

*That's what you say, Mr. Hitchcock. But I do, Mr. Hitchcock. With all your cordial humor, your nice round face, your nice innocent paunch, you are the most wicked, cruel man I have ever met.*

# Alfred Hitchcock on His Films

## HUW WHELDON/1964

HUW WHELDON: *This was the forty-ninth occasion on which, to use your own words, you had "done your best to make your audience scream in agony." This, despite the great variation of your films, is the constant factor—the Hitchcock speciality, so to speak. Do you think, Mr. Hitchcock, that audiences are frightened today by features or factors any different from what frightened them forty years ago when you first started?*

ALFRED HITCHCOCK: No, I wouldn't say so, because after all they were frightened as children. It is all based on Red Riding Hood; so what they're frightened of today are exactly the same things they were frightened of yesterday.

WHELDON: *Do you think, when making films, that women are frightened by different things from the things that frighten men?*

HITCHCOCK: Oh I would say so, yes; after all women are frightened by a mouse; you don't see men jumping on chairs and screaming.

WHELDON: *When you make a film, are you setting out to frighten men or women?*

HITCHCOCK: Women, because 80 per cent of the audience in the cinema are women. Even if the house is fifty-fifty, half men, half women, a good percentage of the men have said to their girls: "What do you want to see, dear?" So men have very little to do with the choice of the film.

From *The Listener*, August 6, 1964, pp. 189–90.

WHELDON: *When it comes to audiences in different parts of the world—take American audiences as against British audiences, instead of men as against women—bearing in mind your Red Riding Hood point that we are all frightened by the great simple thing, are American audiences frightened by different things from European audiences?*

HITCHCOCK: I would say no. You've got to remember the American audience is the global audience. I once said to an Englishman: "You don't understand America, because you think they are Americans, but they are not. America is full of foreigners. They are all foreigners since 1776." So whatever frightens the Americans frightens the Italians, the Rumanians, the Danes, and everyone else from Europe.

WHELDON: *Do you think it does an injustice to you, simply to think of you as a man who above all else has frightened the wits out of audiences?*

HITCHCOCK: Yes; you have to remember that this process of frightening is done by means of a given medium, the medium of pure cinema. The assembly of pieces of film to create fright is the essential part of my job, just as a painter would, by putting certain colours together, create evil on canvas.

WHELDON: *You are a master, aren't you, of the unexpected?*

HITCHCOCK: That's only because one is challenged by the audience. They are saying to me "show us," and "I know what's coming next." And I say: "Do you!" They're expecting the cliché; and I have to say, we cannot have a cliché.

WHELDON: *When you talk about putting bits of film together, and then creating, in terms of what you call pure cinema, the sequence that you are going for, I can imagine that it must have been a bit of a shock to you personally when talkies came. Because in a sense you are talking almost about a classical technique, aren't you?*

HITCHCOCK: The only thing wrong with the silent picture was that mouths opened and no sound came out. Unfortunately, when talk came in, the vulgarians, the money-changers of the industry, immediately began to cash in by photographing stage plays. A lot of films one sees today are what I call photographs of people talking, and they bear no relation to the art of the cinema. The point is that the power of cinema in its purest form is so vast because it can go over the whole world. On a given night a film can play

in Tokyo, West Berlin, London, New York, and the same audience is responding emotionally to the same things, and no other medium can do this. The
theater doesn't do it, because you have different sets of people; but in a film
they are the same actors. In translating a film, in what they call dubbing,
there is liable to be a loss, and therefore when one is thinking of a film glob-
ally the talk is reduced to a minimum, and if possible you tell the story visually and let the talk be a part of the atmosphere.

WHELDON: *I imagine it is because of this point of view that your reputation is
so high with the great avant-garde film critics, in France particularly . . . Have you
ever been tempted to make what is nowadays called a horror film which is different
from a Hitchcock film?*
HITCHCOCK: No, it's too easy. I believe in putting the horror in the mind
of the audience and not necessarily on the screen. I once made a movie,
rather tongue-in-cheek, called *Psycho*; and a lot of people looked at this thing
and said, "what a dreadful thing to do," "how awful," and so forth. But to
me it had great elements of the cinema in it. It was a big joke, and I was
horrified to find that some people took it seriously. It was intended to cause
people to scream and yell and so forth, but no more than the screaming and
yelling on the switchback railway. This film had a horrible scene at the beginning of a girl being murdered in the shower. I deliberately made that pretty
rough. But as the film developed I put less and less physical horror into it,
but the tension in the mind of the viewer was increased considerably: I was
transferring it from film into their minds. Towards the end I had no violence
at all, but the audience by this time was screaming in agony, thank goodness.

WHELDON: *You mentioned a switchback railway. You do see yourself as a
switchback-railway operator?*
HITCHCOCK: I am possibly in some respects the man who says, in con-
structing it, "how steep can we make the first dip?" If you make the dip too
deep, the screams will continue as the whole car goes over the edge and
destroys everyone. Therefore you mustn't go too far, because you do want
them to get off the switchback railway giggling with pleasure: like the
woman who comes out of a sentimental movie and says, "It was lovely. I had
a good cry."

WHELDON: *But what is a good cry as opposed to a bad cry?*
HITCHCOCK: I think it's the satisfaction of temporary pain. It is the same

thing when people endure the agonies of a suspense film. When it's all over they are relieved. I once committed a grave error in having a bomb from which I had extracted a great deal of suspense. I had the thing go off and kill someone, which I should never have done, because they needed the relief from their suspense. Bad technique: never repeated it.

WHELDON:  *Bad technique, yes. Mind you, perhaps it came nearer reality, because bombs do go off.*
HITCHCOCK:  That's probably true. I don't think many people want reality, whether it is in the theatre or in a film. It must look real, but it must never be real, because reality is something none of us can stand, at any time.

WHELDON:  *Would it be accurate to say that the tradition of your films on the whole is the tradition of the English adventure story which takes us back to John Buchan?*
HITCHCOCK:  John Buchan had a big influence on me, but more than that, I think that the attack on the whole of the subject matter is strictly English. Where sometimes one gets a little into difficulties with the American people is that they want everything spelled out; and they worry about content. I don't care about content at all. The film can be about anything you like, so long as I'm making that audience react in a certain way to whatever I put on the screen. If you begin to worry about the details of what the papers are about that the spies are trying to steal, that's a lot of nonsense: I can't be bothered about what the papers are, what the spies are after. I often fall foul of critics who criticize content instead of technique.

WHELDON:  *And the technique is the technique of Philipps Oppenheim, and John Buchan, Mrs. Belloc Lowndes, and Conan Doyle?*
HITCHCOCK:  It comes into that area, but you see the English have always had a fascination for crime as such.

WHELDON:  *Is it true that you are yourself a great expert on crime?*
HITCHCOCK:  As a detective, do you mean? No. But I suppose one has at one's finger-tips all the details of the famous cases of the past. For example, in the film *Rear Window* there are two passages in it which come from famous English crimes. The Crippen case—I used a bit of that; and the Patrick Mahon case—a man who killed a girl and then cut her up into pieces and threw the

flesh out of the window of a train. But his great problem was what to do with the head, and that's what I put in, in *Rear Window*, with the dog sniffing the flowerbed. I made the movie years ago, and I employed as the technical adviser a man who was one of the big four at Scotland Yard, and he was on this case. It was near Eastbourne. Mahon did not know what to do with the head, so he put it into the grate and put a fire under it. There was a big storm going on outside; the thunder and lightning were terribly melodramatic, and the heat under the head caused the eyes to open. So this poor man ran out into the storm, and never came back until the morning when the fire had done its job. This ex-superintendent of Scotland Yard told me that he went to the butcher's and got a sheep's head, and put it in the grate to test the time it would take to burn. So the head business went into this picture.

WHELDON: *May I ask you about some films that you made in this country, and films that you subsequently made in America? Do you yourself see any distinction between these? One is thinking of* The Lady Vanishes, The 39 Steps, *and* The Man Who Knew Too Much, *for example, which you made in both countries.*
HITCHCOCK: Well, as the French say, the early English period is quite different from the American period; there was much more spontaneity, I suppose, and more instinct at work in the English period, but more calculation in the American period. That is the main difference.

WHELDON: *Have you ever made a film without regard to any audience?*
HITCHCOCK: Yes, I made one called *The Trouble with Harry*, and it lost, I suppose, about half a million dollars, so that's an expensive self-indulgence. And here we come to the question of ethics with other people's money.

WHELDON: *Let us take the ethics of the film itself; why do you think it lost money?*
HITCHCOCK: It was outside the usual run of pictures. It was a little comedy—an English book, strangely enough, although I laid it in Vermont. It was a typically English comedy of the macabre, a story about a dead body. A little man, played by Edmund Gwenn, while shooting rabbits, was responsible for a man's death. So he buried the body, and then he found out next morning that he wasn't responsible, so he dug it up again; and then someone else came along and they had a reason why the man should be buried, so he was buried again. The whole film was about the burying and the pulling out

of this poor body. It was rather amusing, but I'm afraid the people who run cinemas, and those people who distribute films, my natural enemies, couldn't see it as an attraction for the public.

WHELDON:    *You thought well of it yourself?*
HITCHCOCK:    I enjoyed it, definitely.

WHELDON:    *What frightens you personally, Mr. Hitchcock, if anything?*
HITCHCOCK:    Any trouble frightens me. I was once asked: "What is your idea of happiness?," and I said: "A clear horizon."

# Let's Hear It for Hitchcock

## EMERSON BATDORF/1970

HE SAT THERE LOOKING like a smaller pear on top of a larger pear, the upper pear, or head, decorated with a pendulous lower lip that threatened to drown him in a rain-storm by catching the downpour.

At 70 Alfred Hitchcock remains one of the brilliant raconteurs of our time, and one of the great film makers of any time. His name has stirred pleasurable emotions in movie goers for more than 40 years and in TV watchers almost since the start of the squint box.

He was in a reminiscent mood. True, he was being interviewed about *Topaz*, his latest picture, but not one of his best. The reporters got him going on other things: sex, violence, practical jokes, the reason for being.

He was remarkable, not alone in the brightness of his ideas, but in the rich, thick, sensuous quality of the voice in which he expressed them, and in the fact that he said funny things gravely and never laughed. He approached a smile only once.

"I remember during the making of *The 39 Steps*, I had Madeleine Carroll working late, handcuffed to this actor Robert Donat who was dragging her over some rocks. And waiting on the side to take her out was Randolph Churchill. And he got concerned for this woman because I was letting Donat drag her over the rocks. He said, 'I say, old man, don't you think you ought to be a little careful? She's got high heels on, you know.' I just gave him a look and then went on with the job."

From *Cleveland Plain Dealer*, Sunday Magazine, February 1, 1970, pp. 28–30, 31.

QUESTION: *What do you think of the trend toward nudity in films today?*
"I think they'll eventually tire the audience of all-in wrestling scenes in bed. As I have said before, what are they all waiting for? What is the ultimate of the nudity? It's to dolly in between all those legs to the big closeup. But the point is I've already done it. At the end of a picture called *North by Northwest*, Cary Grant lifts a girl up into a berth and I cut to the phallic train entering a tunnel.

"In *Psycho*, I had a naked girl in the shower. But, you see, the shower scene was made of 78 cuts. It took seven days to shoot. For 45 seconds.

"But you know, some of the scenes I shot in slow motion? You don't see it in the film. In order to cover the breast. I've got the struggle going like this: (gestures). Up comes the arm. Covers the breast. Then we speed it up . . . the actors do it in slow motion, we photograph it in slow motion. Then when it's projected normally you get:" (demonstrates a speedy motion of the hands, with unerring coverage.)

QUESTION: *Would you go to all that trouble today to give the appearance of nudity but not its reality?*
"I might not. Because of the permissiveness. It doesn't alter the fact that I think it's a bore. I have a perfect opportunity in *Topaz* when the Frenchman takes the Cuban mistress to bed. And I just photograph the shoulders up. It's enough for her to drop her robe and him to take the shoulder straps. And I follow the two heads down onto the bed. I don't get back to show the nude figures for a very different reason.

"I prefer the camera to be as intimate as the two people are. By getting back you just photograph a couple of nude people getting into bed. What's the point in that? You know, a man's backside is not particularly attractive.

"Once you've seen the act in big closeup, then where do you go? Then you start on eroticism. All right, so you want me to start on eroticism. You want my first erotic scene? A violinist in love with a girl and he ties a G string or something to the two nipples and plays it with a bow. And also indulges in a little pizzicato. You be imaginative about eroticism! I can start anywhere you like!"

QUESTION: *What's your feeling about violence in movies?*
"Violence is all right where it is necessary. If we want to go back to *Psycho*, there we have a very violent scene, a second less violent scene because I've

already conditioned the audience. But as the film went on I took the violence out of the film and left it in the mind of the audience. By giving them that first horrible example, that's all I had to do. I had to threaten the rest."

QUESTION: *Where and how do you live these days?*
"We live in Bel-Air (Calif.). We've lived there since 1939. We live a quiet life. Don't really give cocktail parties and that sort of thing. Not that we're snobs. You know; when you give these parties, and you have 50 to 100 people all sitting at separate tables. I used to look at them and ask, why don't they go to a restaurant?

"Once at one of the very few parties we ever had, I thought why the hell should we have a lot of tables? So I rented 45 chairs and 45 TV tables, black ones, and put 'em in a big circle. Then I put some grass mats down and I put place cards at every place.

"But not one name corresponded to any of the guests. All Christian names. The first man I watched was Eric Ambler, the author. This is what happened:"

Here Hitchcock got up and trudged around the table counter-clockwise, giving sidelong glances to the left at the imaginary place cards like a pigeon kicker looking stealthily for his quarry, until he got back where he started. There was a simulated baffled look on his face.

"Mrs. Stewart said to Jimmy, 'We're not invited. We're not supposed to be here.'"

QUESTION: *I have heard about your elevator trick. Do you still do it?*
"It works, you know, if you want it to." (Some people hadn't heard of it so Hitchcock obliged by explaining.) "Well, I used to get on the elevator at the St. Regis Hotel in New York, about the 16th floor, and if it were crowded, as we were getting in I'd say to my wife, 'Well, look! I didn't know the gun was loaded! When it went off it tore a piece of flesh right here (gesturing, at neck). And the flesh flapped down over the collar. You could see the white ligaments.'

"The people in the elevator were all listening. Then I said, 'Suddenly I found my feet wet. And after I looked down I was in a pool of blood! They were soaking.'

"Finally you get out. And the people are all standing there looking. I did it once and a woman said, 'Let me get out! Let me get out!'

"The other gag I once pulled was in the same elevator. I got in with my wife. You must stop talking, as you get in. Then I said, 'Do you know she married four times and had a child by each husband? And one day the four children met. And what do you think they said to each other?' And got out of the elevator."

QUESTION: *To what do you attribute your devilish sense of humor?*
"A sense of the ridiculous, I think. I once gave a dinner years ago in London. I happened to have a friend who was the son of the owner of a big chain of restaurants. This was a restaurant called the Trocadero, one of the big ones in London. We had a private room upstairs. I had as guests Gertie Lawrence. Or Mrs. A. Or Star! (Here he twinkled his eyes, a feat I had hitherto thought impossible.) Sir Gerald du Maurier, who was the top man in London, about like what Olivier is today, and Benita Hume, Ronald Colman's wife.

"And all the food I had made up was blue! Even when you broke your roll. It looked like a brown roll but when you broke it open it was blue. Blue soup, thick blue soup. Blue trout. Blue chicken. Blue ice cream.

"There were other things at the dinner. Gertie Lawrence, when she sat down, sat on what is called a whoopee cushion. Vulgar noise. You know, talking of vulgar noise, the origin of the word razzberry as a term of disapproval?

"It is used every day. Razzing. But it comes from 'Giving him the rahsberry.' (Here the difference in British and American pronunciation was distinct). It's rhyming slang. You've heard of English rhyming slang. 'Up and down the apples and pears.' 'Run to Uncle Ned.' Well, it's raspberry tart. Rhyming slang. Isn't it strange that the things that people use as a sort of corruption over the years and they never bother to find out why?

"It's like the word 'bloody' which in England is a very, very bad word.

"It's only because of its religious connotations. It goes back to when they said 'By Our Lady.' It's a speech corruption. And people say, why is 'bloody' such a bad word in England? It's the religious thing."

QUESTION: *Do those devilish ideas come to you full blown or do you stay awake nights devising them detail by detail?*
"They come spontaneously. I also remember walking down the peacock alley of a big English hotel many years ago. My poor wife had to suffer this. On

the benches on each side were these very old ladies. Knitting and God knows what.

"It was a resort hotel. It was back in the days when women were starting to wear slacks. Very few women did. Dietrich started it. And as we were walking I saw very quickly these old girls all were talking about my wife's slacks. Whispering. And looks.

"So I leaned to my wife and said (here he raised his hand and spoke behind it): 'THEY ARE ALL TALKING ABOUT YOUR TROUSERS!' As though she were a deaf person. She jumped out of her skin and said, 'Shhhhh! Wot'chu doing?' 'I SAID, THEY'RE ALL TALKING ABOUT YOUR TROUSERS' and all these women suddenly turned and went back to their knitting." (Here he gave a deft imitation of a little old lady suddenly going back to their knitting.)

QUESTION: *Your jokes are the intellectual type. You don't steal park benches or anything?*

"They are harmless to the people. It's not spilling soup down people's necks and that sort of thing. It creates a bewilderment. It's like one night in Chasen's Restaurant in Hollywood. We had a party in the back garden. And there was a table for 14. Mostly agents anyway, as far as I remember.

"And I decided to put at the head of the table a rather aristocratic old lady with her hair beautifully done and a long black dress. And then disown her.

"People arrived. The first couple arrived and they looked around and they said, 'Who's the old lady?' and I said, 'I don't know. I'm trying to find out.'

"I'd got her from Central Casting. I had never seen her before. All she was to say was 'I'm with Mr. Hitchcock's party' should she be spoken to. And eventually among the guests was Collier Young. He was at that time story department for Myron Selznick's office. He arrived with his wife and said, which I think is always annoying, 'May we bring our house guest?' The house guest was there.

"Said Collier Young, 'Who's the old girl?' I said, 'I don't know. I'm trying to find out,' and Chasen, who was in on it, kept away till everybody had arrived. And now it was the topic of conversation. Who is she? I said, 'I'm waiting for Chasen.' Finally, Chasen arrived and I said, 'Dave, go ask the old lady. She's not supposed to be here.' He went and bent over and came back and said, 'She's with Mr. Hitchcock's party.'

"I said, 'She can't be. I don't know who the hell she is!' So everyone sat down and here was this strange woman. There was a young fellow there, Charles Benyon, a writer, and halfway through the meal he banged on the table and said, 'It's a gag!' And suddenly he looks at the only other uninvited guest and says, 'And you're a gag too.' That was Collier Young's house guest."

QUESTION: *Have you given up not smoking? (He was engaged with about a foot long perfecto from the look of it.)*
"I'm doing this because I'm dieting."

(His dieting brought up the subject of the big diet, the grandaddy of them all, during which he lost 100 pounds while filming *Lifeboat* with Tallulah Bankhead. They both subsisted on a filet mignon for lunch. Miss Bankhead at the time was in a ritual dry spell, having vowed not to allow a sip of alcohol to pass her lips until World War II ended. Did she cheat? "No, she never cheated. Not to my knowledge."

(The movie *Lifeboat* brought up mention of a couple of Hitchcock's astute observations, only one of which will be printed.)

"That was the occasion when Mary Anderson, a little girl who was under contract to Fox, I found stuffing Kleenex into her brassiere to fill herself out. She thought Fox was going to make her a big star. One day she sat in the back of the boat and preened herself. 'Mr. Hitchcock, which is my best side do you think?' I said, 'Mary, you're sitting on it.'"

QUESTION: *What do you do in your spare time, outside of think up tricks?*
"I don't think up tricks. I think those days are over. I find it hard to get any sense of humor going now. Everyone is so painfully serious. Out there (Hollywood), you know.

"I read. Over the weekend I usually read biographical material. I never read fiction. Because that's too much like work. So I read biography, recent history like the Harrison Salisbury book about Leningrad. Nine hundred pages!"

(The questioning shifted to underground films; are we getting anything out of them? Hitchcock the craftsman didn't know, but he had a feeling that nothing about art could really be good and at the same time without foundation.)

"Strangely enough, I personally am not interested in content. I don't give a damn what the film's about. What I'm concerned with is the manner of telling the story and how you put your scenes together, and in consequence create an emotion in an audience.

"That's what I mean by pure film. The way you put it together to create an emotion. Let me give you an example. I consider one of the most cinematic films I have ever created is *Rear Window*. And yet here's a film in one room and one man who never moves from his position.

"But look at the structure. He looks, he sees, he reacts. Purely by this man's reactions you construct a whole murder story. (Here he said he used this example in the *Encyclopedia Britannica*, for which he did the section on motion picture production.)

"We take a closeup of the man (Jimmy Stewart) and cut to what he sees. And what do we show? A woman nursing a baby. You cut back to your face reaction and he smiles. Now what is he? He's a benevolent, nice gentleman.

"Take away the middle piece of film (the mother and the baby) and substitute a girl in a bikini. Now he's a dirty old man. That's what I mean by the purity of montage and the control of film."

QUESTION: *Someone asked about the crop dusting scene in* North by Northwest. *Who had the idea of having the plane dusting crops?*
"My idea. It comes under the heading of what one's life really is: Avoiding the cliché. It was a conventional configuration. Standing a man on the spot. Now, what is the cliché? Stand on the street corner at night. Under a lamp. In a pool of light. Waiting. The cobbles are washed by the recent rain. Then you cut to a window and somebody peering out and the black limousine comes along.

"So I said I won't do it that way. I'm going to do it in bright sun-light. No houses, no trees, nowhere to hide. I show a whole section of the countryside. With nothing. A Greyhound bus comes along. Cary Grant gets off and stands there. Very high shot. Took it high to show the loneliness of the situation. Nothing happens. Suddenly a car comes along. zzzzzzzzZoom. Goes right by.

"Where's the menace coming from? Then another car. And then of course inevitably I brought in the black limousine. And it went right by. Suddenly from a field from the very distant trees a jalopy comes. A man gets out. The jalopy goes by, leaving a man on the opposite side to Cary Grant.

"Is he the menace? I'm making the audience think like hell. The man strolls across. He and Grant speak. Suddenly the man says, 'That's funny.' He looks across the field. 'That's a crop duster dusting a field where there are no crops!' At that moment, the local bus comes and the man gets on before Cary Grant has a chance to question him.

"And Grant's left alone. With the strange crop duster. Sure enough it rises up. And suddenly to his alarm it's diving at him. Suddenly the shots ring out. He runs and it chases him. I had shots where I followed with the plane swooping right at him. He comes to a cornfield. He dives into the cornfield.

"Now comes the important rule that I always insist on: If you're going to have a crop duster, it must dust crops!

"So he's in the cornfield and the plane unloads the dust and smokes him out. He runs onto the roadway and there's a double oil truck. Gasoline truck. And it stops with a screech just as the plane's coming down on him. The plane was going after him but it didn't expect the truck to stop. And they hit."

(Here Hitchcock whammed the table with his right forefinger, which is as carried away as he ever got.)

"Bang.

"A holocaust.

"There you see the avoidance of the cliché. No place to hide."

QUESTION: *Do you think in pictures?*
"Yes."

QUESTION: *Have you been in every one of your pictures?*
"Since 1926. *The Lodger.* With British film star Ivor Novello."

QUESTION: *Why?*
"Oh, as a gag."

QUESTION: *Even the first time?*
"In place of an actor. We ran out of actors. The real *Lodger* wasn't an elaborate one. It was very simple. It was, is the man above in the rooming house Jack the Ripper or not? That's all the story was. But in order to open the audience up, what I did, I opened the picture with a big head of a screaming blonde girl. And I remember to get the blonde hair all out, I laid her head on a sheet of plate glass and lighted it from behind.

"And then I showed a lot of people on the Thames embankment, the policemen and the bodies pulled out of the water. And then I showed the reporter going to the phone. He's a wire service man. And then I showed the dissemination, where it went. BBC, newspaper, teletype in clubs and so forth; running signs. But each time I added a piece of news about the murders. A. he only killed blonde girls. B. he did it on Tuesday night. He'd done so many. And he went around carrying a small black bag and wearing a cloak.

"You picked this stuff up as you went along. And I remember one shot I did was the newspaper van going out with deliveries. And this shot I couldn't get in because we didn't have back projection facilities at the time.

"It was the back of a newspaper van. (He rapidly sketched on the back of a menu the drawing that appears with this story. He started his career doing art work.) A back view like this, and it had back doors, double doors. Just like that. It had oval windows. And sitting in front were two men and I put black caps on them and the result was that the black caps make the windows look like eyes. As the thing moved from side to side, so the black caps move from one side to the other.

"And I show the effect of the news on different girls. Brunettes didn't care. Blondes who worked in hairdressers stole black curls and put 'em under their hats. I showed girls coming off the stage into dressing rooms of a musical show. And I followed one home. And she lived in Bloomsbury. She lived down in the basement of the house. The local detective, her boyfriend, was there with her mother and father. They chided him for not arresting the Ripper, being tardy or something.

"While they're all talking, the room gradually gets dimmer and it gets darker and darker until the mother says, 'Dad, put a shilling in the meter, would you?' And RAT TAT TAT at the front door! Mother goes to answer the door. And I cross cut quickly. And as she opens the door the shilling goes in. As the door opens the lights come up, like that! And there is a man with a cloak and a black bag! It ran about 11 or 12 minutes before the man made his entry.

(Hitchcock started writing titles in silent movies after entering pictures through the advertising department as a layout man. This was in London.)

"I'm American trained. Paramount started a London studio. When you walked in the door you might as well be in Hollywood. They were all imported people. They didn't have producers in those days. They had an editor. Like a newspaper. When the film was finished it came to him again and by the use of titles he could polish up the film, change the character and everything by the use of titles. And that's where I learned my business.

"I never learned in the British studios. As a matter of fact, the first picture that I worked on as a writer and as art director (he did both simultaneously)—of course this was in the day when everything was exaggerated; sets were enormous, people lived in cathedrals and God knows what—was called *Woman to Woman* and although it was an English director I remember the *London Daily Express* review headline: "Best American Film Made in England." That was me. Sets and story. Which I had learned from American people."

QUESTION:  *Someone asked, what about rating pictures?*
"There have been ratings in England for at least 40 years. U for universal. A for adults. And they added many years later two other categories: H for horrific and X uh, uh . . . I always call it X for breakfast.
    (There were groans.)
    "Don't you know that old gag? (It is best to say these rapidly and let the sense seep through. I have been able to discover tricky meanings in all but three and I'm working on those. One of the unclear ones is B for Brooks, which I believe is because this system was devised by a Charles Brooks. Anyhow, this is what Hitchcock rattled off:)
    "A for ism, B for brooks, C for Ilander, D for dumb, F for vessence, H for pension, I for Novello (that'll tell you how old it is!), J for orange, K f'rancis (I like K'Francis!), L for leather, M fa size, I've forgotten what N's for. O for the wings of a dove. P for relief. Q for food. R fuh mo! S for you. T for two. U fa films. V va la France. W. I can't remember W. X for breakfast. Y for God's sake. And Z f'r winds.
    "I used to have a game years ago of an imaginary cast in a film. And all the names are technical terms. Did you ever hear that? Well, the leading lady's name is Dolly Shot. The leading man is Ward Robe. The heavy is Mike Shadow. The German spy in this film is called Herr Dresser. The character woman was Mae Kopp. The cameraman was Otto Focus. Then we had a little child actress called Faye Doubt. There was a ballet-dancer called Pan Over. The director's name was Manny Takes. The cutter was Eddie Tor. Strangely enough, the art director's name was Art Director. There was a chief electrician, Xavier Arcs.
    (It was during this recitation, which was rapid fire, and the previous alphabet proclamation that I feared Hitchcock was about to lose his cool and actually smile. He didn't, but the tape displays an actual beginning of a chuckle.)

"I remember one night sitting with Chaplin. And I started on this thing. And do you know his face went blank for the rest of the evening trying to think of other ones and he never thought of one. Absolutely blank all evening."

QUESTION:  *Did you think of all?*

"Yes, except for Xavier Arcs. Do you know who gave me that? Grace Kelly."

(The subject of other people's movies came up and *Phantom of the Opera* was mentioned. About this Hitchcock, as usual had an interesting story.)

"This'll interest you! *Phantom of the Opera* with Lon Chaney was never shown in England. Never shown in England! Because the head of Universal (the company that made it) in England at the time was a man called Bryson. And they were bringing the *Phantom of the Opera* over on one of the big ships and he managed to get the local military to turn out a guard of honor to greet the film cans!

"As the ship docked in Southampton they dropped a banner over the side, 'Welcome to England, *Phantom of the Opera*.' And the guard came down the gangway carrying these tins of film. And the military in uniform, they presented arms like they do to the queen! Present ARMS! And they all went like that (rigid posture) as the film cans came down the gangway.

"It created such an outcry. Questions in Parliament. The film never was shown."

All good things must end. Hitchcock had to leave to make a TV appearance. After that he had more cities to go to so he could talk such sprightly talk to people that he could get a lot of space in newspapers. He walked off toward the elevator, a rather small, Buddha-shaped figure in a black undertaker suit and white shirt, smoking a long cigar to keep his weight down.

The elevator wasn't crowded. He didn't perform.

# Dialogue on Film: Alfred Hitchcock

## AMERICAN FILM INSTITUTE/1972

ALFRED HITCHCOCK VISITED the Center for Advanced Film Studies in February of 1970, soon after the Center had opened. Mr. Hitchcock was at the end of a nation-wide speaking tour discussing *Topaz*, which had just been released. The occasion of his visit brought out, in addition to fellows and faculty of the Center, many other members of the film community. His film *Rear Window* had been screened for the fellows, but as it usually is with Mr. Hitchcock, the questions ranged over his vast fund of film knowledge.

STANTON KAYE: *In* Sabotage, *when somebody suddenly kills Oscar Homolka there's a film about a bird being shown—Who Killed Cock Robin? In* Psycho, *Tony Perkins stuffs birds and also his mother. In* The Birds, *in the cross-cut shot of the mother grabbing at the son and also the girlfriend grabbing at the son, he's surrounded by all these birds. Birds are often used for women.*

ALFRED HITCHCOCK: Well, I don't know. I think women are referred to as chicks, aren't they? That's the only connection I can think of at the moment. The *Who Killed Cock Robin?*: there, you see, they ran a small movie house and Sylvia Sidney's little brother had been killed, so it seemed necessary to comment on it by using the cinema. The Disney cartoon *Who Killed Cock Robin?* seemed to lend itself to that association. It's a personal thing with me to utilize the setting and the circumstances and relate them to the situation.

---

From *Dialogue on Film*, no. 5. American Film Institute: Center for Advanced Film Studies, 1972.

JIM SILKE: *Could you elaborate on what you call your personal rule for utilizing the setting and the circumstance and relating them to the situation?*

ALFRED HITCHCOCK:  Well, it's really a matter of utilizing your material to the fullest dramatic extent. For example, in the picture *Rear Window*, James Stewart is a photographer, so naturally he fends off his attacker with the use of photographic material, such as a flash gun. That's only because it is indigenous to him. As much as I possibly can, I always insist on using those elements that belong to the character and involve them in the actions of the story. For example, in the picture *North by Northwest*, Cary Grant is trapped in an auction room. He can't get out except one way, and that is bidding, crazy bidding. He gets himself thrown out. But the essential point is that he is in an auction room and you must use the auction room. Now, in that same film there was a final sequence on the faces at Mt. Rushmore. Due to the objections of the government, we weren't allowed to have any of the figures over the faces. We were told very definitely that you could only have the figures slide down between the heads. They said this is the shrine of democracy. What I wanted to do, and was prevented from doing, was to have Cary Grant slide down Lincoln's nose and hide in the nostril. Then, I wanted Cary Grant to have a sneezing fit. That is a typical example of utilizing your material to the fullest. This is a personal thing with me. As often as I can I incorporate, down to the last detail, the elements of the scene into the film.

TIM HUNTER: *This reminds me a little of the opening of* I Confess. *In order to get to the window, where we see the murdered man, you have all the street signs. Do you also do this kind of thing with geography?*

ALFRED HITCHCOCK:  Yes, any use you can put it to. In the opening there, you see what we were doing was using the street signs which said, "Direction, direction." They point and point, and it was a way of leading the audience right to the dead body.

HUNTER: *One way or another, in quite a few of your films, you open with an exterior shot that cuts in closer and closer to a window. Examples of this would be* Shadow of a Doubt, Psycho, *and* I Confess. *I just wonder what you think of when you go back to that opening every once in a while.*

ALFRED HITCHCOCK:  I think the main value of it is that you orient your audience to the locale. If you open on a window, then you've got the audience wondering. In my particular genre of work, there is a great confusion between the words "mystery" and "suspense." The two things are absolutely miles apart. Mystery is an intellectual process, like in a "whodunit." But suspense is essentially an emotional process. You can only get the suspense element going by giving the audience information. I dare say you have seen many films which have mysterious goings-on. You don't know what is going on, why the man is doing this or that. You are about a third of the way through the film before you realize what it is all about. To me that is completely wasted footage, because there is no emotion to it.

HUNTER: *So in your own terms, have you never made a mystery?*
ALFRED HITCHCOCK: No. Not basically, to say, this is a mystery because I found that it is like a whodunit. I've only made one whodunit, and that was many, many years ago. Before you arrive at the five second revelation, there is no emotion from the audience. When you are reading a book, you are terribly tempted to turn to the last page all the time, but that is merely an emotion of curiosity. The mystery form has no particular appeal to me, because it is merely a fact of mystifying an audience, which I don't think is enough.

HUNTER: *I was thinking of* Under Capricorn. *At the end it is revealed that Margaret Leighton has been fostering Lady Henrietta's alcoholism all along. We learn things that we didn't know before. It's almost as if we have been watching a mystery, but we didn't know it was a mystery.*
ALFRED HITCHCOCK: Well, you can apply that to *Psycho* as well. There you have a revelation at the end, but that is merely a momentary thing. It doesn't alter the fact that you've been through a lot of suspense wondering when the figure is going to strike.

JAMES BLUE: *You say that suspense requires giving the audience information. I wonder if you would enlarge on that.*
ALFRED HITCHCOCK: Well, let's take a very, very simple childish example. Four people are sitting around a table, talking about baseball, five minutes of it, very dull. Suddenly a bomb goes off. Blows the people to smithereens. What does the audience have? Ten seconds of shock. Now take the same scene. Tell the audience there is a bomb under the table and it will go off in five minutes. Well, the emotion of the audience is different because you give them the information that in five minutes time, that bomb will go

off. Now the conversation about baseball becomes very vital, because the audience is saying: "Don't be ridiculous! Stop talking about baseball! There's a bomb under there!" You've got the audience working. Now, there is one difference. I've been guilty in *Sabotage* of making this error, but I've never made it since: the bomb must never go off. If you do, you've worked that audience into a state. Then they will get angry if you haven't provided them with any relief. That is almost a must. So a foot touches the bomb and some-body looks down and says, "My God, a bomb!" Then he throws it out of the window and it goes off. That is an example of information given to an audi-ence. You can't expect them to go into any kind of emotion without the information.

BLUE: *Does there arrive a point in that interim, before it is discovered and then thrown out the window, when we first learn of its presence? Does there arrive a point where, if the discovery of the bomb is not made at that moment, the audience could lose interest?*

ALFRED HITCHCOCK: No, I don't think so.

BLUE: *Can you stretch it out?*

ALFRED HITCHCOCK: There's a limit. If you stretch it out too long, they will start to giggle. They'll relieve the tension themselves. They'll do it for you, if you don't do it for them.

GEORGE SEATON: *Do you feel that example is the same as the sight comedy gag? Chaplin always said you show the banana peel first, and then you cut to the man approaching it.*

ALFRED HITCHCOCK: Well, in that case, George, I think you are quite right. If it's the man wearing the top hat who is walking towards the man-hole, the nicest shot you could do would be to put the camera on the ground, have the manhole in the foreground, and see the man approaching the hole wearing the top hat. Now, the next cut ought to be the head and shoulders of the man. You dolly with him and he drops out of the picture. You don't have to go back to the manhole any more. He walks along and suddenly whoomp, he goes! Now, to complete this, if you want satisfaction, you should now cut down to the manhole. He is lying there bleeding; the blood is pouring from his head. A policeman looks down, calls an ambulance. He's lifted up and taken to the hospital. The wife is brought to the bedside, and they say, "I'm afraid there is no hope." There is a fine line between comedy and tragedy.

SILKE:  *You indicated in the Truffaut book that if you don't give them the who, what, where, and when—the journalistic musts—that it interferes with the suspense and the emotional process. An audience will intellectually be trying to figure it out anyway.*

ALFRED HITCHCOCK:  Let's say that you set up a suspense scene and you happen to have two characters who look the same. You're going to have the audience say, "Which man is that? Is that the other man?" You are going to distract them from the emotions. Keeping our mind on one thing involves many things, such as clarification, locale, who is what, making sure the characters are not wearing the same suit. There are many elements that you have to clarify, so that you leave room only for the emotions.

BLUE:  *A scene that is not classical suspense, but simply a scene where you must have a certain amount of interest, a certain amount of information, and a certain amount of exposition, what do you look for to make that scene play? Would you attempt to use the suspense device in that?*

ALFRED HITCHCOCK:  Well, exposition before you start. The exposition should be dealt with and set to one side of the picture.

BLUE:  *Let's take an example,* The Man Who Knew Too Much. *You open in the back of the bus. Could you describe to me what you were doing in terms of the audience?*

ALFRED HITCHCOCK:  I think that was the introduction of the character. There are moments where you have to use a certain amount of footage to introduce the character. In that particular case you just didn't introduce them by small talk. You have a little boy playing and accidentally pull the veil off. You need some piece of action that would be interesting to look at rather than just, "This is John Smith. This is his wife, and this is his son." In other words, it's like all exposition: it's a pill that has to be sugarcoated. In other words, you are telling the audience something, giving them some piece of information, but at the same time it must appear to be something else.

HUNTER:  *In* North by Northwest, *there is a scene in the FBI building. It is the first time we see Leo G. Carroll, where they let us on to the fact that George Kaplan doesn't exist and Roger Thornhill is substituting for him. That is a scene of pure exposition. Without very much sugarcoating. Granted, it sets up the audience for a good solid hour before you ever have to do any further exposition. How do you feel about shooting scenes like that?*

ALFRED HITCHCOCK: Well, these scenes are a must, but don't forget that it does not come at the opening of the picture. It's when it comes at the opening of the picture that it is difficult. But that scene came at a point when you were accounting for a number of strange bizarre events that involved an average man.

JIM KITSES: *Is it important for you to have characters that have some kind of conflict or problem or characteristic that relates to the drama, so you can use that in the same way you use the background?*

ALFRED HITCHCOCK: Yes, in certain stories, very much so.

KITSES: *Is it important that Grant is an advertising man in* North by Northwest?

ALFRED HITCHCOCK: Well, in that he is an average man. As a professional, you see, he is not a detective, not a criminal. He is everyman. That helps involve the audience much more easily than if he was unique. I have never been interested in making films about professional criminals or detectives. I much prefer to take average men, because I think the audience can get involved more easily.

KITSES: *How about the girl in* The Birds?

ALFRED HITCHCOCK: In *The Birds*, the girl is a nothing. She just represents complacency and smug satisfaction, in order to contrast that with the ultimate happening.

KITSES: *You are on record in many interviews of bewailing the difficulty of finding the right material. What is the right material in your terms?*

ALFRED HITCHCOCK: It is very difficult. It would depend upon which direction you were going. You may be making a psychological murder story or a chase story. I make many, many different kinds of pictures. I have no particular preference, to be quite honest. Content, I am not interested in that at all. I don't give a damn what the film is about. I am more interested in how to handle the material so as to create an emotion in the audience. I find too many people are interested in the content. If you were painting a still life of some apples on a plate, it's like you'd be worrying whether the apples were sweet or sour. Who cares? I don't care myself. But a lot of films, of course, live on content.

KITSES: *But aren't there any general rules about what makes appropriate material? You've had problems with writers, for instance, who wouldn't give you what you wanted.*

ALFRED HITCHCOCK: Well, I have had problems with writers because I find that I am teaching them cinematics all the time. You have got to remember that with a lot of writers you have to go by the page, what is written on the page. I have no interest in that. I have that square, white rectangle to fill with a succession of images, one following the other. That's what makes a film. I have no interest in pictures that I call "photographs of people talking." These have nothing to do with cinema whatsoever. When you stick up a camera and photograph a group of people, and pick up the close-ups and two-shots, well, I think that is a bore. I'm not saying that you've got to make every film without dialogue, because you have to have dialogue. The only thing wrong with silent films is that no sound ever came out of the mouths. But at least it told a story visually and pictorially. So many films are an extension of the theater. Now, I've made them. But if I pick a subject like *Dial M for Murder*, well hell, I don't even have to come to the studio. I could phone that one in, because there is nothing for me to do. Years ago I made a movie of Sean O'Casey's play, "Juno and the Paycock." For the life of me, I couldn't figure out what to do with it, except photograph it in one room, with the Irish [Abbey Theatre] Players. The film was very successful, and I was ashamed to read those laudatory notices for which I had done nothing except photograph the Irish Players doing their job.

SILKE: *Are you saying that when you see the material, you can visualize the entire movement of that film?*
ALFRED HITCHCOCK: Yes, definitely.

SILKE: *The whole film?*
ALFRED HITCHCOCK: Beginning to end.

SILKE: *Could you do that in 1922?*
ALFRED HITCHCOCK: Yes.

SILKE: *Is this kind of visual response something that is just innately in you, or is it something that came through being an art director, and so forth?*

ALFRED HITCHCOCK: I think one of the biggest problems that we have in our business is the inability of people to visualize. What I am about to say is hearsay, but I remember Selznick, the producer, when he was talking about Irving Thalberg, the great name in our business. Selznick used to say, "Thalberg is great with a finished picture." When you examine those words, they mean that the man lacked any visual sense. The film had to be made as quickly as possible, in eighteen days or twenty-one days. Then they looked at it on the screen and remade it. To me that seems to be an awful thing. Imagine a composer sitting down with a blank music sheet in front of him, and a full orchestra. "Flute, give me a note, if you please. Yes, thank you very much," and he writes it down. It's the same thing, but a man can compose music directly on paper and what's the result? It comes out as gorgeous sounds or what have you. The visual, to me, is a vital element in this work. I don't think it is studied enough. Go back to the early days. Go back to Chaplin. He once made a short film called *The Pilgrim*. The opening shot was the outside of a prison gate. A guard came out and posted a wanted notice. Next cut: a very tall, thin man coming out of a river, having had a swim. He finds that his clothes are missing and have been replaced with a convict's uniform. Next cut: a railroad station, and there coming towards the camera dressed as a parson with the pants too long is Chaplin. Now, there are three pieces of film and look at the amount of story they told. These are the things that I think are so essential, especially when you send your film into a foreign country, Japan, Italy, or wherever. If you send a film which, as I mentioned earlier, is "photographs of people talking" all the way through, and that gets to a foreign country with subtitles underneath, the poor audience will spend the entire evening reading. They won't have time to look at the pictures.

HUNTER: *Back to character for just a moment, and the fact that Roger Thornhill in* North by Northwest *is Mr. Average Man. In his ability to deal with espionage and kidnappers and the world he is thrown into, does he come out differently than what he was before?*

ALFRED HITCHCOCK: I don't think so. I think the situation was so bizarre that it made him forget his mother, his wives, and everything else. He was much too preoccupied in getting himself out of the mess that he was in.

HUNTER: *But he goes to get Eva Marie Saint out of the mess that she is in.*
ALFRED HITCHCOCK: But that particular element would apply much
more to a psychological story than it would to a chase story.

BLUE: *Why did you select those particular characters and what was their value
in your story, in* North by Northwest?
ALFRED HITCHCOCK: First of all, you have available to you a film star by
the name of Cary Grant. Don't lose sight of that element. You are actually
playing a character, but you are also playing the personality of Cary Grant.
The value of having Cary Grant, the film star, is that the audience gets a little
more emotion out of Cary Grant than they would from an unknown,
because there is identification. There are many members of the audience who
like Cary Grant, whether they know about his character in the scenes or not.

JACK WEINSTEIN: *Talking about Cary Grant, I feel that it was a mistake not
to have him as the murderer in* Suspicion.
ALFRED HITCHCOCK: I thought so, but I wasn't in charge at that time. I
had to be more or less compromising. I was loaned out to RKO by Selznick
and they had the whole thing set up. The whole subject of the film is the
woman's mind: is my husband a murderer? The ending, on which I had to
compromise, was that he was not. But the real ending that I had for the film
was that he brings his wife a fatal glass of milk. She knows that she is going
to be killed, so she writes a letter to her mother: "I'm in love with him, I
don't want to live anymore, he's going to kill me, but society should be pro-
tected." Folds the letter up, leaves it by the bed. She says, "Would you mind
mailing that for me?" She drinks the milk, he watches her die. Last shot of
the picture is Cary Grant whistling very cheerfully, going to the mailbox and
popping in the letter. But that was heresy, to do that to Cary Grant in those
days.

KAGAN: *In that very film, it seems the psychology, the deep motivation of the
characters, is part of the film: her questioning herself, her surroundings. To what
degree do you think it is bad to an audience that that character you created has a
great deal of psychological interest?*
ALFRED HITCHCOCK: Well, I think that if you take the central figure of
Tony Perkins in *Psycho*, you have a very complex individual. It would depend
on the story and the yarn that you are telling. After all, in the picture *Marnie*

you had a very complex character, which I don't think really came across sufficiently. You had a man with a fetish. And his fetish was that he wanted to go to bed with a thief. With a bad character. You know, it's like a man having a taste for oysters. There was a case which I'm reminded of which took place in the English about three or four years ago, where an armless woman sued another woman, who had no legs, for alienation of her husband's affection. That's a true case and it was tried in the court. By the time the husband got into the witness stand the whole thing was unravelled: he had a fetish for maimed women. So the case was lost. There you have a very complex character.

KAGAN: *What is your idea about what a heroine should be?*
ALFRED HITCHCOCK: Well, in the first place, I've never been very keen on women who hang their sex round their neck like baubles. I think it should be discovered. It's more interesting to discover the sex in a woman than it is to have it thrown at you, like a Marilyn Monroe or those types. To me they are rather vulgar and obvious. I think it is much more interesting in the course of the storytelling to discover the sex, even though the woman may look like a school teacher. Anything could happen to you with a woman like that in a taxi.

Q: *How do you translate your own personal understanding of the emotion fear?*
ALFRED HITCHCOCK: Well, there are many ways of doing it. I mean, when I gave the example of the bomb, I was specifically talking about suspense, not so much fear itself. Fear comes after suspense. In other words, one of the main, in fact the main constituent of suspense is fear. I mean, people will, for example, go to a fairground, pay money to go into the haunted house, because they want to scare themselves. It's there in everyone. A mother, when she holds a three month old baby in her arms, says "Boo!" and why she does that I don't know. When the child grows up and goes on the swing it gives itself a different kind of fear. And then later on, has money to go on the roller coaster and pays to be scared, providing, as I explained, the relief, providing they can get off giggling. Or come out of the haunted house, giggling.

Q: *You say that you have to have that as part of your picture?*
ALFRED HITCHCOCK: If you have the suspense, if you create the fear,

you've got to relieve it. In other words, you have to have a climax where you have had a lot of suspense and fear, in a picture like *Psycho*. Perkins comes in dressed as a woman with the knife, you have to stop it there. Let's assume you didn't, and he came and he stabbed the next girl to death—you know, where do you stop? You've got to let the people out sometime.

KEN LUBER: *Could you explain to us, once you have a script set and you have your actors, how do you go about it? Do you have rehearsals with them, do you talk about characters with them?*
ALFRED HITCHCOCK: Yes, privately in the dressing room. Not demonstrably so.

LUBER: *Is that before production or afterwards?*
ALFRED HITCHCOCK: Before.

Q: *You do not rehearse the scene?*
ALFRED HITCHCOCK: No. Oh, with dialogue scenes you can, a duo can be rehearsed, but if you've got very competent actors you can get them to go off on their own.

Q: *If you pre-visualize all of your films, then what kind of joy do you get out of directing?*
ALFRED HITCHCOCK: I don't, I'd just as soon not do it. The moment the script is finished and the film is visualized, that, as far as I'm concerned, is the end of the creative part. I'd just as soon not shoot the picture.

Q: *Why don't you let someone else shoot the picture, after you've got that joy out of it?*
ALFRED HITCHCOCK: They might screw it up.

Q: *Then once you have this picture visualized, how much do you ever change, other than casting?*
ALFRED HITCHCOCK: Not too much. You see, it is very, very essential that you know ahead of time something of the orchestration, in other words, image size. What I mean by orchestration is, take the close-up, well, that's like in music: the brass sounding brassy, loud sound before you need it. Sometimes you see films cut such that the close-up comes in early, and by

the time you really need it, it has lost its effect, because you've used it already. Now, I'll give you an example where a juxtaposition of the image size is also very important. For example, one of the biggest effects in *Psycho* was where the detective went up the stairs. The picture was designed to create fear in an audience and then gradually transfer from the screen into their minds. Hence the very violent murder to start with, another one less violent (and more frightening), and they've got that thing in their mind. Then as the film goes on there is no more violence. But in the mind of the audience, and in the anticipation of it, it is all there. Here is the shot of the detective, simple shot going up the stairs, he reaches the top stairs, the next cut is the camera as high as it can go, it was on the ceiling, you see the figure run out, raised knife, it comes down, bang, the biggest head you can put on the screen. But that big head has no impact unless the previous shot had been so far away. So that is just where your orchestration comes in, where you design the set-up, that's why you can't just guess these things on the set.

HUNTER: *I understood why you cut to the close-up of Martin Balsam after he's just been stabbed from the high angle. What intrigues me is why you introduced him in such a strange way. When we first see him in Sam Loomis's hardware store, he's brought right into the camera. We've never seen him before and therefore I wonder why you used the close-up.*

ALFRED HITCHCOCK: You bring him in like that because you are bringing in a new possible menace.

BLUE: *I almost have the feeling that I could recognize a shot from your films if I should see it out of context. I wonder if you would care to comment on the placing of the camera.*

ALFRED HITCHCOCK: Well, I think mainly it is a matter of the interest in the composition. I have a horror of what I call the passport photograph: shooting straight in. It's dull, it's not interesting, and a slight variation on that is not so much the desire to get anything in the way of sharp angles, low or high or what have you, but merely to avoid the standard level shots.

Q: *Very often we think of your staging in depth. I remember a shot in* Strangers on a Train. *A character we see is in the dark in a hallway and we see all the way back into a study where there are people. I thought it was made with a wide angle, but as I began later to look at it I noticed that you were in fact using a rather long*

*lens, or at least a 50 mm, to make that shot, and therefore you raised the light level*
*a great deal. I was wondering, does this represent anything thematic in your*
*approach, to use a longer lens even in depth staging?*
ALFRED HITCHCOCK: If you use a wide angle lens, of course, you naturally change your perspective considerably. As a matter of fact, if you use a
short focus lens, say 100 mm, you foreshorten; your standard view is about a
50 mm. That would give you what the eye sees.

BLUE: *Is your tendency to stage with the formal 50 mm?*
ALFRED HITCHCOCK: Yes. Sure. Otherwise you make a room look too big
and you send the back wall too far away. If you use a wide angle lens, you
make the set much bigger than it really is.

BLUE: *Does this have something to do with the emotional quality, the fact that*
*you would stick with the normal perspective?*
ALFRED HITCHCOCK: No, it would depend, it would depend. You see,
sometimes you get involved with the whole question of the depth of focus.
There is a whole group of people who think everything should be sharp in
front and equally sharp at a distance, which in actual fact is almost impossible in real life. I remember at Paramount, when they first introduced Vista-
Vision. They did their first test out in the desert. They were making a film
with Martin and Lewis and when they saw the first results, they were over-
whelmed and ecstatic that a hand in the foreground was sharp as a figure
half a mile away. And what the hell that's got to do with picture making I
don't know, but they were delighted. They all thought this was a wonderful
system. Of course, what the camera department failed to tell them was that
if you shoot the desert then you have to stop down to a pinhole and it will
make everything sharp, including five miles away. But the camera department was afraid to tell them. So they let them think it was VistaVision. I was
doing this picture *To Catch a Thief* at the time and I remember the head of
the studio, who shall be nameless, comes to me and says, "Look, in these
close-ups of yours everything's blurred, that's not VistaVision." I said: "So?
The audience is not going to look round the head, they are going to look at
the head we've got on the screen." "Yes, but in VistaVision everything is
sharp!" So the camera department secretly went round to each cameraman
and said pile up the lights, so as to continue to deceive the front office. They

went around to every cameraman on the lot and made him pile up the light so that everything was sharp.

GEORGE STEVENS, JR.: *Could you talk about the problem of getting a set the way you want it?*

ALFRED HITCHCOCK: Yes, about the set dressing. As I was explaining earlier, one of the biggest problems that we have is in terms of atmosphere, as I call it. We have a very strange system in this industry, and that is that the man that is called the art director leaves the set the moment it is painted and finished but not dressed, not even the carpet. And the new man walks on, called the set dresser, and he is the man who reads the script and then proceeds to dress the set: goes out and picks furniture, carpet, goes into the prop room, gets ornaments, paintings, and this man is in charge of what is the most vital element of the decor, the atmosphere. Instead of being a set dresser he should almost be a writer, because he ought to know the character of the person who lives in that room. But he doesn't, and that is why you see so many films that have an artificial look. It is because they are very badly dressed. And the only way I have ever gotten around it is to send a photographer with a color still camera. In *Vertigo*, Stewart was playing a retired detective who went to law school and who lived in San Francisco. So I said to the photographer, "Go to San Francisco, find out where a retired detective lives, make sure he went to law school, and go in and photograph his house. Get all the detail and bring it back and dress the set that way." This is a very big problem.

Q: *If you care so much about the authenticity of the sets, in making it look real or feel real on the set, then why do you use rear screen projection and things like that that look fake?*

ALFRED HITCHCOCK: That's a decision that you have to make quite a bit. It depends. If you are shooting a long dialogue scene and you go outside and you shoot it in an open car in the street, you've got to dub the whole scene because of the external sounds. Now you've got to do that or you can do the best back projection you can get. And it can be well done, and it can be badly done. At least then you can let the players have the comfort of being able to play the scene naturally and spontaneously.

Q: *Well, wouldn't they be playing it naturally and spontaneously in a studio with a background mirror or if they were driving the car?*

ALFRED HITCHCOCK:  Yes, but I think they'd be distracted. They'd be distracted by traffic, the guy driving the car. There have been a lot of pictures made that way, with the camera strapped on the front and the windshield taken off, but you do run the risk of having to re-dub the whole thing. No, when you're dubbing a whole long dialogue scene, you're not going to get the necessary emotion into it. That's the risk you run.

WEINSTEIN:  *Do you in fact storyboard your films?*
ALFRED HITCHCOCK:  Sometimes, not always. It can be done. You can storyboard key scenes.

WEINSTEIN:  *I see, it's the less important shots that you let go.*
ALFRED HITCHCOCK:  They're nothing. Where you storyboard is the thing I just described in *Psycho*, the man coming up the stairs, to make sure that you get the contrast in the size of the image.

WEINSTEIN:  *In* Vertigo, *where they're climbing up the stairs in the tower, there is a very strange effect.*
ALFRED HITCHCOCK:  That effect took thirty years to get. It really did. When I was making *Rebecca*, I had a scene where Joan Fontaine is supposed to faint. I explained to Selznick I wanted to get the effect of her looking and everything seeming to go far away. Where I got the idea from was at the Royal Chelsea Arts Ball in London on New Year's Eve. I remembered at a certain time during the evening everything seemed to go far away. And I asked for this effect and they said they couldn't do it. I tried again about five years later. For *Vertigo* they tried different effects and finally it was arrived at by a combination of a dolly shot and a zoom lens crossing each other. Dollying in and zooming out. When the head of special effects came to me I said how much was it going to cost. He said $50,000 to put a camera high and take it up and zoom it, because of the enormous rig. I said, "But there is no one in the set." Why didn't they make a miniature and lay it on its side? "Oh, I hadn't thought of that." So they did it and it cost $19,000.

MICHAEL BARLOW:  *The last time I saw* Vertigo, *I tried to concentrate on the camera movements, which I think are extraordinarily beautiful. But as hard as I tried, I can't verbally express what those camera movements meant. When you plot out a story like* Vertigo, *do you think of a specific emotional effect you want the camera to arrive at?*

ALFRED HITCHCOCK:  Yes, there were moments when you need that, but you don't necessarily storyboard all of those, because it's very hard to do camera movements. Your artist usually draws a big arrow, which doesn't really convey where the camera is going. I think you more or less have to leave that till you go on the set. But you have it in mind.

JEREMY KAGAN:  *The sequence in* Psycho, *the first murder, is integrally cut. To what degree did you conceive the editing of it beforehand, and was this story-boarded?*

ALFRED HITCHCOCK:  To some extent, yes. Actually, there were seventy-eight set-ups and it took forty-five seconds on the screen. First of all, the leading lady was a bit squeamish about revealing herself, so I had to get a nude stand-in. It was made up of all those tiny pieces of film because the knife never touched the body at any time. Just an illusionary thing.

KAGAN:  *So you did the storyboarding beforehand, but in the editing it did change.*

ALFRED HITCHCOCK:  Oh, we tightened it up and got the tempo going. Sure.

SILKE:  *That use of pieces of film to create violence as opposed to actually depict-ing violence, you've used it in* Psycho, *the end of* Rear Window, *and* Torn Cur-tain.

ALFRED HITCHCOCK:  There's no question that for any kind of violence that you want to portray on the screen, that's the way it can be done best. Let me see if I can give you a comparison. If you stand in a field and you see a train going by half a mile away, you look at it and it speeds by. Now go within six feet of the train going by; think of the difference in its effect. So what you are doing is you are taking the audience right close up into the scene, and the montage of the various effects gets the audience involved. That's its purpose. It becomes much more powerful than if you sit back and look. Say you are at a boxing match and you are eight to ten rows back: well, you get a very different effect if you are in the first row, looking up under those ropes. When these two fellows are slugging each other, you get splashed almost.

SILKE:  *In the sense that you used the proportion of the head in* Psycho, *the preceding shot far away to create a contrast in proportion, now you are creating a contrast in the length of the footage. Preceding violence you have a long lengthy . . .*
ALFRED HITCHCOCK:  No, not too long. No, once that figure comes in and starts to stab, you're in it. Oh, you're absolutely in it.

SILKE:  *Well, at the end of* Rear Window, *you go through several sequences which are quite lengthy of Jimmy Stewart preparing himself.*
ALFRED HITCHCOCK:  Ah yes, but the moment the man attacks him, I mean, to legs, arms, head, then at that moment, the moment of contact, then you are into your pieces of film. You involve the audience right in the sense of the violence.

SILKE:  *But you purposely slow it down preceding that moment to provide better contrast.*
ALFRED HITCHCOCK:  I think that comes automatically. The distance of the figures, you see. That's why I think barroom brawls in Westerns are always a bore for me, because one man hits the other, the table collapses and he falls back over the bar. If they would only do a few big close-ups here and there, it would be much more exciting, instead of looking at it from a distance. But you see, they make a mistake, they think it creates a greater air of reality by seeing it at a distance and in fact they are doing the wrong thing.

BLUE:  *To return to the discussion of structure; the last few films you've made, your pictures have seemed to divide up into almost two stories:* Topaz, Psycho, *and* The Birds; Torn Curtain *perhaps less so. I wonder if you could explain to us what your fascination is with this device, the double story. What are you attempting?*
ALFRED HITCHCOCK:  Well, I think if you take a picture like *The Birds*, you'll find the personal story is rather a thin one because traditionally it's an event story, like the early H. G. Wells stories, like "War of the Worlds." In all Wells's famous stories, the personal story is very, very secondary to the events. Otherwise you wouldn't get the effect. Whether it is Martians or what have you, they take it over and almost swamp the personal story. So the personal would tend to be on the thin side. In that type of picture.

BLUE:  *But is there a definite reason, in terms of dealing with the audience, of starting with this kind of story?*

ALFRED HITCHCOCK: Well, the first thing, you see, you have to remember the audience goes in anticipating something. They've read something about it in the ads, so it's a question of how much of the lightweight story you put up in the picture in the beginning. I believe it was Fellini who said, "Hitchcock made them wait for the birds to come on. I wouldn't have the nerve to do that." But I think it is a matter of figuring it out and then gradually, one bird just hitting the girl. And the gradual slow buildup.

DAVIDS: *Did you see the film* The War of the Worlds *before you made the film? Did it influence your thinking?*
ALFRED HITCHCOCK: No, it's rather vague in my mind, the "War of the Worlds" film. I once had breakfast with H. G. Wells on the blue train and we were discussing "War of the Worlds" and I was talking about making it into a picture and he said in his high piping voice: "Oh no, you couldn't do that today, I'd have to invent all new devices." So it didn't relate to *The Birds* at all.

BLUE: *In* Topaz *you had a double structure there, could you tell me how you related to the various parts?*
ALFRED HITCHCOCK: For example, they had a whole section of the Russian defector that was dropped. There was a whole section about stealing the Cuban trade packet. That was completely isolated, and the French section was another, so it was a matter of pulling those together.

BLUE: *Was there anything particular you had to do to pull it together?*
ALFRED HITCHCOCK: No, you just let everything emanate from the Russian defector. He provided the information.

KITSES: *You say you don't like the notion of filming theater, but a lot of your films do fall into acts that peak at certain points.*
ALFRED HITCHCOCK: I think that that is true, because in order to sustain an audience's interest you have to give them a series of climaxes. Otherwise, you have to have a very powerful yarn to hold them from the beginning to the end. In a sense it is almost like, which is out of date now, what we used to call the well-made play. That ran into three acts: proposition, argument, and resolution.

HUNTER: *You generally structure your climaxes in terms of montages. In* Psycho *and* The Birds *you push that kind of montage to its limits, you get in as many kinds of shots as you possibly can. In* Marnie, *the climaxes expressed in terms of montage are just the opposite. You slowed them down. In* Topaz *and even* Torn Curtain, *there is much less of that. Are you becoming less interested in that kind of montage?*

ALFRED HITCHCOCK: No, I think it would really depend upon the situation, you know. After all, that is the beauty of film; there are so many ways to go.

BRUCE LANE: *Could you tell me a little bit about training the birds for* The Birds?

ALFRED HITCHCOCK: Training? Well, we had a bird trainer and he was able to train a certain number of seagulls, and I think about thirty or forty well-trained ravens and crows. A lot of it of course was double and triple printing. In fact, the last shot in *The Birds* was composed of sixteen separate pieces of film.

LANE: *Are any of those birds stuffed?*

ALFRED HITCHCOCK: No, I'll tell you what we did. We rented five hundred ducks and sprayed them gray. We started off with chickens but the neck movement gave them away.

LANE: *When the seagulls attack at the windows, were you throwing them at the windows?*

ALFRED HITCHCOCK: Oh yes, sure. We had men on ladders, and the gulls were trained to be thrown and land on the flat table top nearby the camera. And, for example, the little girl with a gull at the birthday party: we built a little platform on her shoulder and a gull was put there, but its beak was bound, and she had a little wire and as she ran up the dunes she was told to pull her hand up and down so that you got the effect of its pecking.

LANE: *In the shots where you throw a seagull at a window, for instance, why would you use a trained seagull instead of a wild one?*

ALFRED HITCHCOCK: Well, because the wild one may go half way there and say, "Where the hell am I going?" and turn round and come back. I don't trust them.

KAGAN: *Is there a film where you really like the music? Is there a film of yours that you really feel is the best use of music or silence that you've ever had?*
ALFRED HITCHCOCK: I can't think of one offhand.

BLUE: *What about the sort of sweeping lyrical moment in* Vertigo *under the green neon lights?*
ALFRED HITCHCOCK: You see, here you had a man who was really a necrophile, i.e., he was going to bed with a dead body, hence the green light. He was waiting for the girl to complete her hair and everything, and he was in love with a dead woman. So you want to help that, and the music helped it, because he was going to bed with a dead woman.

BLUE: *You would say that the music did more than simply repeat the image.*
ALFRED HITCHCOCK: Sure. It, shall we say, intensified his necrophilia.

BLUE: *I notice that in* Torn Curtain, *and it is possible that we can find it in other pictures of yours, that you have got the audience interested and have used suspense to discover something which all of a sudden you reveal before the maximum has been developed. In other words, we learn that Paul Newman is in fact not defecting very early.*
ALFRED HITCHCOCK: You're forgetting another value. What will the girl say when she finds out? I'll give you a specific example. In *Vertigo*, it was the end of the book before it's revealed that it is one and the same woman. I decided halfway through to blow the whole thing, tell the audience the truth and not wait until the end. People were horrified. "What are you doing? Giving it all away?" I replied that if I didn't I'm starting another story. Jimmy Stewart has lost one woman. She's dead, she's gone, he was crazy about her, and she even drove him into a nursing home. Now he sees a girl on the street, he sees some resemblance, and he gets hold of her, gets into her room. From that point on in the book, he endeavored to change the girl back into the image of the dead woman he wanted to renew. The reason I gave the whole thing away was to give additional values. First, we know who she is; added value, what will Stewart do when he finds out? We know something that he doesn't know. Now there is an element of suspense. Second, why does the girl resist him? If you haven't told the audience who she really is, you won't understand her behavior. Why she doesn't want to wear a gray suit, why she doesn't want her hair made blonde.

KITSES: *Do you differentiate between fear and horror?*
ALFRED HITCHCOCK: Well, horror is really an extreme of fear. It's as far as you can go.

KITSES: *Many of your films operate almost like dreams or nightmares.*
ALFRED HITCHCOCK: They are. That's the theory of it. That's why a picture like *North by Northwest* is a nightmare, but it behooves you to be realistic. Because when you have a nightmare and you are being led to the electric chair, it is so vivid that you are glad when you wake up.

KITSES: *When you said the theory of it, do you think of it that way?*
ALFRED HITCHCOCK: No, but I think it is very, very vital that the detail be accurate however bizarre the situation may be, as part of the nightmare.

KITSES: *And what are your ends in putting nightmare on the screen? What do you want to do to the audience?*
ALFRED HITCHCOCK: Give them pleasure. Same pleasure they have when they wake up from a nightmare.

# Alfred Hitchcock

## JANET MASLIN/1972

THE FIRST FIVE MINUTES in the lobby of the St. Regis, waiting to reach Alfred J. Hitchcock on the house phone, feel very much like an opening scene in one of his pictures. Every detail is important, the air is one of taut anticipation, and, since everyone knows Hitchcock likes to do his walk-on early in every picture (so as to keep his audiences from getting too distracted looking for him), the only question is where is he hiding? The desk clerk seems too humorlessly cosmopolitan, the bellhops are much too spry to be approaching their 73rd birthdays. The most likely candidates are a group of visiting Oriental scientists, all chattering busily in one corner of the lobby, but it's a well-known fact by now that Hitchcock no longer likes to do his cameos in costume.

His suite is number 1401, on what would really be the 13th floor if the hotel had no qualms about numbering it that way. He will certainly lumber slowly to the door and open it with his famous, much-televised "Good Evening," even if it is 9:30 A.M. on a sunny Monday. But when the door finally does swing backward, the figure at its handle is entirely too natty and youthful to be his. This is the Universal Man (Hitchcock refers to Universal as "our company"), whose assignment it is to supervise the current publicity tour, which begins with a week of solid interviews *(Time, Life, New York Times, Dick Cavett Show)* and an honorary Columbia degree in New York, then proceeds to Boston for *Frenzy's* American premiere. The Universal Man is plainly amazed at Hitchcock's stamina in matters of promotion. "I've seen men in their twen-

From *Boston After Dark*, 3, no. 24 (June 12–June 20, 1972), pp. 1, 12, 13, 23.

ties do this kind of thing for three days and get surly," he remarks. "He's going to do it; for two weeks, maybe longer."

In the suite's sitting room, which is positively littered with bouquets of congratulatory flowers, there stands a formidable sight. The main thing he suggests at first is a giant cookie, the big bakery kind that's iced in two matched semi-circles, the top half vanilla and the bottom one chocolate. He is very round, much more so than ever before, and he has grown so jowly that there's no longer any neck visible. But he stills looks ruddy and imposing, sturdy as a boulder. He decides to cover up the white shirt with his suit jacket at the prospect of being photographed.

*Frenzy*, the new picture about a psychopathic rapist who strangles women with neckties, is anywhere from 51st to 57th in the roster of Hitchcock's films (there are several dubious early entries, like the unfinished *Number Thirteen* in 1922). It is slated for a June 20 American premiere in Boston (it has already opened in Paris), and Hitchcock himself has been scheduled to give out everything from a *Frenzy* Cup at one racetrack to *Frenzy* margarita mixes (the drink figures peripherally in the picture). He has long been reputed to have a keen interest in commercial considerations (he is also an infamous practical joker), and so his willingness to perform such stunts is more characteristic than it might sound.

The director and Alma Reville Hitchcock, his former script girl and tiny, bird-like wife of forty-odd years, have both come from Los Angeles, where they have recently been living. She waits patiently in the bedroom while her husband, propped up immobile in an armchair, his posture powerfully reminiscent of Humpty Dumpty, complies with the demands of his busy schedule. He is one of the most over-interviewed people imaginable (François Truffaut's exhaustive sessions took 50 hours to complete), and yet he never fails to be both articulate and interesting—even though some questions, by sheer force of probability, are bound to seem repetitious to him by now. However does he manage to maintain his spontaneity?

"Ah," he says. "The trick is to always be able to give a different answer."

BOSTON AFTER DARK: *Is the new film,* Frenzy, *more closely related to your earlier pictures than it is to the other things you've done in the sixties?*
ALFRED HITCHCOCK: No, that's a sort of a misconception. The earlier pictures were English in their setting mostly, and this once happened to be that way.

B A D : *Yes, but people have already started to compare it to pictures like* Psycho *and* Strangers on a Train.

A H : Oh, it's a different picture than *Psycho—Psycho* had no humor, except mine. To me, *Psycho* was a big comedy. Had to be.

B A D : *Why a comedy?*

A H : If I were doing *Psycho* as a serious picture, it would be done in terms of a case history. It certainly wouldn't be done in terms of the haunted house and the mysterious figure. They're all comic—they're bound to be. When you're designing a picture of that kind, you're laughing up your sleeve when you can hear the audience screaming.

It's no different from a man who designs a roller coaster. He may hammer the nails and the screws in seriously, but the total result is going to be screaming.

B A D : *Do you see the rape sequence in this picture in that same vein?*

A H : No, the rape scene comes under the heading of "What Is Worth Doing Is Worth Doing Well." In other words, that's a technical thing. If you have to show the one scene in the picture that is the basis of the whole story, it has to be done right and well.

B A D : *Was that a difficult scene to do?*

A H : It took time because, after all, it's composed of many pieces of film and montage and it's a very very slow construction. The man comes in and it's a long time before he ultimately kills her.

It's done very realistically on that account.

B A D : *For instance, the strangulation scene looks as though she really is strangling—her neck starts to get red, and . . .*

A H : Oh, that's all done with little pieces of film. You shoot along this way and along that way; you shoot the knot, you shoot the head. . . . It's composed of a tremendous number of different pieces of film. It's like the bathroom scene in *Psycho*. There, it's purely illusionary—the knife never touches the body at any time. It's composed of 78 pieces of film that go through in 45 seconds.

B A D : *How many pieces are there in the strangulation?*

A H : I would say there would probably be about 50 or 60. But they're so fast, and that is the whole point—you indicate, you *suggest* violence by the rapidity of the cuts. You *must* be very intimate with it. To make you feel the effect of that strangulation, it's done in very close shots. The closeup of the man straining, his individual hands . . . what effect do you want to have on the audience? Do you want to have the effect of scaring them, or making them feel the horror of it? If you'll notice, that's the only one in the film. The film is about multiple murders, but I don't show the others. They're all done with discretion, except the one.

BAD:  *About the more psychoanalytic orientation you seem to be leaning towards lately, with* Marnie *and* Psycho, *and now with this film, I wonder what you see as the killer's motivation here.*

AH:  Two men explain it in the pub, don't they? He's a psychotic, he's definitely a case, because he's impotent. That's the whole basis of it. A man who is impotent and only gets satisfaction out of killing. You have the prime example of the Christie case—he killed eight women and buried them all over the house. And you also have an echo of the Evans case tied into the Christie case in *Frenzy* because you have the wrong man picked up. In the case of Christie-Evans the police, mind you, *hanged* Evans, and he was an innocent man. The only recompense ever given to him was to take the body out of prison grounds and put it in consecrated grounds three years later.

The amazing thing about the case is that Christie was a necrophile. In other words, he killed women to get sexual satisfaction. I remember reading the transcript of the trial, and the prosecuting attorney cross-examining Christie said something like this:

"And you say there were three steps down to the kitchen?"—"I think so."

"And you say she fell?"—"Yes."

"And then you found she was dead?"—"Yes, I think so."

"Did intercourse take place?"—"Yes, I think so."

"Did it take place before, at the time, or after her death?"—"At the time, I think."

Now there you get an example of the sexual killer who only becomes potent in the moment of killing. This is no make-believe—I'm telling you actual facts in a courtroom transcript.

BAD:  *In the film, why does Rusk say his mother used to quote Robert Frost to him? That line he quotes from "The Death of the Hired Man"?*

AH: He probably heard it somewhere. I'm sure he didn't know who Robert Frost was, either. Like any more than when he says "My mum always used to say 'Beulah, peel me a grape.'" That's Mae West, a well-known Mae West quote.

BAD: *Is there a MacGuffin in this picture?*
AH: If you can call it a MacGuffin, it's the act of murder by the Killer. Actually, the term really only applies to a spy story—it's whatever the spies are after. It's something that the characters on the screen care about but the audience doesn't exactly understand it. The papers, the plans of the jet engine, you can make it anything you like.

BAD: *Was there a conscious effort to Americanize the dialogue? Because it seems not at all idiomatic, and with the accents very clear.*
AH: We had two different versions. In the English version we say lorry instead of truck, and the guy says "I live on the first floor." In the American version, it's "I live on the second floor." Because in England it's ground floor, you see, and then it's first floor.

BAD: *So were ALL these scenes shot twice, or is the sound just different?*
AH: Twice, twice. There's an English version, and an American version.

BAD: *Which scene did you have to do the most times?*
AH: None. All done right then and there, out of the head.

BAD: *Did you use story-boards for this picture? [detailed sketches of every scene]*
AH: No, I didn't, I carried it in my head. For example, the potato truck sequence? I dictated that one lunchtime. Hundred and eighteen shots.
In fact, to help the cutter, not only did I list out the hundred and eighteen, but I had a special number put up for each one, because I realized the cutter would be confronted with a whole lot of film—close-ups of the killer and potato sacks behind him—and he would get awful confused which was which. So I had special numbers made, yellow cards with black figures on them, and each shot was numbered according to my dictated sheets.

BAD: *Do you supervise your cutters ordinarily?*
AH: Well, I shoot a pre-cut picture.

BAD: *You didn't have to do any retakes on anything this time?*

AH: No, because the picture's already cut, you see. I don't shoot all kinds of angles. That would be like a musician trying various kinds of notes for one particular note. Well, that's ridiculous—for me, there's only one note needed, and that note is the right one. And so it is with the cut.

BAD: *Did you have any particular problems with the actors in this picture?*

AH: None whatever, no.

BAD: *Why did you decide to do it this way, to use no stars and a cast pretty much unknown in America?*

AH: I wanted as much realism as possible. But they are *all* leads in the London theatre. For example, the man who plays the sergeant, the one who sips that drink—he was playing the lead in the most successful play in London. I think it was called *Forget-Me-Not Lane*, by the same author who wrote *Joe Egg*. Nichols is his name. And the wife of the detective is Vivien Merchant, a very famous actress on the stage there.

BAD: *They're all extraordinary, but I just wondered if you were worried about the commercial prospects of not having any stars in the picture.*

AH: No, because stars don't sell pictures any more. Only stories.

BAD: *So does that mean all the things you've said in the past about the star system no longer apply?*

AH: Well, it's been proven, hasn't it? The star system is not an insurance. The star is good if the picture's good.

BAD: *I meant that in the past, in the forties, stars like Cary Grant and Jimmy Stewart were unwilling to play villains.*

AH: You can't make Cary Grant a murderer, that is true. That would apply today with those particular men, because you've got to remember they've grown up to be stars over a number of years. You can take Cary Grant all the way back to Mae West. You didn't turn those people into villains until you got your rough fellow like Humphrey Bogart. He broke the mold, shall we say.

BAD: *Was it your effort or the production company's effort a couple of years ago to make a star out of Tippi Hedren?*

AH: It was my effort, because we had such a shortage of women.

BAD: *How did you find her?*
AH: In a commercial. I think it was for some face cream. I later turned her over to Universal, because you can't have the same woman in every picture. But nothing ever came of her.

BAD: *Why not?*
AH: They offered to renew her contract if she would agree to do television, which she didn't want to do. So she lost out on it.

BAD: *Would you consider doing that again if you found somebody in another commercial?*
AH: Well, I don't know, it takes a lot of . . . you know, to build a person up it costs a lot of money. With the Hedren girl, I had a special wardrobe made by Edith Head, special tests. I even brought Martin Balsam in from New York to play opposite her, just for a test, and I took a scene out of *To Catch a Thief* for that test. Building a girl up, it takes a lot. We don't have the system any more—in the old days of MGM, boy, they put them through school practically, they had a whole roster of stars. But those days are gone.

BAD: *Do you find it easier to work with actors who don't think of themselves as stars?*
AH: Well, I find it easier to work with actors who don't give me any trouble. You can never tell with actors—what happened to our company the other day?

Dean Martin walked off the location and they're suing—it was in the papers—for six million dollars. And he walked off because he didn't like the location.

BAD: *You've never had that kind of problem?*
AH: If an actor gives me trouble, I just tell him "You do what you like. There's always the cutting-room floor. And when you're on the cutting-room floor, you get trodden upon."

BAD: *I wonder if you considered using Michael Caine in* Frenzy, *because he looks so much like one of the actors you did use.*

AH:  If you did, then you'd have to have just as big a man in the other part. You couldn't have that part played by Caine and a lesser actor as your leading man, you'd have to balance them out. Otherwise, you'd give the story away the moment Caine came on the screen.

BAD:  *So then, in other words, you think this is a Hitchcock picture and it doesn't need anybody else in it, it still can be a big success?*
AH:  Yes, but it needs people, that's what we have in the picture, we have a whole host of London top players. Can't get any better.

BAD:  *I understand that there are feminist groups that have already been offended by the picture's view of women. Were you at all prepared for that while you were making it?*
AH:  I've never heard . . .

BAD:  *I was told there'd been reactions at the New York screenings to the whole thing with cooking, that kind of a wife, the marriage bureau, these women who seemed very repressed—that was found to be sort of offensive in some quarters.*
AH:  I think they're stretching a bit. After all, women do go to the Cordon Bleu, to learn how to cook.

BAD:  *I guess. But not pig's feet, do they?*
AH:  Sure, *pied a pork*? Very famous French dish.

BAD:  *Did you deliberately use recognizable parts of animals in those dishes?*
AH:  No! They're genuine French dishes! Soup's a kind of bouillabaisse, soup de poisson, and *everybody* has had quail aux raisins. That's about 100 years old, that dish.

BAD:  *I understand you're—I don't know if you're a cook, but I understand you're quite a gourmet.*
AH:  Good supervisor, anyway. I've always agreed that you should eat at home better than you can in a restaurant.

BAD:  *Why don't you like Margaritas?*
AH:  I didn't dislike Margaritas, the character in the film disliked them.

BAD: *I thought it might be personal.*

AH: No, no, I'm a professional. I don't put my personal feelings into pictures. I don't indulge myself—I don't make pictures to please me. I make them to please audiences.

BAD: *Not even after all these years?*

AH: Why should I please myself? That, I think, is an indulgence which too many directors do. They sacrifice too many people's jobs, and the studios get closed down because they make pictures to suit themselves and then it doesn't make any money. They do that a lot in England, and then you read in the paper about how Shepperton Studios may have to close down. It's like a man I had once to lunch—an English man came over once with a note of recommendation that I should see him—and I said to him "what's your business?" He said, "my business is financing films." I said, "I always thought films were financed from the receipts of the previous film."

BAD: *Have you ever made a picture that didn't make money?*

AH: Probably one or two, but I've always been guaranteed a minimum of seven or eight or more million dollars.

BAD: *How well can you gauge these things before the picture comes out?*

AH: You can't, really. You take a picture like *The Birds* that was a big, successful picture, it did about eleven million. Who knows? It might have done more, but a lot of people don't like birds, they're scared of birds. A play was once put on in New York, called "Guest in the House," and in it the leading girl was terrified of birds in a cage.

BAD: *Do you think people like seeing things they're afraid of?*

AH: No, some people are really scared of things like birds. It's like some people don't like snakes, others pick 'em up and hang 'em round their necks.

BAD: *Do you set out deliberately to scare people?*

AH: No more than the man who builds a haunted house at Disneyland. He sets out to scare people, and they pay money to go in. They scream, and they come out giggling.

BAD: *Are you ever frightened by these things yourself?*

AH: Not at all.

BAD: *Truffaut once said to you something about how the man who makes all these pictures about fear is himself a very fearful person.*

AH: No, as I say, I'm no different from the man who builds a haunted house where the skeleton jumps out. Scares the bejesus out of the customers, but they always like it.

BAD: *But mightn't that man have nightmares about his own haunted house sometimes?*

AH: I don't think so. I should think he'd be more concerned with painting a good skeleton.

BAD: *It seems, with* Frenzy, *that you've painted an extraordinarily good skeleton, and the little details are about as carefully worked out as they've been in any of your films. Did you put any more effort than usual into this one?*

AH: No, I think it's really when you have a good collaborative writer. (The collaborator here was Anthony Shaffer, author of *Sleuth.*) That helps an awful lot.

As for detail, the sets we used were actual copies of wherever we had to build. Like the Hilton Hotel—we had the Hilton Hotel people down to the studio, and they were amazed to see the lobby of the room a dead copy of one of their own rooms. You know that scene—with the woman up on the balcony. Where human nature is put to the test. Would *you* help a man on the run, or not?

BAD: *Are you asking me, or is it just a question?*

AH: Well, I'm asking you.

BAD: *I guess it would depend who the man was and what he was running for.*

AH: Well, you see, this is a big question! Most people don't want to get involved when they see a street accident, maybe two cars, even though they've seen it they take a look and drive on. Because right through their minds flash interviews with lawyers, appearing in court, and they think "I don't want any of that."

BAD: *Is that why you have those two working girls who come along and don't hear the scream after the body is discovered?*

AH: Oh, they just happened to be passers-by. The reason I did that scream was because I took away the cliché. How many times have you seen the scene where the body's discovered? Same old scene. So I do it differently. And this way, what the audience is seeing is that girl going upstairs. Opening the door. Looking around. Hanging her hat up. Then opening the other door and seeing the thing.

So I make the audience visualize these things. And therefore, they get more out of it than if you just laid it on the line for them.

BAD: *This picture seems so much warmer and more sexually explicit than anything you've been doing lately. Why is that?*
AH: I think you can lay that down to the playing of the actors.

BAD: *I assume you supervised their casting in the first place.*
AH: Yes, but you can have the same man and . . . I wanted Sergeant Spearman to be a nice, decent cop or detective. Now, did you see *Clockwork Orange*? He was in that. He played a prison guard, barking the conventional . . . same man! And in *Frenzy* he's a warm, nice man. He doesn't go yelling all over the place, he's very quiet. Look at the way he extracted that look as he watched the breakfast being eaten by the other man. This is what I call a maximum of effect with a minimum of effort.

BAD: *You mentioned* Clockwork Orange. *I'm curious what you thought of that.*
AH: I thought it was an interesting picture.

BAD: *Are there any new directors who you think are especially promising?*
AH: No, I haven't seen any particularly . . . I like Buñuel's work. Did you see *Tristana*? Catherine Deneuve. That was very good. He's simple. I don't like these films where the flowers are out of focus in the foreground. I'm *bored* with those. I'm also bored with Fifth Avenue, Park Avenue traffic, all on top of each other, and then the crowd's walking. They don't walk, they bob. What for?

BAD: *How do you feel about Hitchcock imitators, of which there seem to be many?*
AH: Oh, there are plenty of those. It's like when I decided in *North by Northwest* that Cary Grant was to be put on the spot. Now what is being put on the spot? The cliché is that he stands at the corner of the street under a lamp,

the cobbles are washed by the rain, it's night, a black cat slithers along the wall as somebody peers out of a window. This is the cliché for that sort of a scene. So I said no, I'm going to do it with *no* shadows, bright sunshine, not a tree or a house in sight, nothing. And out of the sky comes a crop-duster. And cases him. Well, what did you see? I did that to avoid the cliché.

But that in itself becomes a cliché. Because the next time I saw it was in a Bond film, and instead of an airplane they had a helicopter chasing Bond. Then the next film was *That Man From Rio*, where they had a motorboat chasing a man in the water. Then we came to an automobile in the street chasing a man up onto the sidewalk. *That* became a cliché. So we're just about through with the mechanical instrument chasing the man.

BAD: *Have you seen anybody do anything that you think of as improving on what you do—not improving, but doing interesting things with it. I'm curious if you saw* Le Boucher, *for instance. That's been described as sort of neo-Hitchcock.*
AH: Chabrol picture? No, I didn't see *Le Boucher*. But I know Chabrol quite well. He wrote a book on me, you know.

BAD: *What do you think of all the things that have been written about you? Do you have anything as a special favorite, or do you discount it all?*
AH: No, it's all right. . . . Truffaut is writing a piece on *Frenzy* for next week's *Paris-Match*.

BAD: *What about Robin Wood? Have you ever seen his book?*
AH: Haven't met him for years. He was a very profound young man.

BAD: *Do you have any particular feelings about auteur criticism, or film critics in general? Do you ever pay any attention to them?*
AH: Well, I don't know. There was an article, I think it was in one of the papers in Cannes where Anthony Burgess said he got 500 pounds for *Clockwork Orange*. He felt directors were getting too much.

BAD: *Do you think very many of the young people who are starting to make films now have an innate sense of what they're doing?*
AH: No, I think a lot of them work purely by accident. I saw there was one on the plane by our company, isn't it, called *The Hired Hand*, by Peter Fonda.

Wasn't he in *Easy Rider*? (Universal Man: "Yes. But this didn't cost much, and it was his first directorial effort.")

AH: Oh, was it?

BAD: *You didn't like it much?*

AH: Well, it's not doing well, is it? I only speak as a stockholder. Gets me worried.

BAD: *How much did* Frenzy *cost to make?*

AH: I think just over two million. The reason I'm able to keep the costs down is because I know the technical means to do so. I've been an art director. I've been a script writer. Back in 1923 I used to write the script and be the art director on the same picture! I've even turned the camera.

BAD: *Why did you give up all those sidelines you had a couple of years ago—the books and the TV show?*

AH: Oh, the books are still going, and the mystery magazine.

BAD: *But the television show?*

AH: Well, I did 273 half-hour shows—not personally, I did about 19 myself all told—and 90 one-hour shows. They're still in circulation now. If I started in television again, I'd be in competition with myself. Did ten years of it. And I've done hour shows in five days.

I did the best half-hour show with Barbara Bel Geddes—it was called "Lamb to the Slaughter." It's about a woman who kills her husband with a frozen leg of lamb. Most successful half-hour I've ever had. She kills him and then, in a daze, she puts the lamb in the oven to cook.

Then she upsets the room and calls the police—"there's been a fight, someone's attacked my husband." The detectives come, and the doctors come, and the detectives ask about the shape of the weapon, and the doctors say it was shaped like that (traces leg of lamb). "You've got to have a handle to hold it, and the nature of the wound is a flat one." So this goes on, and they look everywhere for the weapon—finally, two detectives come along and tell the woman she's got a dinner cooking, and she says "Oh, my God, I forgot all about it." And she opens the oven where the leg of lamb is now cooked, and she says "Look, I can't possibly—why don't you fellas have it?"

So the final scene is they're all sitting around the table still discussing the case, and now they're down to the bone. And the last line is one of the detectives saying "Well, I don't know, doctor—it might be under our very noses."

I shot that in two days. Whole thing in two days.

BAD: *As we don't have much time, the one last thing I'd like to know is what do you see as the main difference between* Frenzy *and your other recent pictures?*

AH: I'd say that the story, and the nature of the subject matter, gave me more opportunity. See, in a picture like *Topaz*, how can I make the jokes? Because I have got Frenchmen talking English, Cubans talking English, and it's very difficult to get to the core of what one's after. And then again, in *Torn Curtain* you've got East Germany with English being spoken, so there's a kind of an underlying untruth to those kinds of things. Whereas if you take *Frenzy* it's true all the way through—true in its setting, true in its characters, and true in its humor.

This is what the difference is. It's the opportunity.

BAD: *Why did you want to make* Topaz?

AH: Well, the company bought the book and I was desperately short of material. I had worked on a couple of scripts and they didn't turn out well, so I just dumped them.

BAD: *Do you have anything new in mind now?*

AH: No, no, I'm going to look around. See about some new forms of murder.

BAD: *Do you think you'll ever get tired of making pictures?*

AH: Noooooo. Not a-tawl!

# Hitch, Hitch, Hitch, Hurrah!

## RUI NOGUEIRA AND
## NICOLETTA ZALAFFI/1972

ÉCRAN: *What to do when one has only an hour to interview one of the pillars of cinema history and several hundred questions to ask him? Where to begin? What to choose? The answer to this dilemma is implicit in the interview that follows.*

HITCHCOCK: I never think of the films I make as being *my* films. I'm not that vain or egotistical. If I were to make films for my own satisfaction they would certainly be very different from those you see. They would be much more dramatic, more realistic, possibly without humor. The reason why I have specialized, so to speak, in suspense is strictly commercial. The public expects a certain type of story from me and I don't want to disappoint them.

The "director-author" instinctively takes up a certain type of subject. For me this constant is my specialty. I know very well that when the public goes to see a Hitchcock film, they will be very disappointed if they don't find one or more crimes in it. That is a rule that even critics can't escape. Some years ago, in 1949, I agreed to make a film that was a vehicle for Ingrid Bergman, *Under Capricorn.* Well, it didn't work. When it first came out a Hollywood critic wrote, "We had to wait 104 minutes for the first shiver." I didn't want it to be a "shivers" film. For reasons of the story there was in fact at a certain point a scene with a shrunken head on a bed, but that was all. If that remark has remained engraved in my memory, that is because it shows how the public and critics think about my work. One day Fellini made this comment about *The Birds:* "I would never have had the courage to make people wait

From *Écran* no. 7 (July–August 1972), pp. 2–8. French translation by Nogueira and Zalaffi. Translated into English by James M. Vest.

so long before showing them the first bird!" Even people in my field of work can be disappointed at not immediately finding my trademarks: knives, slit throats, "shivers."

ÉC R A N :   *One may find your theory on "auteurs" in the mouth of Joan Fontaine in* Rebecca: *"My father always painted the same flower because he thought that when an artist had found his subject he had only one desire—to paint nothing else."*

HITCHCOCK:   Yes, that is very evident with painters. We can see it clearly when we visit a museum. Looking at paintings by different masters, we notice that each of them has his own style. We recognize at one glance a Rousseau, a Van Gogh, a Klee. So I ask myself why one should not always recognize the mark of a director or a filmmaker (I do not like the word "director" because I find this term incorrect and prefer the label "filmmaker"). I believe that one of the main reasons for this difficulty in identifying the stamp of a director is that most of them do not have a particular style. The quality of the film they are making generally depends on the quality and importance of the subject matter. As for me, the content of a story, the plot, does not interest me at all. It's the manner of recounting that fascinates me. What attracts me is to discover what will provoke a strong emotion in the viewer and how to make the viewer feel it.

Moreover, I think that in all artistic domains we attempt to create an emotion. The importance of a work of art, no matter what sort, is to evoke a reaction. It doesn't matter what sort of reflex is stimulated. As soon as one says "I like" or "I hate" that signifies that one is no longer indifferent. I very much like the story of the young couple in a museum of modern art. They stop, perplexed, in front of an abstract painting. Suddenly a hand with a finger pointing at them emerges from the frame and says, "I don't understand you either."

A filmmaker can repeat himself just like a painter. If you were to ask me, "Why did Boudin always paint the seashore and never the zoo?" I would answer "Simply because he never had any more desire to paint a zoo than I have to make a musical comedy."

When a critic is not very deep—which is the case less rarely than one might think—he limits himself to retelling the story of the film that he sees. He considers relating the events as equivalent to doing "criticism." That strikes me as a very lazy attitude, unless it is a way of hiding profound ignorance. Why should it be different for a film critic than for an art critic? It is accepted that an art critic must know his subject, right? He must know, for example, that Cézanne is one of the precursors of the modern movement in art and that the most important thing for him was to translate visual sensations. Similarly for me, when I take on a screenplay I feel the same needs.

Often when I have just finished a film, I ask myself why I did it and wish I hadn't made it. Perhaps that's because I don't like being obliged to go to the studio every morning to say that it's not the right color and we have to have another and to correct everything that is wrong. For me the entire construction of a film has already been done during the elaboration of the screenplay. One often says, concerning the theater, that a play does not exist when it is not being presented before an audience, that it's at the moment when the public and the creator come together that the play becomes a whole. But I am too deep this morning, don't you think? Ask me another question.

ÉCRAN: *What I like about your films is the precision of your* mise-en-scéne. *Even in minor films like* Dial M for Murder *(1954) and* To Catch a Thief *(1955) you succeed in a few seconds with the opening shots in plunging us fully into the subject matter.*
HITCHCOCK: Certainly. Just look at *Frenzy:* in the first scene one sees a body floating on the Thames and one understands immediately that this is not a drawing room comedy.

ÉCRAN: *A genre that you tried only once, in 1941, with* Mr. and Mrs. Smith.
HITCHCOCK: Yes, that's true. But you must understand that it was not really a film for myself. I had just finished, in rapid succession, *Rebecca* and *Foreign Correspondent* when Carole Lombard, who had become my friend, said to me, "Why don't you direct me in a film?" I accepted her suggestion. The script had been written by someone other than me, but since my profession was filmmaking, I took it, I went on the set, I yelled "Roll it" and "Cut," and I made it. As simple as that. You find it a sad comedy? Perhaps. That must be reflected on the face of the owner of the little restaurant where Robert Montgomery and Carole Lombard go.

## Ben Hecht and Raymond Chandler

Yes, Ben Hecht worked with me on *Spellbound* and *Notorious*. He was an extraordinary screenwriter and an exceptional man. We would talk together at length before putting anything on paper. Sometimes he would become very lazy and would say, "Well, Hitch, write the dialogues you want. Then I'll correct them." Ben was like a chess player. He could work on four scripts at once. Then he had four helpers who wrote for him.

As for Raymond Chandler, our collaboration [on *Strangers on a Train*] was much less happy. After a while I had to give up working with him. Sometimes, while we were trying to find ideas for a scene, I would make a suggestion. Instead of seeing whether it might be good, he would remark, with annoyance, "If you can do this all alone, why the devil do you need me?" He refused all collaboration with the director.

ÉCRAN: *The late Fernand Gravey related the response that you gave Paul Newman concerning the scene of the struggle near the oven in* Torn Curtain.
HITCHCOCK: Here's the whole story. I was unhappy with the screenplay. I wanted to delay production, but that was impossible because of Miss Andrews' schedule. Concerning Miss Andrews, by the way, I'll tell you that I had tried to dispense with her services on the strength that she was a singer and not a serious actress, in vain because the studio considered her a sure box-office draw.

Meanwhile, Newman, who had read the script and found it poor—which I already knew—sent me a letter to ask me certain questions that he considered vital. Among these questions there was one that was particularly stupid, that proved to me once again that actors are "cattle": "When I fight with Gromek (Wolfgang Kieling) near the oven, why does the farm wife, who is standing at the other end of the kitchen, suddenly think to turn on the gas to help me kill him? And when exactly does this idea dawn on her?" Later, when we met, Newman explained to me that it would have been more normal for such an idea to germinate in the head of the young woman if she were near the stove, since she would only have to lower her head to discover the "weapon" near the two men who were fighting. Dumbfounded, I turned my back on him and walked away. When I arrived at the studio the next morning I told him, "Paul, I've solved the problem of the farm wife. Do you know when the idea of putting Gromek's head into the oven came to her? In her car, coming to the studio!"

ÉCRAN: *What actress would you have preferred to Julie Andrews?*
HITCHCOCK: Eva Marie Saint. She was wonderful in *North by Northwest.*

Helen Rose, the costume designer for the film, had done her wardrobe, but when I saw her screen tests I immediately realized that it was not possible to use her. Helen Rose had fitted her out without taking into account the character she was playing, a woman kept by a rich man. Accompanied by Eva Marie, I went to a famous dressmaker and I acted exactly like a rich man who keeps a woman: I supervised the choice of her wardrobe in every detail.

ÉCRAN: *Just as James Stewart does with Kim Novak in* Vertigo?
HITCHCOCK: Yes, except that James Stewart did not argue the price of the dresses, whereas I tried by every means at my disposal to get a reduction, citing the needs of the film. But they dryly replied that I would have to pay the same price as Mrs. Henry Ford! That's what I did.

ÉCRAN: *In* Vertigo *you had other problems with Kim Novak, didn't you?*
HITCHCOCK: Yes, it was very difficult to obtain what I wanted from her because Kim's head was full of her own ideas. But as long as I'm pleased with the result . . . In any case, the role was intended for another actress, Vera Miles, whom I had already used in *The Wrong Man*. We were ready to begin filming, her wardrobe was finished, the different hair colors had been studied and selected, etc., when, instead of seizing the opportunity of a lifetime, Vera became pregnant! She was going to become a star with this film, but she couldn't resist her Tarzan of a husband, Gordon Scott.

ÉCRAN: *She didn't know about the pill?*
HITCHCOCK: She should have taken a "Jungle Pill!"

ÉCRAN: *How did you film the splendid circular travelling sequence in* Vertigo, *when James Stewart feels that there is in Judy, the girl he's embracing, something that reminds him of Madeleine, the woman he loved? The present and the past fuse with the setting.*
HITCHCOCK: First of all, I wanted to prove that if a man remembers something, he *experiences* that memory, he doesn't *look at* it, as we have seen in so many films, under the guise of traditional "flashbacks." I wanted a man with a woman in his arms experiencing a sensation identical to that of the original moment. To do that I built a set of a hotel room and also of a stable, then I put them side by side on the same stage and made the backdrop we see on the screen, with hotel room and stable linked together. Then I placed the actors on a small turntable and coordinated the two rotating movements.

## *Topaz*

HITCHCOCK:  This is a very complex film that doesn't have a conclusive ending. The best scene in the film, namely the sequence shot at Charlety stadium, does not appear in the final version. When the hero arrives at his home to tell his family that Piccoli wants to fight a duel, he is told that it's idiotic because it's outmoded. The son-in-law is asked, "When was the last duel in Paris?" He answers, "Four or five years ago, between the Marquis de Cevas and Serge Lifar." Then the principal actor [Frederick Stafford] explains to his family that this is not to be a traditional duel where once the first drop of blood is drawn everything stops, because the man who has challenged him really wants to kill him. A long, long time ago I remember seeing in a magazine—perhaps in *Paris-Match,* but I can't be sure—a photo of a duel in an empty stadium. The image of those two men surrounded by the rows of empty seats, alone in the middle of the field, at the far end of which one could clearly see ads for Dubonnet, fascinated me. I shot that scene for *Topaz* at Charlety. High up in the stands I had placed a guy with a high-precision rifle, watching the field. At the moment when the two men were about to fire he took aim at Piccoli's back and shot, then disappeared. The hero said to the panicked witnesses: "The Russians got him. He wasn't useful to them any more." That was the true end of the film. And do you know why it was cut? Because the producer's wife didn't like it! (Laughter) No, I took it out after a preview in the States. The end that you have seen, where Piccoli kills himself, is a compromise conclusion. A horrible compromise.

ÉCRAN:  *Where did you film the sequence of the Cubans' hotel in New York?*
HITCHCOCK:  Entirely in the studio. I wanted to film it in the real Hotel Teresa on Seventh Avenue, in the heart of Harlem, but it had been turned into an office building. I was thinking about using the exterior of the building, placing Hotel Teresa signs at the entrance and making over the front desk, but at the last minute, when everything was ready, John Lindsay, the Mayor of New York, refused us permission to film on site. He thought it would have been impossible to protect us from any number of difficulties that could have befallen us. So we were constrained to rebuild everything in the studio. But we kept the same dimensions as in real life. We avoided the trap of miniatures. To reproduce the interiors faithfully we used photos and postcards from the period when Fidel Castro stayed at the hotel.

ÉCRAN: *How did you conceive the scenes between Castro and Che?*

HITCHCOCK: We found a 16mm documentary that showed all the main figures of the Cuban revolution. I had a platform built—absolutely identical to the one visible in that film—and I asked my director of photography to use a 16mm camera himself and to film the actors I placed on my platform in compatable conditions. Afterward I mixed my scenes with those from the documentary and enlarged it all to 35mm.

ÉCRAN: *When Juanita (Karen Dor) dies, it's like a flower opening.*

HITCHCOCK: Yes, indeed. Just before John Vernon kills her, the camera travels upward very slowly and stops at the moment she collapses. I had attached to Karen Dor's dress five cotton threads that were controlled by five men placed out of camera range. At the moment when she collapsed, the men drew the strings and the dress spread like a flower that was opening. It was a counterpoint. Even though it depicted a death, I wanted it very beautiful.

Do you know why, ever since *Topaz*, I always fear taking a plane in the States? Because I'm afraid it will be hijacked. I would not like to find myself in Cuba, even though I might be better welcomed there than in Russia, where I am banished. Do you know that my films are banned in the Soviet Union? It appears that there Mr. Hitchcock is considered an anti-humanist! Funny, isn't it? Maybe now that Nixon has given Breshnev a Cadillac things will change a little. (Laughter)

ÉCRAN: *To get back to* Topaz, *how did you make the scene of the birds that carry the pieces of bread left by the Western spies?*

HITCHCOCK: To make that scene I hired Ray Berwick, the man I'd used on *The Birds.* He attached the pieces of bread to the birds' lower beaks. As simple as that.

ÉCRAN: *Richard Blaney (Jon Finch), the main character of* Frenzy, *is, like all your heroes, accused of crimes that he has not committed. But, unlike the protagonists of your previous films, Blaney is not very sympathetic to the public. Why?*

HITCHCOCK: Because he's a born loser. I want the public to be with him only in the last part of the film. Blaney is an angry, violent young man: we need time to sympathize with him. Life has been very hard on him. Misfortune has brought him to be condemned to twenty-five years in prison even though he is innocent. Knowing that he's lost and aware of the true identity of the criminal, he decides to justify his condemnation and to resort to a nearly biblical law: "An eye for an eye, a tooth for a tooth." And he escapes from prison to go kill him. But all these elements are secondary in the film. My goal is to amuse the public and not to depress them. Going to the movies is like going to a restaurant. A film must satisfy both body and mind.

ÉCRAN: *In* Frenzy, *Bob Rusk (Barry Foster) is not the only base character. I'm thinking, for example, of the owner of the pub, "The Globe," Forsythe (Bernard Cribbins).*

HITCHCOCK: Yes, that's true. He's particularly horrible. But one must not forget that he is in love with the barmaid and that his feelings guide his conduct. As for the murderer, it is normal that he should appear personable and nice. Otherwise he could not approach any of his victims. Many directors commit the error of making the villain a rather ugly man with a ridiculous black moustache who doesn't think twice about kicking a passing dog. All that is from the past when the face of the evildoer was habitually bathed in green light. Cinema has progressed past those early halting steps. The profession has evolved and we now have a completely different conception of how to handle drama. Formerly, it was always necessary to warn the public of which side the main characters were on, who were the good guys and who were the bad. Now we have become more realistic and we can deepen our characters and give them another dimension. In my story it is evident that the murderer must be rather personable, even charming. If I had given him harsher traits and the air of a sex maniac, all the girls he met would have run away. I didn't make all that up; it's the result of a deep analysis. I studied numerous cases concerning murderers of this type. Everyone knows that one of the most captivating of predators, as far as its victims are concerned, is the spider. To better illustrate this idea, there is an expression: "Will you come into my parlor, said the spider to the fly." Children's stories, too, often put us on guard against false appearances. So in "Little Red Riding Hood" we have the kindly grandmother who is a wolf; in "Snow White" the little old lady with the apples is the witch. And isn't there also the expression "a wolf in sheep's clothing"? All these considerations led me to make my murderer a charming being that a girl could be delighted to follow into his apartment.

ÉCRAN: *Don't you think that Mrs. Brenda Blaney's secretary might have made Bob Rusk happy, if she had been his kind of woman?*

HITCHCOCK: That's entirely possible. In any case that would have made for a very interesting scene to see them make love together.

ÉCRAN: *After the murder of Mrs. Blaney and of Babs the barmaid, the camera remains alone for a while. In the first case it waits downstairs for the secretary of the victim, whom we have seen enter the building, to cry out to announce the discovery of the body. In the second it backs down the empty stairs that lead to Bob Rusk's apartment after having left him at the door, through which he had taken Babs with the intention of killing her.*

HITCHCOCK: In the first instance, I say to the public: "You have seen many films where someone discovers a corpse. Invariably the woman who finds the body screams out her terrible discovery in a close-up. This time, things will be different." I counted on the public, thoroughly aware of events, to imagine the horror of the secretary and to calculate approximately when they would hear the scream. For the second crime, I wanted viewers to notice that when Bob follows Babs up the stairs, he is no longer smiling. "He's deciding how to dispatch her," we should be thinking to ourselves. "Will he first offer her a drink?" As he goes through the door with the barmaid, we hear him utter the same phrase that he used with Mrs. Blaney, "You are my kind of woman," and from that moment on we know with certainty that the young woman will not emerge from his apartment alive. At the instant of this revelation, I, the "maker," address the audience: "You all know what is going to happen. You can do nothing to stop what is going to occur. You can't get up out of your seats, run toward the screen, climb the stairs, break down the door and cry 'Stop! Don't kill her!' You can't do anything and your powerlessness becomes part of the suspense. Let's get out of here!" What to do? So we tiptoe out. As soon as we get into the street, we raise our eyes toward the window of Bob Rusk's apartment, waiting for a cry for help, but in the street we discover that the traffic is so noisy (I turned up the sound at that moment on purpose) that we realize that even if Babs cries it will be useless: we'll hear nothing!

ÉCRAN: *Your murderers are often psychopaths and latent homosexuals.*
HITCHCOCK: Normally a psychopath is sexually impotent. He manages to make it with women only when he strangles them. There was a famous case in London, a man named Christie, accused of killing eight women and hiding their bodies under the floor of his house. During the trial, when the

prosecutor asked him whether the sexual act had occurred before, during, or after the death of the victims, he replied, "During, I believe."

ÉCRAN:  *What interested you in Arthur La Bern's book?*
HITCHCOCK:  Potatoes!

ÉCRAN:  *Very fine response!*
HITCHCOCK:  You see, for my own creative satisfaction, if I have as a backdrop a produce market, it must serve a dramatic function. The story *must* emerge from the backdrop. In the case of *Frenzy*, it unfolds from potatoes. From that given I constructed the various segments of the story: the sequences with the truck, the truck stop, etc. Thanks to the potato dust one says to oneself that perhaps the police will discover a trail that will lead them to the true criminal.

Madame [Zalaffi], looking at the three buttons securing your pants, I cannot help but tell you a funny story: One Sunday morning the famous playwright George S. Kaufman shows up at the apartment of the equally famous Broadway producer, Jed Harris, to talk about a new play. Harris comes to the door completely naked. Kaufman doesn't miss a beat. He enters, sits, has a drink, and in all seriousness discusses the play with Harris. When he is leaving, before the door completely closed behind him, Kaufman turns, sticks his head through the opening, and says: "Jed, your fly is open."

ÉCRAN:  *It must be difficult for you, having worked with so many great actors, to find young people capable of filling their shoes.*
HITCHCOCK:  That's partially true. But what troubles me most is finding original stories and especially new ways of killing.

ÉCRAN:  *Why have you not made* Titanic, *the film that was to have marked your debut as a director in the U.S.?*
HITCHCOCK:  I abandoned that project to make *Rebecca*. In *Titanic* there was only one scene that engaged me, and if I had made that film I would have made it for that scene: a group of men playing cards at a table. On the table there is a glass of whisky. Close-up of the glass. We see the liquid start to tip. We hear someone laugh!

# Alfred Hitchcock

## CHARLES THOMAS SAMUELS / 1972

SINCE NO OTHER FILMMAKER has been interviewed so usefully or at such great length as Alfred Hitchcock (in François Truffaut's *Hitchcock*), I was at a special disadvantage in this case. Although I prepared my questions to ensure novelty, duplication turned out to be unavoidable. Directors who are artists—individual sensibilities rather than faceless craftsmen—exhibit characteristic themes and techniques; logically, their comments about themselves must show a similar confinement. I should not have been surprised to find Hitchcock answering my questions by so frequently referring to anecdotes he had offered Truffaut.

As a consequence, however, I omitted from the transcript much of a talk that ranged over a five-hour period in the well-appointed quarters of Alfred Hitchcock Productions at the Universal studio. Because his general remarks reflect confrontation with a view of Hitchcock's talent distinctly different from that of Truffaut's, I retained most of those. Since comments on individual films proved less original, I render the summary of his career rather sketchily.

Additional description is also unnecessary for the corpulent figure that is Hitchcock's well-known trademark. But I can report that the dour voice and manner of his television appearances are clearly fabricated. "Agreeable" and "almost avuncular" come closer to describing his behavior—at least, as interviewee. Perhaps "imperturbable" might complete my impression. In

From Charles Thomas Samuels, *Encountering Directors*. New York: G. P. Putnam's Sons, 1972, pp. 231–50.

responding to questions or objections, Hitchcock has the air of a man wholly confident of his credo. This he expressed in our talk, emphasized in minor revisions he asked to make in the transcript and summarized in a personal letter with which he accompanied its return.

SAMUELS:  *Your long distinguished career has taken you through every technical revolution in cinema. Were there any you would have preferred to miss: sound, Technicolor, Vista Vision, etc.?*

HITCHCOCK:  So far as screen size goes, I never liked what is commonly referred to as the letterbox screen. It leaves you with a good deal of empty space that causes the audience to wonder what it's there for. A painter is able to choose the canvas size that fits his subject. (I happen to own a Dufy that was painted on a long, narrow canvas; but the subject is a harbor and therefore suitable.) Filmmakers, on the other hand, are bound by the screens available throughout the world. You can't compose for a New York screen only; you've got to think, say, of the screen in Thailand. I've always believed in film as the newest art of the twentieth century because of its ability to communicate with the mass audiences of the world. In any case, I suppose that oversized screens were devised when the industry was searching for novelty, which, of course, led to Cinerama. But I can even remember films, in which, out of pure showmanship, the screen size was altered to produce a climax.

S:  *As in De Mille's* Samson and Delilah?

H:  Yes, or *Portrait of Jennie*, where there was a lighthouse and lots of water that lent themselves to the process. But I don't think it enhanced the story.

S:  *Isn't it generally true that technical impediments are useful? For example, you seem to me to change vistas without an expansible screen in a film like* The 39 Steps, *and therefore, to excite us by your skill. Through your editing, you alternate open and closed spaces.*

H:  You can do anything you want with montage. Cinema is simply pieces of film put together in a manner that creates ideas and emotions. The tragedy is that people don't make films that way now. Because I'm bound by consensus to make thrillers—

S:  *May I interrupt for a moment? Would you have liked to release yourself from this binding?*

H: I'm not sure. The cobbler should stick to his last, you know.

S: *However, you began your career with a variety of films. Why did you narrow your focus later?*

H: Unfortunately, one's employers expect certain things from you, so I've been more or less forced to stick to my genre. But, you know, people confuse what I do with mystery. I don't believe in mystifying an audience. I believe in giving them all the information and then in making them sweat. It's no good devising a film to satisfy only yourself. The subject doesn't count either. You get your satisfaction through your style of treatment. I'm not interested in content. It disturbs me very much when people criticize my films because of their content. It's like looking at a still life and saying, "I wonder whether those apples are sweet or sour." Cinema is form. I see many good films that contain very fine dialogue. I don't deprecate these films, but to me, they're not pure cinema. Trying to make them cinema, some new directors find odd angles to shoot from, but they still only produce what I call "photographs of people talking."

S: *I agree with your objection to weird angles. That's why I was puzzled in* Spellbound *when you shoot Gregory Peck drinking a glass of milk by aiming the camera at the glass that's being drained.*

H: I was playing with white there, in preparation for the denouement, which had to do with snow. Throughout the film, I wanted to make a sort of leitmotiv of that color.

S: *In view of your characterization of yourself as a formalist who just happens to work in the thriller genre, why have you, on occasion, made something like* Under Capricorn?

H: *Under Capricorn,* I made to please Ingrid Bergman, who was a friend of mine. I was looking for a subject that suited her, rather than myself.

S: *You've said you like to achieve your effects through editing. What do you think of directors who don't rely on it so much, like Antonioni and Bergman?*

H: Antonioni is almost a surrealist.

S: *But he's as visual as you are.*

H: No question!

S : *Bergman is rather more complicated because he relies so much on words.*

H : And yet he has indicated on one occasion that he learned a lot from Hitchcock. He uses the visuals as much as he can, whether in the form of gigantic close-ups or natural objects; you know, the sapling trees against the sky and so on. What Truffaut appreciated from my technique was the use of the subjective treatment. A typical example is the film *Rear Window*, where the central figure is a man in one position whose viewpoint we study. His viewpoint becomes his mental processes, by the use of the camera and the montage—and this is what I actually mean by subjective treatment. The objective treatment, however, is also used when necessary; but for me, the objective is merely an extension of the theater because you are a viewer of the events that take place in front of you, but you are not necessarily in the mind of the person. Subjective shooting puts the audience in the mind of the character.

S : *You obtain your best results, I think, by creating sharp intrusions of the subjective in an otherwise objective narrative. For example, I'd instance the change to subjective camera angle in* Notorious *when Ingrid Bergman has to meet all of her husband's Nazi friends and convince them she's a Nazi, too. By making the camera her eyes, you convey the intensity of the threat.*

H : Yes. I wanted to say visually, "Here is Ingrid in the lions' den; now look at each lion!"

S : *These alternations we've been discussing—between open and closed vistas, subjective and objective camera work, etc.—indicate what I believe to be the essential musicality of your films.*

H : I, myself, use musical terms when I direct. I say, "Don't put a great big close-up there because it's loud brass and you mustn't use a loud note unless it's absolutely vital." Cinema is the orchestration of shots.

S : *In* The 39 Steps *you orchestrate not only shots, but music itself. You begin and end with natural music in the music hall, have a bit more of it in the Salvation Army Band scene, and use background music very sparingly: a bit in the moor chase and a few romantic bars when Madeleine Carroll returns to the inn room after learning that Donat has been telling her the truth. Yet in your American films you tend to use background music more generally. Why the shift?*

H : A matter of conventions. Moreover, when I first came here, I didn't have the complete freedom I'd had in England. One had to conform. Don't forget, I came in a period when the producer was king. I suppose the most flattering thing ever said to me—not immediately after *Rebecca*, but two or three years later—was Selznick's: "You're the only director I'd ever trust a picture with." In those days—although I'm now speaking heresy—I never understood how, for example, Selznick could say, "Thalberg's great with a finished picture." A producer like that used to take a finished film, rewrite it, reedit it, and so on. I first experienced this when I started *Rebecca*. I'd rehearse a scene, but before I could get ready to shoot it, the script girl would come up and whisper, "I have to phone Mr. Selznick now." He had to okay the final rehearsal before I could shoot! That's how heavy the hand of the producer was in those days. Another example is retakes. When I used to complain of a technical defect and ask to reshoot a scene, he'd say, "No retakes!" "Why not?" I'd ask. He replied, "It may not be in the picture." The producer used to assemble the film, arrange the credits, even outfit it with a temporary score taken from the music library. Within three weeks of the last day of shooting, you'd have the sneak preview.

S : *How did you manage to become invulnerable to this kind of interference?*
H : Very simply: I was loaned out. As soon as I was working for someone I wasn't under contract to, the supervision was lessened.

S : *I had understood that you evaded interference by shooting things out of order.*
H : No, I just normally work that way. To me, a picture must be planned on paper. People are always asking me why I don't improvise on the set, and I always reply, "What for? I'd rather improvise in a room with the writer." My method is very simple. I work out a treatment with my screenwriter. In order to do this, you've got to have a visual sense. I never look through the camera; I think only of that white screen that has to be filled up the way you fill up a canvas. That's why I draw rough setups for the cameraman.

S : *You're making live-action animated films.*
H : You could say that. If I wanted to, I could draw every frame of the finished picture. But when I have a good cameraman, I don't need to go that far. I simply tell him what elements I want to include or exclude in any shot. What I do with the writer is involve him in the direction of the picture and have him collaborate in the creation of the story line, including dialogue.

After having completed this process, I leave it to the screenwriter to write his dialogue within the framework of the finished, agreed cinematic story line. I know every shot we'll end up with because the planning stage has been so complete. What mystifies me is why so many other filmmakers need to see things on the screen before they edit, whereas a musician can hear his music simply by looking at the notes and lines of his score. Why shouldn't we do the same?

s : *Can't you plan so carefully and definitely because of your genre? After all, your films work precisely because they manipulate the spectator. Yet there are other sorts of films. André Bazin argued, for example, that deep focus and long takes left the spectator free to choose the elements he wished to pay most attention to and thus were to be preferred.*
H : Is a listener allowed to choose the notes he'll hear? If you free the spectator to choose, you're making theater, not cinema.

s : *I'd like to talk about a different kind of freeing the spectator. What do you think of the disinterested quasi-documentary style of neorealism—a film like* The Bicycle Thief, *for example?*
H : It's very good, but it's no different from any chase story.

s : *But the emphasis is not on effect. Rather it is on the social realities reflected in the situation.*
H : Yes, but De Sica takes the audience into whorehouses, soup kitchens, homes. . . .

s : *But not so as to produce a sharply defined emotion in each case. A panorama is created. That's not your intention.*
H : I go further than a film like *The Bicycle Thief*, which shows a man and a boy walking in front of a panorama. I believe that your backgrounds must be involved in the story. For example, in *North by Northwest*, when Cary Grant gets trapped in an auction room, I use this setting by making Grant start crazy bidding.

s : *What I'm driving at, however, is my suspicion that you're not interested in documenting a social reality without regard to evocation or the solving of an esthetic problem.*

H : Where else is the dramatic impact for the ordinary spectator? You've got to remember that *Bicycle Thief* wasn't a success with the Italian audience. It's funny you should instance this picture. We have a home in Northern California, and in the period of *The Bicycle Thief*, we happened to have an Italian couple working for us who spoke not one word of English. One day my wife and I took the mother and her daughter into San Francisco, where my wife and the girl had to do some shopping. Since I didn't know what to do with Mrs. Chiesa, I decided to take her to see *The Bicycle Thief*. It was an Italian movie, I thought it might interest her. There was a knot of about twenty people in the theater—it was a road show, I remember, at the Geary—and we watched the film. Do you know, she only gave one exclamation the whole time: when the father cuffed the little boy. So when we got outside, I asked her how she'd liked it. She said, "Okay. But why didn't he borrow a bicycle?" Of course, she demolished the whole thing. So I said, "Mrs. Chiesa, what films do you like?" "Ah," she said, "I like a Betty Grable musical."

S : *You may direct your films at the Mrs. Chiesas, but your style seems to me to require some sophistication in anyone who wishes to appreciate your work.*
H : Yes. I don't expect the average spectator to go beyond his emotional reaction; then, if the others like to examine the way. . . . You know, this may explain why occasionally one of my films is indifferently received and then, a year later, it becomes a classic. I never understood the delay.

S : *Can you give me an example?*
H : *Psycho.*

S : *But wasn't the first response to* Psycho *due to a brutality unexpected in a Hitchcock film? Your films aren't usually brutal. Why, in* Psycho *and* The Birds, *did you suddenly change that?*
H : But *Psycho* was designed to throw a violent moment on the screen and then reduce the violence as the film progressed, while keeping its effects alive in the minds of the audience. Furthermore, brutality was inherent in both subjects. It's like *Frenzy*, which is the story of a man who is impotent and therefore expresses himself through murder. I only show one of the women being murdered; the rest I leave to the audience. I show a second murder this way: I bring the man and his victim along a corridor through an extended shot that takes us up the stairs, around the turn of the stairs, along the pas-

sage; then, I show them entering the room as the door closes, and he says something to the effect that she's his type. Then I cut and take the camera back the very way we've come—I had to have a special rig built for this—until we reach the street. As we're coming down, the traffic noise has been getting louder. Then I take us all the way out into the busy Covent Garden Market until we can see the full facade of the building. I then deliberately bring the street noises up to such a volume that the audience must say to itself, "No one will ever hear the poor girl's screams." I'm not interested in showing brutality. I made *Psycho* in black and white purposely to avoid the blood. Red would have been unpleasant, unnecessary; I wouldn't have been able to treat the blood cinematically, as in the editing of its flow down the drain and so on, had the sequence been in color.

S : *Since you've raised the subject, what do you think of working in color?*
H : Color should start with the nearest equivalent to black and white. This sounds like a most peculiar statement, but color should be no different from the voice which starts muted and finally arrives at a scream. In other words, the muted color is black and white, and the screams are every psychedelic color you can think of, starting, of course, with red. Years ago I answered this question by describing a murder in a park, where you'd pan down to feet struggling in a flower bed full of white asters. Since it's night, you still haven't gone much beyond black and white. Then you dolly in to one petal of the white aster till it fills the whole screen; then suddenly there's a slash of red.

S : *I understand Chabrol does something like this in* The Butcher, *where a sandwich suddenly has blood dripping on it.*
H : Has he?

S : *Is it true that you regard your actors only as elements of composition?*
H : Well, the actor must be an element because film is montage. But I do explain the cutting to him so he knows why I've asked him to cooperate.

S : *Do you let your actors see rushes?*
H : Certainly.

S : *You don't try to make your actors become other than what they are, do you? I mean, you seem to me to select your performers for qualities they inherently possess.*

H : Well, if you take what I call a fantasy chase picture like *North by North-west*, it's good to cast a known personality in the role of the endangered hero. That way the audience worries more about the character. We always are more deeply concerned by what happens to someone near to us than by something we might, say, read in the paper.

S : *Am I not right, however, in thinking that the acting in your films is generally low on the list of your priorities?*

H : No. The tiniest role is just as important as the bigger roles.

S : *Your minor characters always seem better to me.*

H : In *Frenzy*, for example, I have more character parts than I've had in years because the London stage actor is willing to play a moderate size part. So, I've got Vivien Merchant, Alec McCowen, Bernard Cribbins, Anna Massey, and so on. They're all leading players, you see. Vivien Merchant actually brought the character to me.

S : *In view of the technical brilliance of most of your films, I wonder why you so often settle for bad backdrops. I think, for example, of the mother's street in* Mar-nie, *where you show an obviously painted ship and an obviously painted sky in the background.*

H : That was a technical mixup, and something of which I did not approve. We were very pressed for time, or I would have scrapped the whole thing and started over. I wanted to show something that had always fascinated me—I think I'd seen it in Copenhagen and London, as well as in Baltimore, where *Marnie* takes place—a row of houses and suddenly a ship looming above them.

S : *You would shoot on location whenever you could, then?*

H : Of course. On the other hand, some location shooting has become terribly cliché. I mean, if I see any more people walking along sidewalks and made to appear as if they were dancing because of the use of a long focus lens! We've got an awful lot of people nowadays who'll say, "Ah, I must symbolize the traffic." So they use a ten-inch lens that makes the cars all shimmer. If I see any more out-of-focus flowers in the foreground!

S : *Your films constantly show respectable people secretly attracted to crime. Why?*

H : Can you give me an example?

s :  *Remember that little woman in* Strangers on a Train *who is so excited to learn that her cab is being commandeered by policemen chasing someone. She's a very minor character, but your films are full of touches indicating the same generalized attitude.*

H :  I think this is a little quirk; there's no deep significance in it.

s :  *But you often show that people find crime sexy. I think, for example, of the Peggy Ashcroft character in* The 39 Steps. *She is attracted to Donat, of course, because he's from the big city, which she longs for; but she is even more attracted when she learns he's a fugitive.*

H :  I think this must have something to do with my being English. Crime is much more literate in England than in America. In England, unlike America, crime novels are first-class literature. Not only are the English more attracted by crime, but the crimes themselves are more bizarre.

s :  *English eccentricity?*

H :  They are eccentric, especially the intellectuals. I remember what happened, for example, to the poet Lascelles Abercrombie when he was challenged to a duel. Offered his choice of weapons, he chose steamrollers. I'll tell you how deeply interested the British are in crime. There's a group in London called Our Society. It meets regularly on Sunday evenings at a fashionable restaurant in a private room. The members include lawyers, writers, journalists. When they meet, they rehash a recent cause célèbre, effectively trying the case among themselves. They borrow exhibits from the trial and so forth.

s :  *What do you think differentiates the British interest in crime from the American?*

H :  The British interest is esthetic.

s :  *Did you then change your style of treating crime when you moved from England to America?*

H :  I'd say that until *Frenzy*, and setting aside *North by Northwest*, I haven't had as much opportunity to introduce the British type of humor in my American pictures.

s :  *So* Frenzy *takes you back to something like* The Lady Vanishes?

H :  Except that that was a fantasy and *Frenzy* isn't. The closest I think I came in my American films to the humorous portrayal of character along with the crime was in *Shadow of a Doubt.*

s : *I think that film also comes rather closer than usual to having content.*

H : That's true.

s : *I'd like to hear what you think of my version of this content. Aren't you showing that the girl in the film isn't quite so superior to her murderer-uncle? When he first comes to town, she's happy to have the relief he brings her from small-town bore-dom, but when she realizes that he threatens the status of her family, she pretty ruthlessly tries to get rid of him.*

H : She switches from adulation so suddenly that she becomes paranoid. The horror of learning what he is makes her switch loyalty almost viciously.

s : *Aren't we meant to find her ruthless?*

H : She is ruthless. She comes down those stairs wearing that ring and thus tells him he must leave or be executed.

s : *Our sympathy is split between them. He's a murderer. . . .*

H : But a very attractive man. That's something I always insist on. Movies usually portray murderers as tough and unsympathetic. That always makes me wonder how they ever got near their victims.

s : *You wouldn't be interested in a murderer who didn't get close to his victims, would you?*

H : No. I've never been interested in professional criminals. The audience can't identify with their lack of feeling. I'm also not interested in the conven-tional detective. That's why, for example, in *Frenzy* I invented the chief inspector's wife so as to permit myself to place most of the discussion of the crime outside a professional context. And I get comedy to sugarcoat the dis-cussions by making the wife a gourmet cook. So this inspector comes home every night to discussion of the murders and overrich meals.

s : *In the early scene of* Shadow of a Doubt, *when Joseph Cotten is being chased, why do you select such a high-angle shot?*

H : For clarity of effect. It was like saying, "Here we are above a maze, where you can see both the exit and all the people who are trying to keep him from getting there."

s : *Why did you have the niece fall in love with the detective at the end of the film?*
H : I think that was a commercial concession, really.

s : *You do, occasionally, introduce a love element that isn't strictly necessary. Why don't you resist this convention?*
H : I'm not self-indulgent where content is concerned; I'm only self-indulgent about treatment. I'd compare myself to an abstract painter. My favorite painter is Klee.

s : *But can't a commercial concession in content hurt the form? After all, the end of* Shadow of a Doubt *is corny.*
H : It is corny. In *Frenzy*, I have dared—because times change—to kill off my love interest.

s : *Speaking of daring, why do you so often show lovers, who are forced by circumstance to bed down for the night, behaving like virgins, even though it's quite clear that they've had plenty of experience? This happens, among others, in* Rear Window *and* Foreign Correspondent.
H : Well, the Laraine Day character was a Quaker. And, in *Rear Window*, I think the audience is thinking about another problem; I mean, how did they do it with his leg in a cast? Anyway, we weren't as permissive in the period when those films were made as we are now.

s : *Yet* The 39 Steps, *which is earlier, is also more risqué.*
H : In Hollywood, we had the Breen Office. We couldn't even show a husband and wife in bed together.

s : *Well, let's go back then to* The Lodger, *which you've claimed was your first characteristic film. In connection with the subject I've been interested in, your detective in this film is inferior to the criminal: he's stupid, lascivious, uncharming, etc.*
H : He's a local; he hadn't the lodger's finesse. He's a constable off the beat, that's all. Since those days, however, as you'll see in *Frenzy*, the level among inspectors has gone up. They've a police college now.

s : *How did you get the idea for that marvelous shot of the lodger's hand moving down the banister?*

H : All such touches were substitutes for sound. I wanted to show, by means of that shot, that the woman downstairs was probably hearing a creaking noise.

s : *You repeat this sort of shot several times, as in* Foreign Correspondent *and, most famously,* Vertigo.

H : Staircases are very photogenic.

s : *Why do you make the young girl in the film so sexually aggressive toward the lodger?*

H : She's goaded by the idea that he might be Jack the Ripper.

s : *Another instance of the attractiveness of crime. Aren't you attributing to your characters your own delight in excitement?*

H : I must refer again to the English attitude. Did you ever read *We the Accused* by Ernest Raymond? It's based on the Crippen case, although he alters the locations and circumstances. Raymond shows the whole process of English law. He shows the police to be kindly, but also the murderer, who did nothing worse than rid himself of a bitch of a wife. He takes us right up to the hanging, when the governor walks into the condemned man's cell and says, "Good morning." Then the hangman steps forward and says, "Put your hands down at your sides, old chap." And then his hands are strapped, and the procession starts. The white cap goes on, the noose goes on, and the assistant executioner straps the ankles. Then the hangman gives the condemned a friendly tap on the arm and pulls the lever. On the way to prison, when they were originally arrested, the murderer was asked what type of tobacco he wanted, and the girl for whom he killed was offered a choice of magazines.

s : *In* Blackmail, *you've said that you wanted the first sequence to illustrate duty, but doesn't this throw us off a bit? The film begins almost as if it will be a documentary about a day in the life of a policeman; then it becomes a thriller.*

H : I wanted the whole film to have that effect, but I was prevented. I wanted the film to open with an ordinary criminal being apprehended by detectives who behaved like men working in an office, just doing a job. In the last sequence, the detective's girlfriend was to give herself up, and then I would have repeated the same routine as I started with. The whole idea was to show his conflict between love and duty, with duty winning out.

s :  *But that isn't thriller technique; that's content.*
H :  Yes. The only thriller technique in the film would have been the girl's suspense about whether or not her murdering a rapist will be discovered.

s :  *Doesn't this alteration suggest that you might not have become so totally a director of thrillers had things worked out differently?*
H :  I think you'll find that the real start of my career was *The Man Who Knew Too Much.*

s :  *But might you have gone on to make films which, though effective and cinematic, had a more thorough grounding in the complications of real life?*
H :  Well, I did make a film out of Galsworthy's *Skin Game.*

s :  *But you're not fond of it.*
H :  Because it's too theatrical.

s :  *Do you think you would have branched out beyond thrillers more often had you written your own scripts?*
H :  No, I'd probably have narrowed down.

s :  *Why don't you write your own scripts?*
H :  I do.

s :  *But not the dialogue.*
H :  I do now and again, but you can't be jack-of-all-trades. Dialogue writing, out of which comes character, is a job of its own. I'm busy enough with the cinematics. I work with the writer, as I've told you, very closely. You know, our first treatment can run as long as one hundred pages.

s :  *In the murder scene in* Blackmail, *did you allow Cyril Ritchard to sing because he was a singer or because you wanted him to?*
H :  Because it was my first talkie and the producers wanted it. It's like that

old talkie *In Old Arizona*, which thrilled everyone so because it allowed them to hear bacon frying.

s: *The opening of* Murder! *is notable as a forecast of your later combinations of suspense and comedy. You pan across a sinister street but then show the inhabitants doing funny things: In one apartment, a man is taking his teeth out of a glass; in another, a girl tries unsuccessfully to get into her bloomers, always putting both her legs through the same opening.*

H: That last detail was taken from a night when I went into my mother's room during an air raid in World War I. The whole house was in an uproar, but there was my poor Elsa Maxwell plump little mother, struggling, saying her prayers, while outside the window, shrapnel was bursting around a search-lit zeppelin—extraordinary image.

s: *Do you make references to your own experience often in your films?*

H: Odd bits here and there, but very rarely. *Murder!* was an interesting film, though, because I intended it as a satire on the theater. In those days, the actor-manager was king: Sir Henry Irving, Sir Herbert Beerbohm-Tree, Sir Gerald du Maurier. Du Maurier used to have an office over His Majesty's Theater, called the Dome, where he conducted his business. That's why I dressed Herbert Marshall, who plays the hero, in black coat and striped pants, like a cabinet minister. They never went into the provinces. So, when my actor-manager does, he finds himself experiencing conditions which, up to then, he had disdained. When he starts investigating the murder there, he feels he's suffering the indignity of a lower order of actor.

s: *In the finished film, doesn't the comedy get restrained by the thriller element?*

H: Yes. But I still keep the theater business alive with the play within a play, when Marshall makes the murderer read from a play dealing with the crime, like Hamlet making Claudius witness his own crime to see if the man will expose himself. You know, I modeled the murderer on a circus performer of the period. He used to enter the ring, dressed like a woman, accompanied by a trim maid, and then go into his trapeze act. Oddly enough, the girl who plays the thief in *To Catch a Thief* did a high wire act in the circus, too.

s: *Since the murderer is a homosexual in this film, why do you make his motive shame at being a half-caste? It hardly seems the more serious problem.*

H: He was a half-caste homosexual. In those days, being a half-caste was very serious. Being a Eurasian in India, for example, meant you belonged to neither side, so that you weren't accepted. But the element is surely dated now.

s: *In* Rich and Strange—
H: One of my less successful pictures.

s: *But it has many good things in it.*
H: Yes, I like it.

s: *Is the opening sequence with the umbrellas what gave you the idea for the umbrella scene in* Foreign Correspondent?
H: Two different purposes; in *Rich and Strange*, I simply used the umbrellas to express the life of ordinary clerks in the city of London.

s: *Do you ever reuse a device deliberately, though?*
H: Can you give me an example?

s: *In* Rebecca, *Joan Fontaine's employer puts out her cigarette in a jar of cold cream; in* To Catch a Thief, *Jessie Royce Landis puts hers out into an egg.*
H: I was aware of that repetition; the second example was used to show my utter dislike for eggs.

s: *Why did you use place-name titles in* Rich and Strange? *Wasn't that a rather anachronistic device?*
H: Oh, you had to. You've got to remember that some people in the audience won't be able to identify a remote place just by seeing it. In *Frenzy*, I've got a shot of London taken from five thousand feet up, yet I put a crest over it as though it were a map. I want to make certain that everyone realizes we're in London.

s: The Man Who Knew Too Much *has a great deal to do with place.*
H: You know how I wanted to start the original version of that film? I wanted to show the hotel window in St. Moritz, which reflects the beautiful Alpine scenery, suddenly shattered by a bullet, so that the whole window

cracks and smashes to the ground. But I was told that a bullet would go right through and simply make a hole.

S: *Why do you precede the killing with the comic bit of the unraveling sweater?*
H: To show that death comes when you least expect it.

S: *Isn't the final episode, in which the kidnapped child is rescued, rather anticlimactic, coming as it does, after the Albert Hall sequence?*
H: No, because the film is about the kidnapping; the assassination is just my MacGuffin. The characters in the film are worried about the MacGuffin, but the audience isn't.

S: *What made you decide to use Doris Day in the remake?*
H: I'd seen her in a film called *Storm Warning*, where she gave a good non-singing performance.

S: *Didn't this produce the same problem that you have in* Blackmail, *where an inappropriate musical number is forced into the film because your star is a singer?*
H: No, here the singing becomes part of the story.

S: *One of the most charming scenes in the remake is the dinner in the Moroccan restaurant. Was that improvised?*
H: Yes. That place is brick for brick, fabric and all, exactly like a restaurant in Marrakesh. I let the actors improvise their behavior with the unusual food, though, as you say.

S: *Why did you change the dentist's office in the original into a taxidermist's in the remake, particularly since the latter turns out to be a false lead?*
H: Dead right. I don't know. That was a mistake.

S: *Although* The Man Who Knew Too Much *was your first success in the thriller form, wouldn't you agree that* The 39 Steps *is a better film?*
H: Yes. The speed was perfect. You know, people say that you can cut a film and make it go fast. I don't believe that. Speed is preoccupation. In *The 39 Steps*, there was no dead footage, so the audience's absorption creates the impression of speed.

s :   *One small thing that bothers me in this film is the superimposition of the dead spy's face—talking to Donat in the scene right after she's murdered.*

H :   I don't remember why I did it, but I wouldn't repeat it today. What was the last scene in the version you saw?

s :   *Donat and Carroll, who were handcuffed together, now clasp hands in love, with the now useless handcuffs dangling between them.*

H :   You know, originally, I'd shot another scene. They drive away from the theater in a cab. Donat says, "Now that's all over, and I can start paying attention to my wife." "Your wife?" she says. "Are you married?" "Yes, I'm married to you." "How?"—and he tells her that the rule in Scotland is that if you declare yourself man and wife in front of a witness, you are man and wife, so they'd been married while hiding at the inn.

s :   *It's a good thing you cut that. The present ending is much better. Why did you make a film of Conrad's* The Secret Agent? *I thought you disapproved of turning literary masterpieces into films.*

H :   It was a project I was assigned by Gaumont British. I only read the book once. We go to all sources for material, don't we?

s :   *Were there any complaints at the time that you were making a thriller out of what was originally a political satire?*

H :   The question never came up.

s :   *Why did you change Verloc into a theater-owner? Did censorship keep you from showing his seedy little shop with its pornography?*

H :   No, I just thought there would be more dramatic opportunities this way—as there were—for example, in the scene when his wife comes home after her brother's death and sits in that flea pit of a movie house, where they're playing the cartoon *Who Killed Cock Robin?*

s :   *Would you agree that* The Lady Vanishes *is your best British picture?*

H :   Well, it did have that guaranteed movement provided by a train. Gilliat and Launder had written the script, but I wanted to make several changes. Their script ended when the lady is removed on a stretcher. I added the whole last sequence where the train is held in the woods and also the bit in the middle about the illusionist. I don't think that Launder and Gilliat were too pleased when, after the film came out, it was referred to as a "Hitchcock picture." I believe that's what made them decide to produce and direct their own scripts, which they've done with great success ever since. They had written the two English comics as silly-ass types. I decided to cast the roles against type. I found Naunton Wayne and Basil Radford, who were used to playing absolutely different parts. Later they made a career out of their combination.

s: *You also provide a strong patriotic motif. The British eventually come through with characteristic grit.*
H: That's the way they would have behaved.

s: *In general, your British heroes seem to me to result from more acute social observation, whereas the characters in your American films seem almost allegorical. Is that true, and is it a consequence of your expatriation?*
H: I think you'll find the answer to that in *Frenzy*, which has all the social detail you're talking about. That film is full of characters who belong to their background.

s: *Is the relative abstractness of milieu in your American films a response to your sense of being foreign?*
H: I guess so. I'll give you an extreme example—though it comes from my British period. When I made *Murder!*, I made a German as well as an English version. In the German version, Alfred Abel played the Herbert Marshall part. When it came to directing that, the producers wanted to change so many things it would have made for two separate pictures. I had a scene in the original where Herbert Marshall is brought a cup of tea by the landlady. Her kids come into the room, climb all over his bed, even let their kitten get under the bedclothes. Meanwhile, Marshall sits there trying to preserve his dignity. The German actor wouldn't do it. He insisted that you couldn't make fun of so important a man. He wouldn't allow himself to be dressed as Herbert Marshall was—in tweeds and a raincoat—when visiting the suspected murderess in jail, either. I'd already satirized the black coat and striped pants and wanted to show him now in the role of amateur detective. Abel demanded that he be allowed to wear the more formal costume to visit a young lady. What we British would have found funny, the German found improper.

s: *In your American films, the humor does seem to lie not in the character, but in the lines.*

H: I think my British films use humorous understatement. You'll find the same kind of understatement in *Frenzy*.

s: *It seems to me that your American characters are quirky without respect to their national origin. Your humor in these films is more psychological than sociological. I think, for example, of Bruno in* Strangers on a Train. *You even use the setting, which is clearly American (Washington), rather allegorically. So we have Bruno standing in black before a white pillar of the Jefferson Memorial.*

H: Bruno becomes sinister, standing in front of all that white.

s: *Then, to get back to* The Lady Vanishes: *What was Michael Redgrave like to work with?*

H: It was his first screen part. When we started, we rehearsed a scene, and then I told him we were ready to shoot it. He said he wasn't ready. "In the theater, we'd have three weeks to rehearse this." "I'm sorry," I said, "in this medium, we have three minutes." But he learned the new way quickly.

s: *Why did you include that single shot of the train hurtling over the viaduct?*

H: That was a miniature. The whole film was made in the studio. I don't recall the reason for that shot, though.

s: *I think it sustains the sense of danger because of the height and so forth of the viaduct.*

H: Yes.

s: *You were very clear to Truffaut on the flaws in your next film,* Jamaica Inn, *but I'm still puzzled by the slowness of its pace. It's almost as if you wanted to accentuate the problem.*

H: Don't forget, I was associated with two extremely difficult men: Erich Pommer, the producer, and Charles Laughton.

s: Foreign Correspondent *is very patriotic; it even ends with "The Star-Spangled Banner." Was that your idea?*

H: That was Walter Wanger and Ben Hecht.

s : *Don't you think it was the wrong package for all your fine thriller ideas?*

H : Got me a telegram from Harry Hopkins!

s : *I'd like to move now to what seems to me an outstanding example of your American period,* Strangers on a Train.

H : I liked it very much, but, you know, I had terrible trouble getting my treatment dialogued. Eight writers turned me down. They couldn't visualize the story. This shows that some writers don't look at the screen. They think only of the written page.

s : *The film is full of brilliant images, like the anonymous feet at the beginning. I wonder whether others were so clearly planned as that one. I think, for example, of the scene in the dining car, where Farley Granger is in clear light, but Robert Walker, the sinister character, is always barred by shadows cast by the venetian blinds.*

H : That's a trick of staging. I remember in *The Lodger* when Novello goes to the window, I made one shadow of the lattice cross his face and the other come down between his eyes.

s : *In the novel, Guy pays for his crime, whereas he doesn't in the film. Do you think the notion that Bruno is the embodiment of Guy's murderous impulse is compromised by this?*

H : You could say that, but after all, what made him guilty?

s : *He willed his wife's death. That doesn't warrant death for him, but in the film, you let him off completely.*

H : If he were punished, I think the audience might leave the theater feeling dissatisfied, and you might lose all that went before.

s : *Don't you think today's audiences would accept a downbeat ending?*

H : No question. In *Frenzy*, the heroine gets killed.

s : *Do you at all regret yielding to commercial considerations of contemporary audience response?*

H : I come back to my previous remark about cinema as a world medium. No other medium can reach so wide an audience. A film can go to South America, as well as Japan. I mean, there is some satisfaction in knowing that ne's cardboard head stands in the middle of a Tokyo marquee with the two stars on either side, even though I'm given Oriental eyes. I'm reaching people a long way off.

s : *You used a double for Farley Granger in the tennis match.*
H : Two. I even had a machine made for that scene that could project balls under the camera. Granger is always hitting right into the lens. We had to have a very strong spring arrangement so that the ball would go way over just before the cut.

s : *Since you've agreed that, in general, you stay away from stories with deep content, why did you choose to make* I Confess *and* The Wrong Man?
H : I guess I was persuaded by the gentleman I formed a partnership with during that period. He knew quite a bit about cinema. He founded the London Film Society, which almost amounted to the introduction of foreign films into English-speaking countries. *The Wrong Man* I needn't have done. I was under contract to Warner Brothers then, for whom I'd made three pictures in a period when I might have made four. The contract was up, but since I'd been paid the equivalent of four pictures, I decided to let them have one for nothing. This script was the available project.

s : *In* I Confess, *why do you allow Anne Baxter and Montgomery Clift not to age very much during the film, though it covers a considerable time span?*
H : It's difficult to do. If you show your characters lined in one scene, you've got to line them through the whole film. If you make them younger in the earlier scenes, you've got to give them such heavy makeup that all their character would be gone in close-ups.

s : *Many people thought* Rear Window *in some sense self-referring. Were you conscious of the photographer-spy as in any sense, a self-portrait?*
H : Not at all.

s : *Why did you use a set rather than a real apartment house?*
H : We had thirty-one apartments across that courtyard, twelve completely furnished. We never could have gotten them properly lit in a real location.

s : *What do you think about the prominence that* Vertigo *has assumed for your European critics?*

H : I think they understood the complexities of the situation.

S : *But do you agree with those among them who say the film refers to you: You change Kim Novak into Grace Kelly, just as Jimmy Stewart changes her from one girl to another?*

H : No, there's nothing in that. Here's a good example, though, of the importance of the subjective treatment we spoke about a while back. You remember the scene when Kim Novak comes out of the bathroom, dressed like the original girl and wearing her hair blond? She comes closer to him, as I lift away the green haze in which the scene is shot, and then he takes her in his arms. Then I pan around from them over a special set I had built— showing the stables where he had last embraced what he thought was a dead woman. I put Stewart and Novak on a little platform and turned them around so that with back projection, I could seem to be moving from the hotel room, into the stables, then back into the hotel room. In this way, I could illustrate Stewart's feeling that the kiss is taking him back into the past. A lot of people would have shot this objectively, dissolving from the hotel room into the stable, but that would have lost the subjective effect.

S : *Why did you shoot the climactic Mission Dolores scene on a set?*

H : Because there was no tower on the spot. I matted the tower in. I remember telling the monsignor that he'd have a lot of visitors to his nonexistent tower after the film came out. You know, he did!

S : *Why do you superimpose the painting of Carlotta when Kim Novak comes out wearing the same jewelry? Don't you think this unnecessarily obvious for the same viewers that are able to understand Stewart's rather complex psychology?*

H : No, because this was a very important detail that would later give the girl away. Audiences' eyes wander. You need to underscore something that important.

S : North by Northwest *seems to me your most consistently inventive film.*

H : Took a whole year to write. Ernie Lehman and I decided, as in *The 39 Steps*, to fill out every inch of the film. We decided to make a picaresque thriller with lots of locales for the chase.

S : *It also seems to be audaciously gratuitous.*

H : That's right. I even reduced the MacGuffin. When Cary Grant asks Leo

Carroll what James Mason is after, Carroll says, "Let's say he's an importer-exporter." "What of?" "Government secrets." I realized by this time that the audience doesn't really care about the MacGuffin; it's the excitement of the chase that counts.

s : Psycho *contains some of your most brilliant effects, notably in the editing of the shower murder, but I'm bothered by bits of cheating here and there. For example, when Norman's "mother" enters the bathroom, she is in total darkness though it is dazzlingly lighted. There's also the business of having "her" lines spoken by an actress in the beginning of the film, and the cut to a high-angle shot when Norman takes her body into the fruit cellar so we won't realize that she's dead.*
H : For the bathroom, you must remember that the bathroom light is shining right into the camera. In fact, we had to use a projector lens to get the right effect. We committed the cardinal photographic sin—shining a light into the lens—but that causes the audience to subconsciously realize why they can't see the face of the assailant. As for the mother's voice, it was a bit of a cheat, but it was necessary to the story and I doubt that Tony Perkins could have produced the right falsetto.

s : *Why did you end the film with the psychiatrist's explanation?*
H : Because the audience needed it. Otherwise, they'd have a lot of unanswered questions. You'd run afoul of the icebox trade.

s : *The "icebox trade"?*
H : The people who get home after seeing a movie, go to the icebox, and take out the cold chicken. While they're chewing on it, they discuss the picture. In the morning, the wife meets the neighbor next door. She says to her, "How was the picture?" and the wife says, "It was all right, but we discovered a number of flaws in it." Bang goes your word of mouth!

s : *In* The Birds, *I'm puzzled by the relationship between the family's situation and the attack of the birds.*
H : I only wanted to show that life goes on with its petty interests even when they are dwarfed by some cataclysm. Substitute an air raid and you'd have the same meaning.

S: *But there's an awful temptation to see the horror as some sort of symbolic emanation from the personal drama. Why did you give us so much of the latter if you didn't want us to feel that the personal situation is primary?*

H: Because I didn't want to bring the birds on too early. You know, I think it was Fellini who said he wouldn't have had the nerve to make an audience wait so long for the birds to make their appearance. But I wanted to show how much was going on of minor importance, before this terribly important event takes place. Great catastrophes tend to wipe out lesser human foibles and troubles. And there was a certain amount of truth in that film. A farmer in Bodega Bay told me that he'd lost a number of lambs to birds. They used to peck the animals to death. In Oceanside, once, a house was invaded by starlings coming down the chimney.

S: *Why did you have so much trouble with the ending of* Topaz?

H: I had a lot of trouble with that. It originally ended with a duel in a huge football stadium at early morning. A little knot of men enters, and the duel starts. Then one of the characters becomes frantic and tries to stop the duel. But the referee refuses. Then, at the moment the two men take aim, at the top of the stands a sharpshooter, with a telescopic rifle, shoots the spy in the back. Someone asks the hero what happened, and he says, "Obviously, the Russians have no further use for him." A lot of the film had problems: You had Frenchmen speaking English to Frenchmen; Cubans speaking to Frenchmen in English. How can you believe that?

S: *Is your dissatisfaction with* Topaz *what sent you back to London?*

H: No. I'd been trying to work out the *Frenzy* story for some time. Last year I had three writers on it, but things didn't go. Then a publisher sent me a book with a totally different story, so I started a new *Frenzy* all over again, with Anthony Shaffer writing the screenplay.

S: *A moment ago you spoke of the need for a subject that led you to* Topaz. *Have there not been times when, in retrospect, you found it would have been better to wait and not make a film?*

H: I've dropped many projects. I brought a couple of writers over from Italy for one project, but unfortunately, there was a language barrier. I wanted to work up a treatment of an idea I've had since 1935. It takes place in a big hotel, managed by a family of thieves, brought over by one of their members from Italy. Now, however, the manager is such a big shot that he doesn't need to be a thief anymore. Suddenly, an important woman arrives with a collection of valuable coins. So the manager is stuck with the problem of putting her up in the hotel and keeping his family away from the valuables. From then on, you have adventures. And while they take place, I'd show the whole workings of the hotel: the kitchen, the laundry, etc. It would have been a comedy-thriller with the whole mechanism of the hotel featured. But the script never worked out for the reason I indicated.

s :  *Have you ever been prevented from making a film by your studio?*
H :  Sometimes.

s :  *Why didn't you do it anyway?*
H :  I'd have loved to make a film of *We the Accused.*

s :  *Since you've had such subjects, why didn't you make an Alfred Hitchcock film, with all the Hitchcock mastery, outside the commercial considerations to which, as you've said, you sometimes made concessions you later regretted?*
H :  What do you mean by "outside commercial considerations"? Films about "the human condition"?

s :  *No, just something made without any worry about the box office.*
H :  Well, the subject would have to offer opportunities to tell it my way.

s :  *Have you never had such a subject?*
H :  I own one now: J. M. Barrie's *Mary Rose,* but at present, it doesn't seem to have any commercial potential.

s :  *Why can't Alfred Hitchcock make anything he wants to?*
H :  That's a privilege I have, but one mustn't take advantage of it. My contract gives me complete artistic control. I can make any film I like, up to three million dollars. But such privileges are a responsibility to the studios, which I obviously cannot, and would not, take advantage of. I don't have the right kind of conceit. I want to please everyone if I can. We live in an industry. A lot of people have jobs here: five thousand of them. If every film we made lost money, where would we all be? Many films never get beyond New York's East Side. I didn't walk into this business without proper knowl-

edge of it. I've been a technician; I've been an editor; I've been an art direc-tor; I've been a writer. I have a feeling for all these people. I fill my responsibility to myself by the manner in which I make films. The subjects I choose, however, are chosen so that I'll not indulge myself at the expense of others. You've spoken of commercialism; I don't look at it that way. We should use the power of film to reach a world audience.

# Alfred Hitchcock: The German Years

BOB THOMAS / 1973

ALFRED HITCHCOCK HAD JUST returned from an exploitation tour, an exercise in which he is as expert as in the direction of suspenseful movies. The journey had taken him to West Germany, Italy, Austria, and Switzerland, for the purpose of publicizing his new film, *Frenzy*. He relished some of the memories of the trip, including his travels in a railroad car designed for Herman Goering. In Zurich, the mayor had conducted the press conference.

"These tours are very important to the success of a film," Hitchcock remarked. "It's essential that they be timed just right—immediately before the opening of the picture in those countries."

Hitchcock was talking one morning in his offices at Universal studio, where he has been working for the last decade. The office is roomy and decorated in the style you would expect of Hitchcock: elegant with a touch of the macabre. On the wall facing his desk is a painting of Mt. Rushmore, the monument he used as a prop in *North by Northwest*. If you look closely enough, you'll note that one of the granite portraits is unmistakable—the cherubic Hitchcock himself.

Hitchcock is rarely nostalgic, but the European trip had brought back memories of his beginnings in films. He had returned to Munich, where he had directed his first two films, *The Pleasure Garden* and *The Mountain Eagle*.

"I got my first training in an American studio, you know," Hitchcock commented. "I started in 1920 at Famous Players-Lasky, which Adolph Zukor had

From *Action*, 8 (January–February 1973), pp. 23–25.

opened in London in an attempt to capture the English market. Then in 1924 I went to Berlin. Those were the great days of German pictures. Ernst Lubitsch was directing Pola Negri, Fritz Lang was making films like *Metropolis*, and F. W. Murnau was making his classic films. The studio where I worked was tremendous, bigger than Universal is today. They had a complete railroad station built on the back lot. For a version of *Siegfried* they built the whole forest of the *Nieblungenlied*.

"I arrived in Berlin knowing not a single word of German. My job was as art director, and I worked side by side with a German draftsman. The only way we could communicate was by pencil-drawing things so we could understand each other. That's how I learned German.

"I don't know why there was such a ferment in the German film at that time. It was just after the war and Germany was beginning to fall into chaos. Yet the movies thrived. That makes it all the greater mystery as to why the German film industry is in such bad condition now."

Hitchcock said that the German experience played an important role in his career.

"The Germans in those times placed great emphasis on telling the story visually; if possible with no titles or at least with very few," Hitchcock said. "In *The Last Laugh* Murnau was able to do that, to dispense with titles altogether, except in an epilogue. I don't believe that was accomplished by anyone else. I think Charles Ray tried it in *The Old Swimming Hole* but he cheated: he used a diary throughout the picture. There was another film made a few years ago without dialogue, *The Thief* with Ray Milland. I didn't see it."

The Germans sometimes photographed their films at odd angles, Hitchcock remarked, and they built their sets at odd angles, too. He recalled the railroad set for *The Last Laugh*. The focus of the set was on a large railway clock. All the lines in the set went to the clock, emphasizing the element of time. The remainder of the set in the background was built in a foreshortened perspective so that it seemed to be a great length.

"The locomotive, a whole stream of coaches, and the glass roof of the railway station were all in perspective," the director recalled. "The set had one drawback: as the perspective diminished there was no light in it. They solved that by putting a real train at the point in the distance where the lines met and had people coming out of the train."

Hitchcock directed his first film, *The Pleasure Garden*, in 1925. Locations were shot in Italy, and the studio work was done in Munich. It was a co-production, with Michael Balcon of England's Gainsborough and Eric Pommer of Germany's Emelka-GBA as producers. It was memorable to Hitchcock mostly because his assistant director and script girl was Alma Reville, who became his wife.

"My next picture was *The Mountain Eagle* which filmed with locations in the Austrian Tyrol and studio work at Emelka in Munich," the director recalled. "Even in those days Britain was trying to get the American market. For the role of the demure village school mistress, Gainsborough sent me Nita Naldi, the American vamp. She was the successor to Theda Bara, I believe.

"Miss Naldi arrived at the location with nails an inch long, and she refused to cut them. She had her boyfriend along with her, an elderly gentleman, she called 'father.'"

Hitchcock returned to England in 1926 to make his third film and the first in the long and distinctive string of his Hitchcock suspense films, *The Lodger*. It showed an enormous influence from his two years in the German studios, he said, and the German influence has continued through all of his films, especially in his emphasis on the visual.

"The only trouble with silent pictures was that when people opened their mouths, nothing came out," he said. "The trouble with talking pictures is that too many of them are merely pictures of people talking. I have seen such pictures in theaters on the Champs Elysee with French subtitles and I feel for the poor audience. They spend their evenings reading.

"I've always believed that you can tell as much visually as you can with words. That's what I learned from the Germans."

Hitchcock recalled that his first talking film was made with a German star, Anny Ondra. It was *Blackmail*, filmed in 1929 for British International Pictures.

"We were already into the movie when it was decided that we should use sound," he said. "I suddenly realized that the leading lady spoke with a broken accent. In those days we knew nothing about dubbing so it was a big problem. I finally solved it by placing a girl at the side of the set and having her speak the dialogue as Anny Ondra mouthed the words."

Hitchcock had one more experience with German film making and it was disastrous. It came in 1930 with another Anglo-German co-production, *Murder!* He recalled: "*Murder!* was a whodunit, a rather sophisticated play which had done well in London. Two versions of the script were written, one in

German and one in English, and I went to Berlin with the idea of making two versions at the same time, filming a scene with English actors and then following immediately with German actors.

"I took the script to Berlin, and the Germans suggested many changes. I objected that if the two scripts were too much different I would end up making two pictures instead of one and we would lose the economic advantage of simultaneous shooting.

"That was a mistake. The English and the German versions could not be so closely paralleled because of differences in customs and language. I ran into terrible obstacles in the German version when I came to direct the picture. Although I spoke German, I didn't know the cadences of speech, and I was lost on the set. The actors sounded colloquial to me but I couldn't really understand what they were saying.

"The hero of the English version was Herbert Marshall, and the German was a well-known actor, Alfred Abel. I had problems with Abel because he would not do certain things which he felt were beneath his dignity. The role was that of an actor-manager like a Laurence Olivier or a Gerald du Maurier, and I laid his office in Her Majesty's Theater. During those scenes he would wear a black coat, as you would expect of such a gentleman. Later on as a private eye he visited the girl in jail and I had him wear a tweed suit for his visit there. I figured that would be natural in the course of his sleuthing.

"'I don't visit a girl in these clothes,' Abel insisted. He demanded to be dressed in a black coat and striped trousers. There was no arguing with him." Abel also refused a comedic scene arguing, "You can't do this to such a man." Hitchcock countered that the "Whole point of comedy is to reduce dignity." Replied Abel: "Not for the Germans."

As a result, said Hitchcock, the English version was a success and the German *Murder!* was a complete bust.

The German influence spread to America, Hitchcock noted, with the advent to Hollywood of such directors as Lubitsch, Murnau, Lang, William Dieterle, Michael Curtiz, and Billy Wilder.

"It's curious that while German directors succeeded in Hollywood the French didn't," he added.

"Julian Duvivier, René Clair, Jean Renoir, and other Frenchman made films here, but never with the success they had in France. Why? I don't really know. Except perhaps it's that German emphasis on the visual which permitted Germans to adapt to American films but not the French."

# Conversation with Alfred Hitchcock

## ARTHUR KNIGHT/1973

H ITCHCOCK'S THEORY ON MOVIEMAKING is simple: "I don't care about the subject matter; I don't care about the acting; but I do care about the pieces of film . . . all the technical ingredients that make the audience scream." On his identification with crime, he says: "By and large, I feel that the more interesting work in the field of murder is done by amateurs. They are people who perform their work with dignity and good taste, leavened with a sense of the grotesque. There is polite and wholesome mayhem, practiced by civilized people, and I personally enjoy it."

OUI: *What's the basic emotion you hope to arouse with your films?*
ALFRED HITCHCOCK: The enjoyment of fear. After all, little babies are brought up on fear. When her baby is about three months old, the first thing a mother does is to scare it. Both mother and baby seem to enjoy the experience, the baby recovers from its scare, giggles, the mother laughs, and the cycle is complete.

OUI: *So you think that people want to be afraid?*
HITCHCOCK: Not of real things. They only want to be afraid of things they know are, in a sense, nonexistent. Now, of course, there are individual variations. The arch criminal probably is, in a way, fearless. And we often hear that the bravest man on the battlefield is the coward, not the man who goes and shoots down 20 men and gets the Congressional Medal of Honor. He

From *Oui*, February 1973, pp. 67–68, 82, 114, 116–21.

was probably drunk at the time. The insensitive person can barge through without regard for the consequences.

OUI: *It's really the quality of imagination that you're playing upon in this enjoyment of fear, isn't it?*

HITCHCOCK: Of course it is. Look at the people who pay money to go on the roller coaster, or to see the haunted house; to make themselves scream is a form of pleasure that people will pay for. They go into the haunted house, a skeleton jumps out, and ghosts appear; they'd be terribly disappointed if they didn't get their money's worth and were only quasi-frightened.

OUI: *Would you agree with those critics who say many recent films have gone too far, become too frightening? They put you on a roller coaster and in the end, instead of letting you off the ride, they leap you off the tracks.*

HITCHCOCK: Because, you see, they're too obvious with what they do. There's no imagination. For example, when I made *Psycho*, I made it in black and white for the very simple reason that I didn't want to show the red blood flowing down the bathtub into the drain. The whole scene in the shower was shot as a concept of imagining this woman's being stabbed to death. But if you examine the film frame by frame, you'll find that no knife ever touched the woman's body. The whole structure of a film like *Psycho* is based on giving the audience an early sample of violence. As the film went on, however, I reduced the violence on the screen—but increased it in the minds of the audience.

OUI: *Isn't that true of many of your pictures—the threat of violence more often than the actual fact of it?*

HITCHCOCK: That's true. *Frenzy*, for example, is supposed to be a story of mass murders, but we have only one violent scene. You see only the suggestion of the other killings. But without the one nice—shall we call it meaty—sample, the rest wouldn't have meant anything.

OUI: *Would you say you're interested in scaring people* in *the theater, whereas many new films are interested in scaring people on the way home?*

HITCHCOCK: Yes. They've been screaming at the top of their voices, but they all get off the roller coaster giggling.

O U I :   *How would you have ended* Wages of Fear, *the Clouzot film about the men carrying the nitroglycerin through the jungle? The semi-hero makes it all the way through, and then his truck goes off the road and he's killed. Would you have destroyed this man?*

HITCHCOCK:   First of all, I have to tell you that I nearly made *Wages of Fear* myself. It was offered to me, but the publishing house in Paris screwed up the deal. Now, I've always said, in this kind of story, there's nothing like a good bomb. Fifty percent of the suspense comes from the fact that you can cut to a wheel going over a stone, or you can show the dynamite being shaken. In a film of Joseph Conrad's *Secret Agent*—it's called *The Woman Alone [Sabotage]*—I had a little boy cross London carrying two film tins; inside was a bomb. I showed every obstacle. I think the thing lasted for a whole reel of film. The bomb was to go off at one o'clock, and I had elaborate delays, like the Lord Mayor's show, where the little boy tries to run across the lines and is pushed back. Finally, he gets on a bus—still carrying the bomb. Now, the important thing about this was the fact that the bus had to take on the pace of the procession, so it went very slowly, which added to the suspense, you see. We had the stop sign, the policemen, the cross traffic, people getting on and off the bus. I kept going to clocks—modern clocks, old clocks, seven to one, five to one. Inside the bus is the little boy and a woman with a puppy, and he's playing with the puppy. On the seat next to him is the bomb—this square package in brown paper. Now, when I photographed that package, I didn't shoot 100 feet and keep cutting back to it. I shot the bomb from every angle I could think of, because every time you went to it from a new angle, it jumped. I gave it a vitality. Clocks again—one minute to one. Three minutes after one the thing went off—bus, boy, tremendous explosion.

At the London press preview, a sophisticated reviewer from *The Observer* rushed up to me with clenched fists held in the air, and she said, "How dare you do a thing like that? I've got a five-year-old boy at home." Well, of course, I had committed the cardinal sin, and that was that after putting the audience through the wringer with anxiety, I had not relieved it. That bomb should have been discovered or heard ticking, whatever you like, and thrown out of the bus, and then it should have gone off. Now, going back to *Wages of Fear*, that truck should have gone over, thrown the man out, and as he rolled down the hill, the truck should have exploded violently. Then you would go back to the man watching it, and that should be your ending. Take him right with it until the last minute. If you like, if you could work it, he should have been blown out of the truck to safety.

OUI: *Your friend Truffaut has been largely responsible for a kind of ending that has become almost a cliché now. The film doesn't really end, you simply have a freeze frame and leave the audience suspended.*
HITCHCOCK: He did that in *400 Blows*, yes.

OUI: *What is your feeling about that?*
HITCHCOCK: Well, I think if you leave an audience in mid-air—I'm talking about the mass audience now—they'll be left sitting there. They'll have no chance to give that sigh of satisfaction that most people enjoy. I think films should be tied off, and not necessarily happily.

OUI: *But you do feel that audiences deserve some kind of explanation.*
HITCHCOCK: Very definitely. I've always said that in structuring a film, you may leave certain holes in the early part, so long as you plug that hole before the film ends. You don't have to be so arbitrary as to be what I call "logical," which is very dull, and plug a hole right at the moment it is expected.

OUI: *In* Psycho, *you used a very long scene with a psychiatrist to explain every-thing to the audience.*
HITCHCOCK: Well, that was necessary because you were presenting the audience with an extremely complicated situation involving transvestism, an area unknown to the average audience, and taxidermy, which also had to be explained.

OUI: *On the other hand, in* The Birds, *you leave the audience very much up in the air.*
HITCHCOCK: You had to. Here we have a family in Bodega Bay, 50 miles north of San Francisco, fleeing the area, and one had to leave it to the imagi-nation of the audience that this bird attack was a local thing. Otherwise, where do you stop next? The Golden Gate Bridge? Then you're on a whole new theme. You're on the theme that Daphne du Maurier had in her short story—that the world was being taken over by birds. Well, that's too far to go in a film. In all the accounts that I have read about bird attacks, they were pretty localized, no matter how violent. Oddly enough, when I first arrived

in Bodega Bay, one of the farmers said to me, "It's funny you should come up here to do a film about this. I've been losing a lot of my lambs with the birds attacking and pecking their eyes out."

OUI:  *Is it true that your father had you put in jail for a short while?*
HITCHCOCK:  Oh, yes, that was scary. I was only about five years old, and I had been bad, so my father wanted to teach me a lesson. He sent me down to the chief of police with a note. They locked me in a cell.

OUI:  *How long were you left there?*
HITCHCOCK:  Only around five minutes. But just hearing the clang of that cell door was enough for me. It was terribly frightening.

OUI:  *Experiences like that invariably are reflected in one's work. Do you think that your Catholic upbringing has influenced your films?*
HITCHCOCK:  I'm not conscious of that kind of thing. I can only say that the stringency of the *modus operandi* in the Jesuit school I attended may have instilled in me a kind of fear of authority.

OUI:  *Was all of your formal education under the supervision of the Jesuits?*
HITCHCOCK:  No; after I left the Jesuits, I went to a school of engineering and navigation, studying engineering, electricity, mechanics, the laws of force and motion, and draftsmanship. I had to learn screw-cutting and black-smithing, work on a mechanical lathe, the whole works. One got a thorough grounding there. Then I got a job as an estimator with an electrical company.

OUI:  *So you initially were studying to be an engineer?*
HITCHCOCK:  Well, let's say that was to have been my stable form of endeavor. However, my interest was more toward the arts. While working at the estimating job, I attended the University of London and took a course in art and painting and all that sort of thing. Because of that, I got transferred into the electrical company's advertising department and started designing ads, brochures, and things of that kind. I was about 18 or 19 at the time.

OUI:  *How did you move from institutional advertising to motion pictures?*
HITCHCOCK:  Well, first of all, I found out that a famous play had been acquired by Paramount Pictures, which had just opened studios in London.

I thought I'd get in on designing the art titles. In those days of silent films, all the titles were accompanied by a drawing. Birds flying, hearts breaking, candles guttering. I made up a main title card and took it to the man sent over by Paramount to organize things in England. No charge—nothing; I didn't say, "I'd like to do your titles," but opened up a large, black, paper-covered board with this printed title. And, of course, he was impressed. I don't think he knew much about it, though, because he commented, "That's a nice white paint you're using."

OUI: *You were still with the electrical company while you were doing this?*
HITCHCOCK: Oh, yes, sure. I overlapped the two jobs. In any event, Paramount changed the film it was going to make and did a Drury Lane melodrama called *The Great Day* instead. So I made up another title card and took that along. My demonstrative persistence, of course, eventually got me the job.

OUI: *And you went from there to scripts?*
HITCHCOCK: While I was there, I practiced my hand at script writing. As a matter of fact, I took a story owned by this company and made a script of it and just put it aside. I didn't attempt to sell it. I merely did it as an exercise, you see. And I used to be sent out on odd jobs with a cameraman, to shoot a character going in and out of a door in London somewhere—little tasks like that.

OUI: *Were you still writing titles?*
HITCHCOCK: Yes, of course. The title writer was very important to the success or failure of a picture in those days. If it wasn't a good picture, they'd salvage it with title cards. There was a man named George Marion, Jr., who would completely retitle a picture. I remember the time he took a very, very bad melodrama, *The Cruise of the Jasper B*, and filled it with comic titles. He changed the whole feeling, and the film was an enormous success.

OUI: *What took you from the title cards onto the studio floor?*
HITCHCOCK: Well, Paramount eventually closed down its London operation and brought some people to the U.S. They included directors John Robertson, George Fitzmaurice, Donald Crisp, and big players like Anna Q. Nilsson, James Kirkwood, Evelyn Brent, Norman Kerry, and Eddie Goulding.

Fitzmaurice's writer, incidentally, was his wife, Ouida Bergere, who eventually married Basil Rathbone. But the rest of us who stayed in England were temporarily unemployed. The empty studio became a rental studio, and one hung around for the jobs. Eventually a group came in with a play called *Woman to Woman*. I was hired as assistant director, and they asked me if I could recommend a good script writer. "I'll do it," I said. "You, what do you know about it?" they asked. So I handed them my sample script. They were suitably impressed and I got the job. Then the art director left, saying he had a prior commitment. "What are we going to do for an art director?" asked the executives. I said, "I'll do it." So for nearly three years, I did both jobs—wrote the script and then became the art director and production manager on each picture.

OUI: *And then came the day when you volunteered to direct, too.*
HITCHCOCK: No, I never did. I was the victim of studio politics. Later I was assigned as the writer and assistant director of a play called *The Prude's Fall*, to be shot on the Continent. Unfortunately, the director had picked up with an Estonian girl. He couldn't come to London, because they wouldn't let her into the country. Finally, the whole company crossed the Channel to shoot locations in Venice, St. Moritz, and Lake Como. But every time we arrived at a location, this Estonian girl would say, "Oh, Jeff, I don't like this place," and the director would say, "Don't worry, we won't be here long." We finally returned to London—without a single shot. Not a shot—just because of this girl. The producer, Michael Balcon, eventually said to me, "How would you like to direct a picture?"

I said, "It never occurred to me." And it hadn't. I hadn't any interest whatsoever. He said, "Well, we've got an Anglo-German proposition to make a film in Munich, and we have a story and a half-finished script and a writer." So I left for Munich with just the script under my arm and a couple of English actors; the rest were Germans. The interesting thing, I think, is that when Balcon saw the finished picture, he said, "Well, this looks like an American picture." It had that American gloss on it, you see—it didn't look like a Continental film.

OUI: *Was that meant as a compliment?*
HITCHCOCK: Oh, very much so.

OUI: *Even at this early stage you were making quite a name for yourself as an innovator, were you not?*

HITCHCOCK: I did have a few sequences that had a bit of the visual quality that I think is the basis of cinema. For example, I remember I had a scene where a girl wades out to sea, a native girl—it's all laid in the Middle East somewhere—and the heavy rushed out to save her. She was going to commit suicide. But when he got close to her, he held her head under the water and murdered her. Then he brought back the body and said, "I did my best to save her, but it was too late." You see one thing, but are told another; that's essentially cinematic. Later on in the film, this man got the d.t.s, went berserk, and took a sword from the wall and attacked his wife. So I had the suspense of somebody rushing to get the doctor for help and the doctor arriving with a gun. As the man was about to bring the sword down on his wife, the doctor shot him. And then I went close on the man—the heavy—as he lowered his sword, and he turned round with a look of surprise on his face. And he said, "Hello, doctor." I reverted him to complete sanity for a moment. Whether it was medically right or not, I didn't know; I only cared about the dramatic impact. He looked down at the front of his shirt and there was a big red stain starting. He looked up and asked, "What's this?" and dropped dead.

OUI: *Crime and criminal behavior are the themes of many of your films. Do you have any theory why they've always interested you so much?*

HITCHCOCK: I think it's an English thing. The English have always been very interested in crime. In England, you see, crime writing is considered first-class literature. In America, it's not, and never has been. You can go back to Conan Doyle, you know, or Wilkie Collins. Go as far back as you like, right up to the present day, crime has always interested the English litterateurs. They write books on the most recent *cause célèbre* and it's always taken seriously. Whether you take John Buchan or Mrs. Belloc-Lowndes, Galsworthy's *Escape,* or a playwright like Clemence Dane, G. K. Chesterton's *Father Brown,* all of these serious writers have at one time or another contributed to the literature of crime. I follow in that tradition.

OUI: *Would you also ascribe the Englishman's interest in crime stories to the fact that the papers in England are national in scope—and that consequently a crime story becomes something that involves the whole country?*

HITCHCOCK:  Of course. There is a Sunday paper called *News of the World*, which in its heyday had a circulation of 7,500,000. Its contents are mainly accounts of the various crimes committed all over the country.

OUI:  *Do you find any changes in British crime and attitudes toward it?*
HITCHCOCK:  I would say that there's been a change in England, a general change. You don't get the domestic murder now, because, you see, those took place in the days when people weren't so affluent as they are today. Divorce is slightly easier to get, or a couple can simply part and live separately. The economics of the twenties and even before were very different. Poor lovers could meet only on the park bench or in the tea shop or somewhere like that. Well, now those times have changed, so that crimes in which the husband gets rid of his wife by arsenic poisoning or shooting no longer exist. So most of the crimes in London are usually semi-professional or fraudulent crimes—company directors and people like them.

OUI:  *But you do still have crimes of violence in England.*
HITCHCOCK:  Oh, sure. But they're mostly related to robbery and things like that. There was a period in England when robbery with violence carried a mandatory sentence of 15 strokes of the cat. I think that was given up just before the last war. Usually this cat-o'-nine-tails—it was nine knotted thongs at the end of a short stick—was administered by a guard to a man strapped to a triangle. They had a heavy leather collar around his neck so that the spine would not be hurt, and a doctor would examine him with a stethoscope after each stroke. The doctor would then decide after so many strokes, usually eight or nine, whether or not he'd had enough. Now, for some reason they gave that up. So today you find more robberies with violence.

OUI:  *What do you make of the greater violence in American crimes?*
HITCHCOCK:  Well, the greater violence here is due to the wider possession of guns. Did you see the CBS television documentary *Thou Shalt Not Kill*? It featured two fellows on Death Row. They were gleeful. They were giggling, laughing over what they'd done, you know, as though they'd practiced some practical joke by killing six people. They nudged each other like two school boys as they described their various adventures. I mean, it was a picture of evil at its worst. It was scary.

OUI: *Does that kind of scariness interest you as a filmmaker?*
HITCHCOCK: No, it doesn't. Because it brought out feelings that one shouldn't really have. You would want to see that smiling, grinning face contorted with pain.

OUI: *At the end of a rope?*
HITCHCOCK: Not at the end of a rope—on the rack. Go back to Spain.

OUI: *What do you feel about a film like* In Cold Blood, *which, in a sense, probes the motives of people who murdered for attention?*
HITCHCOCK: The only thing that bothered me was that I didn't get to know the victims. If I had known them and their problems, and then suddenly these murderers come onto the scene, I think it's possible I might have felt a little more deeply about them. I mean, if I were doing it, I would have had some kind of conflict within the family, almost in a Chekhovian way.

OUI: *Do you think that this kind of probing into the minds of killers is valid as entertainment?*
HITCHCOCK: Only if it's colorful. This is the whole point, you see. Because if you take a real case, then you are restricted and bound. As a matter of fact, I think I made an error myself when I made that little film, *The Wrong Man*, in which I had to follow everything that happened in the actual case. I put in certain shots which I shouldn't have. For example, I wanted to show, at the moment when the real man is discovered, that he and the wrong man looked very much alike. I did it by taking a close-up of Henry Fonda whispering a prayer to the figure of Christ on the wall, and then over that big head I double-exposed a real street in Queens—and there's a man walking towards us. He gets closer and closer and comes right into close-up, and I fitted his face over that of Fonda. Fonda's face disappeared and the man turned and went into this general store and tried to hold it up. That's how he was really caught. He was knocked down by the little man who owned the store, while the wife phoned for the police. Now, I should never have done the double-exposure scene, because that never happened in the real story. I was introducing creative elements into a story that didn't need to be improved upon.

OUI: *But if you're taking elements of life and putting them on celluloid in ways that parallel what happened in real life, shouldn't you have the freedom to make such connections?*

HITCHCOCK:  Perhaps.

OUI:  *One of the themes you keep coming back to seems to be the story of the wrong man, the man falsely accused.*
HITCHCOCK:  Well, it happens so often, and I think it creates a rooting interest within an audience, because nobody likes to be accused of something that he wasn't responsible for. Also, in the case of *The Wrong Man,* it was a true story, so there was that fascination again.

OUI:  *How often has the wrong-man theme come up in your films?*
HITCHCOCK:  Well, sometimes it's merely a device. In *The 39 Steps* or *North by Northwest,* it's a way to stop the hero from going to the police. If he's being chased by enemy spies or by the heavy in the picture, the first thing the audience would ask is, why doesn't he go to the police? Otherwise you have no chase story. How do you do that? You make him wrongfully accused. Cary Grant in *North by Northwest* is found holding a knife that he's just pulled out of a man's back. Immediately he panics, and everybody says, "Stop that man!" The same thing with *The 39 Steps.* A woman is stabbed in a man's apartment. He looks down into the street, sees a menacing figure, and fears for his own safety. "They've killed this woman," he thinks, "and they're going to get me because I know." So he disguises himself as a milkman, gets on a train, and decides to carry on the work of the woman because he's got nothing much else on his hands. Then, to his horror, he finds that he's accused of stabbing the woman. So you now have the man on the run, and also in pursuit of an objective. But the important thing is that he cannot and must not go to the police.

OUI:  *Critics have said that one of the extraordinary things you accomplish in* Frenzy *is that in the first 30 or 40 minutes you have the audience so believing in Blaney's guilt that no one thinks he could go to the police with his story.*
HITCHCOCK:  What we were doing was planting the evidence, getting Blaney to behave in such a manner that the police and other people could refer back and say, "I saw him do this, I saw him behave this way and that way," and so on.

OUI:  *We see every circumstance of the circumstantial evidence.*
HITCHCOCK:  That's right. That's what is really going on in the beginning

of *Frenzy.* But you cover it up, you see, with the nature of the man, his character, his hot temper. His behavior towards his wife in the matrimonial agency
is overheard by the secretary, for example, and she becomes the main witness
against him. There's no clear statement made that would imply he was the
culprit. The implication is there by cinematic means. You refer to a tie
around the girl's neck, and then you cut to Blaney putting a tie on in his
room. That's simply the juxtaposition of two pieces of film. I didn't say he
was the murderer.

OUI: *Blaney never betrays himself.*
HITCHCOCK: Well, no murderer ever does. Very often you see the murderer
in movies made to be a very unattractive man. I've always contended that
it's a grave mistake, because how would he get near his victim unless he had
some attraction?

OUI: *Would it ever occur to you in any of these numerous wrong-man stories to
have the wrong man actually convicted, hanged, electrocuted, whatever?*
HITCHCOCK: I don't think audiences would be very pleased. That would
be as bad as letting the bomb go off. There's no relief, you see.

OUI: *What do you consider your more successful moments in making a film
entertaining?*
HITCHCOCK: I suppose one of the high spots was in the picture *Rear Window,* where you see the girl in the murderer's room just as the murderer is
also seen, coming down the corridor to that same room, which makes an
audience, if I may be vulgar, leave not a dry seat in the house. It's emotional
suspense based on previous information. The emotional suspense in *Psycho*
comes from our knowing that there's a woman around the house with a
knife. Anybody who steps into that house may be jumped upon at any time.
That's the apprehension; but without the first murder, you wouldn't have it
at all.

A more subtle example is the suspense of fear. People are in a cable car
and the wire is beginning to shred. What do you do? You cut from inside the
car up to the terminal, then back to the shredding cable wire. Will the car
make it in time? Incidentally, I've more or less abandoned cross cutting in
that type of scene; now I'll only take one cut of the shredding wire and not
go back to it again.

OUI: *Do you think that audiences are grasping things more quickly than they used to?*

HITCHCOCK: No, I think they worry more. For example, in *The Birds,* a girl is sitting on the bench outside the schoolhouse and behind her is a Jungle gym with one bird on it. Then I went closer to her and she lit two or three cigarettes and smoked. I think I shot about 50 feet of film of her just smoking. Then she follows one bird with her eyes, and when it comes down, the whole Jungle gym is smothered in birds. I never showed them arriving one by one. I let the girl and the audience get the shock at the same time. Now she runs into the schoolhouse, takes the teacher to the window, and says, "Look." And there, right outside the school, are a mass of ravens. The teacher says, "Children, I want you all to go quietly out of the school and down the road. You're to go home or go into the hotel if you live too far away, and don't run until I tell you." They go out of the room and I cut as the children file out. I went back to all of the birds on the jungle gym and stayed with them. I never showed the progress of the children; you heard the patter of feet, and the moment those feet pattered, all the birds went up. So the audience was saying, "Where are the children? Are they all out yet? Have they gotten away?" The patter of feet did the trick.

OUI: *Yet you take particular pains to avoid making people uncomfortable.*

HITCHCOCK: I suppose I'm a coward in a way. I never have a row with an actor. For instance, I don't bawl him out or do anything of that kind. As a matter of fact, when we were shooting *Frenzy,* the young leading man, Jon Finch, arrived an hour and a half late one day. All the people on the set were waiting to see how I would react; I remember the actress Billie Whitelaw was livid at being kept waiting. And when he finally arrived, he went around muttering his apologies. I just tapped him on the arm and everybody was astonished that I'd taken it so well. But the point is, what else can you do? What is the value of bawling him out in front of everyone? It extracts nothing from the actor except his enmity. You've made him look a fool in front of everyone. Let it go by and say nothing. I don't like fighting on the set and all that sort of thing.

OUI: *If an actor is not playing the part the way you want him to, what would you say to him to get the performance that you want?*

HITCHCOCK: "Go to the front office and pick up your check. Goodbye."

OUI: *Do you make a mental note not to use that actor again?*

HITCHCOCK: Not really, no. But there are certain actors I've felt uncomfortable with, let me put it that way. Working with Montgomery Clift was difficult because, you know, he was a Method actor, and neurotic as well. "I want you to look in a certain direction," I'd say, and he'd say, "Well, I don't know whether I'd look that way." Now immediately you're fouled up because you're shooting a precut picture. He's got to look that way because you're going to cut to something over there. So I have to say to him, "Please, you'll have to look that way, or else." My kind of picture is made up entirely of looks and reactions. I can tell you a story about Ingrid Bergman, apropos of my behavior toward actors and actresses. We were doing this picture *Under Capricorn*, which *The Manchester Guardian* calls the "forgotten Hitchcock masterpiece." I wanted her to run down the stairs and land on some chalk marks. She protested. Finally, we compromised, and that evening we were having drinks with Joseph Cotten and Michael Wilding and two strangers I didn't know. Ingrid was going off the deep end, saying, "Why do you make me do this—you always are making me do that," etc. That made me a little annoyed, so when her back was turned, I just slipped out of the room. When she found I no longer was there, she was told, "Hitch went back to the Savoy." She retorted, "That's the trouble with him. He won't fight."

OUI: *You may not be a fighter, but you are a very inventive filmmaker. How do you feel about giving away your trade secrets?*

HITCHCOCK: There are no secrets—just problems that need solving. Take the climax of *Foreign Correspondent,* for example. It takes place inside an airliner, and I allowed myself only one shot outside. The rest was shot from inside the plane. Now the problem. We're in the cockpit, looking out. One of the engines is gone and we're diving for the sea. At the final moment, you see over the shoulders of the pilot and the copilot that the plane is hitting the sea, with the water crashing in over the cockpit. Not a soul asked, "What happened to the poor camera crew? Did they all get drowned?" I knew I had to shoot the effect in the studio, so I got a stunt pilot, Paul Mantz, to go out over Santa Monica with a camera attached to the nose of the plane. He did a dive and pulled out at the very last minute, when the camera was practically skimming the water. I brought that film into the studio and ran it on the screen and sure enough, we're diving toward the ocean so close that we practically hit the water. I had the cockpit built as a set, with a big bubble-glass front. Then I had a screen made of opaque, seamless rice paper, eight feet wide by six feet high. Behind the screen was a projector so that we could project the dive on the screen. Also behind the screen were two tanks of water, each holding 2700 gallons. Now, all the propman had to do was pull a bolt on each of these tanks and the water came shooting out. I watched the screen, and the moment the plane touched water, I pressed a button and you saw no screen. The volume of water that came down broke the front of the cockpit and went way over the two men. Tore the paper to shreds, you didn't see any paper at all.

OUI:  *Didn't you use a trick glass of milk in* Suspicion?

HITCHCOCK:  Yes. In order to make a glass of milk that Cary Grant was taking to his wife seem as if it might be poisoned, I started with a very high shot on an upper landing. You, the spectator, very high up, looking down, see Cary Grant carrying a glass of milk on a plate. But it's so far away that you can barely see it. To make the audience fix their eyes on this glass, I had a little battery and lightbulb put in the milk, which gave it a glow. Then your eye went to it, all the way up the stairs until it came past the camera, very large.

In *Rear Window,* there was a character called Miss Lonely Hearts. She lived in an apartment way below and I knew there was going to be a scene later on where she would go in search of a man, she was that desperately in need. You saw her go out of her apartment, cross the street, and go into a café where she would be so far away from the camera that she would normally be lost in all the conglomeration of movement. So I dressed her in an emerald-green suit, and didn't allow anyone else—Grace Kelly or anyone—to wear green in the picture. Not even Kelly green. So that when that green suit went across the street, your eyes never left it.

OUI:  *How about the gun-in-hand scene at the climax of* Spellbound—*didn't that involve camera trickery?*

HITCHCOCK:  Actually, it involved several things. First of all, it involved the tradition, dating back to the silent picture days, that when the star was beginning to show—how do we say it politely?—signs of wear the camera-man would put a square of black gauze in front of the lens. That gauze would soften the whole face because it was so near the camera as to be completely out of focus. In later years, the gauze was replaced by a circular piece of glass which had serrated crosslines molded into it. That became known as a diffusion disc.

I don't know whether it was widely noticed, but I also did some experiments with sound in *Frenzy* which I had never attempted before. If you remember in the early part of the story, two men are talking at the fruit stand and the police sergeant comes up and begins to talk about the latest murders. Rusk says, "Sergeant, have you met my friend?" And he turns, and there is no one there. At that point I cut all the sound off, except for the footsteps of people going by. All the roar of the market was gone; I took it out arbitrarily to emphasize the man's disappearance. And I repeated the same device when the girl Babs quit her job. She came out onto the sidewalk, and then you heard the murderer's voice, "You got anywhere to sleep tonight?" I took every bit of sound off the track then. Dead silence. Of course, it wasn't accurate, but it was an effect which worked. And I used it in reverse: When the camera discreetly retreated down the stairs after Rusk took the girl to his room. It went out into the street, and I brought the traffic up to a tremendous roar so that an audience would subconsciously say to itself, "Well, if the girl screams, no one's ever going to hear it."

O U I : *In* Frenzy *you went further with nudity than you have before. Do you think it might have been too far?*
HITCHCOCK: No, that was the method of the murderer. Because of the nature of his psychosis, he would eventually strip his victims. It wasn't nudity for the sake of it. As a matter of fact, I've always adhered to the feeling that modesty is the best policy. Even in the potato truck scenes where there was a nude corpse being disinterred from a mound of potatoes, I went to enormous trouble to avoid showing complete nudity. I had a bikini made of potatoes—a triangle of large potatoes wired together. This was wrapped around the girl's waist and secured so that even though the potatoes were being scraped away, I knew very well that there would be no pubic hair showing, nothing. And when he got up to the breasts, they were both covered by the girl's hands. She was in *rigor mortis,* of course, but when she was struggling, she was covering her breasts with her hands. I was able to do that because of a very well known fact. If a woman is surprised in the nude, what does she do? She covers her breasts. Why not shield the area between her legs first? Never. Always the breasts.

OUI: *How do you choose your leading ladies? Ingrid Bergman, Madeleine Carroll, Grace Kelly, Tippi Hedren—they are all cool blondes.*

HITCHCOCK: I've never wanted to have the obvious blonde, the one who has her sex hanging around her neck like jewelry, the big-bosomed girl. Neither the Marilyn Monroe type nor the Jean Harlow type was for me, because the statement is there too openly—look, sexy blonde! You've said it right away. I prefer to have the audience discover it. One shouldn't know at first whether she's sexy or not. She probably looks cool, maybe frigid. So what did I do in *To Catch a Thief?* I kept deliberately photographing Grace Kelly in profile, coldish, aloof, then right at the door of the room she turns and plunges her mouth onto Cary Grant's. You've made your statement, but you've made the audience wait for it. I more or less base my idea of sexuality on northern European women. I think the north Germans, the Scandinavians, and the English are much sexier, although they don't look it, than those farther south—the Spanish, the Italians. Even your typical French woman, the provocative one, as I've often said, is not the epitome of French sex. The girl who lives in the country, always wears black on Sunday, is guarded by her parents, wrapped in her family—that's your typical French girl, and it's nothing like what they give the tourists. Therefore, the sexiest women are the ones you get in Ingmar Bergman's pictures, like Ingrid Thulin and those people. My God, you know they are Midsummer Night, a roll in the hay in the barn, like Miss Julie. They'll do anything. After all, there's no one sexier than Ingrid Bergman herself. A very sexy woman, although maybe not outwardly. But the point is that they are all terribly sexy. Oh, I guess Madeleine Carroll, for example, has been married about four times.

OUI: *But you have a way of discovering things in your actresses that no one else ever finds. I keep thinking of Eva Marie Saint, who never looked more sparkling, attractive, or seductive than she did in* North by Northwest.

HITCHCOCK: I watched every hair on her head. She had two wardrobes made for her and I discovered when we screened them that the wardrobe designer was dressing her up as a waif. She was dressing up the Eva Marie of *On the Waterfront.* And I finished up behaving like the character that James Mason played in that film. I went along to Bergdorf-Goodman's myself and sat with her as the mannequins paraded by. I chose the dresses for her.

OUI: *In creating the script, do you ever work backward from some idea that seems to be tremendously useful and unusual, and then try to create the story around it?*

HITCHCOCK: No, I wouldn't say that. But I do feel that if you have a background, just using it as a backdrop is not enough. You've got to do more with it. It's like when I did *North by Northwest*. The Department of the Interior wouldn't let us work on the faces of Mt. Rushmore. They said we must work between the heads. I wanted Cary Grant to slide down Lincoln's nose and then hide in the nostril and get a sneezing fit. That would have been, for me, the completion of Mt. Rushmore; now it's just a monument with big heads, which isn't enough. In that same film, Cary Grant was trapped in an art gallery and couldn't get out any way at all. But he did by one device. He started bidding. That's the thing you have to do when you go to an auction. And by crazy bidding he got himself arrested and out of that particular situation.

OUI: *You were very fortunate in your choice of locations on* Frenzy. *Everything around Covent Garden worked for you.*
HITCHCOCK: Oh, yes, it did. People were actually living in those flats along Henrietta Street, across from the market. Another interesting thing, Wormwood Scrubs prison is right next door to the Hammersmith Hospital. That's actually correct. The prison and the hospital are next door to each other. That was the unique situation that attracted me at the end of this picture. And, of course, the use of the fruit and the vegetables was another attraction, especially the potatoes.

OUI: *Do you ever think of yourself as a film* auteur?
HITCHCOCK: Does that mean that the director writes the whole screenplay?

OUI: *The way the French critics use the word, it means that the director not only writes it, it's his complete concept from start to finish. It really is Alfred Hitchcock's* Frenzy, *rather than* Frenzy, *directed by Alfred Hitchcock.*
HITCHCOCK: Well, I suppose that's true of my work. Who is it that once said that self-plagiarism is style? I think that sums it up in a way. One has a certain instinctive way of doing things. Whether or not that constitutes part of the function of the *auteur*, I don't know. I can only explain why I do something a certain way. It's like the opening of *Frenzy*. I decide that we will now enter London through its gates, which open up for us. Now we come to the leitmotiv of the film. It's going to be about a series of murders, so we

make that into a joke. We cover that leitmotiv by having the man say, "Well, the Thames is not polluted anymore. And from this point on it will contain no more foreign bodies." And at that moment the body of a girl floats in. Now, the reason for the girl's body is to establish something of the nature of what the film is going to be about. This comes in what I call the cinematic writing of the picture. You see, a film, when you put it down on paper, must carry with it a complete visual picture of what's coming on the screen. So I always insist on sitting with the writer from the very beginning and creating about a 100-page outline of all the details from the first shot to the end; then I let the writer go away and complete the dialogue and character. The first stage is really involving the writer into making the picture cinematically, so that when he goes to see it he doesn't have to be surprised, because he should know it all, just as much as I do. That's why I never look at the script again once it's written, because it's all been done. The best way I can describe this outline—it's as though you'd looked at the film and cut the sound off. You would then see just the visual elements. When people ask, "Don't you ever improvise on the set?" my answer always is, "With all those electricians around and all the set dressers and so forth, you're going to start to compose a scene or rewrite a scene?" Now I say, if I'm going to improvise, I prefer to improvise in an office.

OUI: *What's your relationship with the director of photography?*
HITCHCOCK: Complete understanding. I know his language. I've turned the camera myself; I've lit scenes myself, back in the late twenties and early thirties. I remember I shot a whole day's work when the cameraman went sick. So it's a matter of my knowing his language and his knowing mine. He's got to light the scene, of course; but on the other hand, the setup is what you give the operator, and I can sketch that out. You see, I never look through a camera. And I don't understand why people do. Is it to surprise themselves or something? What they should be looking for is a rectangular white screen.

OUI: *So many of the people who come in as directors, especially from theater and television, have no knowledge whatsoever of the lenses and what they can do. They're completely in the hands of the cameraman.*
HITCHCOCK: That's the tragic thing about a lot of the new people coming into our business. Because they don't know their medium, they make what I

call "accident" films. For example, many of these new directors allow themselves to be governed by the conditions on the set. By that I mean, you have an office scene. The boss is seated at his desk. An underling comes through a door and goes up to the desk. Now you set up the camera to photograph the underling from just above his head down to, say, the top of the desk—which means that you've got to be far enough back for the camera to take that in. And you say to yourself, this is too far away for the drama. Nor do I want to do individual close-ups of the two men; the scene is too short. So immediately I say to the propman, "Lift that desk eight inches." So they bring in blocks and lift the desk eight inches higher, as well as the chair in which the boss is sitting. You see what's happening? I'm bringing the desk and the face of the boss higher and nearer to the standing man. Then the camera can move in tighter, because you've built the scene for the camera. Instead, I'm afraid, most directors today would say, "Well, I've got to be back here because that's how it is." But that isn't how it is.

OUI: *Many critics have commented that* Frenzy *is your first film in a long time that hasn't used established stars. Do you have any special feeling about the use of stars in your films?*

HITCHCOCK: If you have a certain kind of a film, a star is helpful. *North by Northwest* is a good example of that. Where you want an audience to have a very specific rooting interest in your hero, you'll get more if the figure is familiar, like Cary Grant. On the other hand, the unknown cast is ideal because the audience comes in without preconceptions. I've always said that the best casting director is the novelist, because he can describe in words every facet and every thought of his characters. He doesn't have to compromise at all, but we do. When we're casting, there's always the compromise, because you might say, "Well, let's have Cary Grant." What are the values? The values are his glamour, his good looks, his box office. Yes, but is he really a stockbroker, does he know figures at all? I wouldn't think so, but he might. Once you decide to go after Cary Grant, the question of suitability takes second place to the question of availability. On the other hand, the virtue of having unknowns is that then there's a greater realism about the whole piece.

OUI: *In* Frenzy, *I think the fact that Jon Finch is an unknown means the audience could really believe that Blaney might have been the murderer, whereas if it were Cary Grant everyone would know he was innocent.*

HITCHCOCK:  Actually, belief is suspended by audiences very much. It swings the other way, because audiences don't like their heroes to be put in any jeopardy. They don't stop and analyze it and say, "Well, he'll never be killed." They still believe he may be killed right up until the last minute. Why they do it, I don't know. But it is a fact.

OUI:  *I know you don't like to talk about people you've worked with, but let me ask if there are any particularly good relationships you recall from your career— with studios, producers, stars?*
HITCHCOCK:  Yes, I would say that working with Ben Hecht was very satisfying because he was a real pro. Even though Ben was a man who played several games of chess at once, worked on several scripts at the same time, he really was a great person to work with. And working with Thornton Wilder—that was also terribly satisfying. Especially on that picture *Shadow of a Doubt*. We didn't start the script until we'd both been to the town, stayed in it, lived in it. The two of us went through Santa Rosa, choosing the house, the locale. Is it the right rent? Would the central character live in this kind of house? All that kind of thing was decided upon before the script was written. So that was very satisfactory. But I miss the things that one did in England, you know, where you could work with someone who was a very good writer of melodrama, say, but who wasn't necessarily the best dialogue writer. I would go through all the donkey work with him and then, having completed the theme, hand it over to a dialogue writer. This won't work in this country, because of the screenplay credit situation. It won't. I've tried it. I remember when I was preparing *Strangers on a Train*, I couldn't find anyone to work on it. They all felt my first draft was so flat and factual that they couldn't see one iota of quality in it, yet the whole film was there if you visualized it. I really believe it's the credit system. You see, at one time we used to have "adapted by" and also "screenplay by," but they got rid of that. Now if there's any dispute, a committee reads all the material and allocates the credits.

OUI:  *I recall your saying that you aren't really interested in mystery films.*
HITCHCOCK:  True. After all, what is mystery film? I know of only two types. There's the one that takes the audience into a setting with lots of mysterious goings on, none of which are explained. The other is the whodunit. Here you find the murder, the police are brought in, and the question is,

who is the culprit? You have, I would say, ten seconds of emotion in a film of that kind. Because it's like a crossword puzzle. It's a wondering film—who, who, who did it? And only at the "Oh" do you get any emotion.

O U I :  *It can have suspense, though.*

HITCHCOCK :  It's not an emotional suspense, it's a wondering suspense. I know, they call them mystery thrillers, but there's no such thing. You can't thrill an audience; you can't put an audience through an emotion without information. You tell them that it's a bomb. You don't conceal it from them. Look at the number of mystery films you see with strange goings on, one thing after another, until about a third of the way through, when gradually it begins to unravel. Well, I think that first third should be thrown away. It's done nothing emotionally for the audience whatsoever. For me, cinema is essentially emotion. It is pieces of film joined together that create an idea, which in turn creates an emotion in the mind of the audience. Not through spoken words, but through the visuals. It's a visual medium. And montage is the main thing. All moviemaking is pure montage.

O U I :  *Yes, but you also have a lot of long takes in which the emotion is conveyed primarily by dialogue.*

HITCHCOCK :  That depends upon the nature of the scene. But one of the worst things a writer can say to me is, "Well, I'll cover that point in a line of dialogue." You should stay as visual as you can.

O U I :  *Yet perhaps the funniest, cleverest scenes in* Frenzy *are the two sequences in which the inspector has gourmet dinners with his wife. And, of course, you get a great deal of verbal information across while everybody's laughing at the poor fellow and the concoctions he's forced to eat.*

HITCHCOCK :  Well, here we go again. This comes under the heading of avoiding the cliché. Now, the cliché is the Scotland Yard officer and chief inspector discussing the case with one of the underlings. And what do you get? You get a scene that you've seen on television a hundred times. You are putting over certain plot elements, but it seems to me that creatively you have to think of a substitute for this. And the substitute must be something that will have some quality to it. The quality of character, with an additional factor of humanizing the chief inspector. You see, you can do several things when you avoid the cliché.

OUI: *The impression seems to be, though, that you have some kind of aversion to food in general. One also remembers Jessie Royce Landis stubbing out her cigarette in an egg in* To Catch a Thief.

HITCHCOCK: Well, that's my aversion to eggs, really. I have a very strong aversion to them. The smell of a hard-boiled egg is the most horrible thing in the world. I also hate bottled sauces of any kind. The most horrible sound in the world is the sound of a hand smacking the bottom of a catsup bottle. As a result of the smacking, some horrible red goo oozes itself out of the neck of the bottle and lays itself over some extremely innocent French fried potatoes that have never harmed a soul in their lives.

OUI: *You seem to have such strength in your own knowledge of so many things. Does it bother you what critics say? Do you pay much attention to them?*

HITCHCOCK: It depends. If the critics are criticizing technique and not content, that's one thing. But very often you find that it's the content that they criticize, not the style. It would be like looking at a painting of a still life, say by Cézanne, and wondering whether the apples on the plate are sweet or sour. Who cares? It's the way they're painted.

OUI: *Or worse, rejecting the painting because the critic doesn't like apples.*

HITCHCOCK: You see, the only question is, what is his qualification as a movie critic, especially if last week on the paper he was the gardening critic? A lot of today's critics are not students of the cinema; and I've often wondered how an editor of a paper or the head of a television station goes about appointing them. I never get disturbed by a bad review from an experienced critic, because that's his job. I always remember Caroline Lejeune, who used to review for *The Sunday Times* in London. At dinner one night in our apartment, her face went a bit red, and she said, "I wasn't very good to you last Sunday, was I?" I said, "Caroline, that's your job. If I took umbrage at it, you wouldn't be sitting at our dinner table here on Wednesday." And it is a fact that I have never written a letter of protest over a bad review to a paper or magazine in my whole lifetime. Never once. This is a funny thing. It's very, very strange, but many of the films that I've made have met with very indifferent critical response. Yet, a year later, there is a complete turnaround. I've never understood this. *Psycho,* for example, was originally dismissed by *The New York Times.* Bosley Crowther reviewed it as merely a low-budget, inconsequential Hitchcock picture. On the following Sunday, he began to see things in it. By the third week, it was a classic. That can be looked up in the files. *Time* magazine also dismissed it as a poor something or other. A year or two later, a film was made called *Repulsion*, and in the ads for *Repulsion* is a quote from *Time* magazine which said, "This is in the classic tradition of *Psycho.*"

OUI: *You say you're more interested in technique than in content, but it seems to me that a number of the pictures that you've made—such as* Lifeboat, Foreign Correspondent, The Wrong Man, I Confess—*have had important themes.*
HITCHCOCK: Well, they vary, you know. It's a question of selecting something that will give you the opportunity to be creative and visualize all the things that you want to do with it. I'm not attracted, strictly speaking, to content. Content doesn't really interest me. It's treatment and technique and creating an emotion in an audience through film that is my major interest. I mean, if it's just content, well, anybody can photograph. Most films that you see are photographs of people talking. They're not pure cinema—not by any means.

OUI: *But at the same time, I think you're doing yourself an injustice to say that a film like* Lifeboat *was simply a study in style.*
HITCHCOCK: No, that's true. The intent of *Lifeboat* truly was the war in microcosm. In other words, at the beginning of the war, the Russians weren't in, the Americans weren't in, and until all these nations could get together, the prospects for democracy were dim. That was the whole symbol of *Lifeboat*. And the people in the lifeboat couldn't get together until they were forced to kill the German. You know, the leading man was a Commie, the businessman was a Fascist—we had all the ideologies, all the nationalities in the same boat, and that boat happened to be adrift. As a matter of fact, a lot of people complained about the picture. They didn't understand it at the time. Dorothy Thompson, when the film was shown in New York, gave it ten days to get out of town. They all thought it was pro-German, which was idiotic. I mean the submarine commander surely knew more about handling a boat than any of the amateurs there. It was as simple as that.

OUI: *Again, one of the first political assassinations I ever saw in a movie came in* Foreign Correspondent. *To say that it's a film that is just a study in style and has a marvelous scene with umbrellas on a staircase—that's inadequate.*

HITCHCOCK: Well, let's say that content is a means to a good end, we hope.

OUI: *Are you really interested primarily in crime films?*
HITCHCOCK: No, except that it's become a thing which is expected of me. If I don't do that, then people are disappointed. It naturally narrows down one's choice of material considerably.

OUI: *Would you like to get off the murder kick?*
HITCHCOCK: Well, if I did, I would be more in the hands of the writer, however good he may be, and I would be practically the equivalent of a stage director who just directs people to pick up that ashtray or walk over there, do this and do that. You often see young directors do what I call photographs of people talking, trying to find angles through the chandelier, under the lamp. They don't mean a thing.

OUI: *Have you considered making a period film?*
HITCHCOCK: A period film? You mean a costume picture? No, I don't like costume pictures, because nobody in a costume picture ever goes to the toilet.

OUI: *Have you ever considered doing a feature-length motion picture for TV?*
HITCHCOCK: No. Why waste all that energy on a television show when you might just as well go into a picture?

OUI: *You did some marvelous television shows, you know.*
HITCHCOCK: Yes, but they were very short.

OUI: *How do you feel when you see one of your pictures on television after it's been cut?*
HITCHCOCK: I don't allow it.

OUI: *Well, after it's had commercials spliced in, then.*
HITCHCOCK: Ah, well, there isn't much you can do about that. You can

only make very definite rules, as I did with *Rear Window,* if you own the picture. That could not be touched at all.

OUI: *The advantage of being Hitchcock.*
HITCHCOCK: They say that a murder is committed every minute, so I don't want to waste any more of your time. Thank you very much.

# Hitchcock

ANDY WARHOL/1974

FRIDAY APRIL 26, 1974, New York City, Park Lane Hotel, 36 Central Park South. Alfred Hitchcock, with his wife Alma Reville Hitchcock, is in New York for a salute on the following Monday from the Lincoln Center Film Society. AW and Vincent Fremont arrive at Mr. Hitchcock's suite, where John Springer, publicist, opens the door. AH is in the middle of an interview by "A Reporter" that will appear the next month in a national weekly magazine. AW and VF walk in quietly and sit in a corner. On the other side of the room Mrs. Hitchcock is sitting on a couch. "A Photographer" is waiting to take pictures when the interview ends. "A Reporter" and AH are seated in front of a large glass window, facing each other, in profile against the background of Central Park. AH is wearing a dark blue suit, white shirt and dark tie. AW is in jeans and a black YSL double-breasted blazer.

AH: *That I haven't got a doorstop?*
A REPORTER: Is that all [the Oscar] means to you?
AH: *Certainly. The studios run those things.*
ARH: They did give him the other one, though. The Legion of Honor. (phone ringing)
A REPORTER: If you could save, say, just a handful of your films, which ones would they be?

---

Originally published in *INTERVIEW* Magazine, Brant Publications, Inc., September 1974. Note at beginning: "Redacted by Pat Hackett." The format of this interview is integral to its meaning and effect, so I have not tampered with it, except to replace all caps for film titles with upper and lower case italics. (When titles are in a section of all italics, I have reverted to roman type for a title.)

A H :   *A Picture called* Shadow of a Doubt, *which I wrote with Thornton Wilder . . .* The Trouble With Harry *. . .* The 39 Steps *. . . for a fantasy, which is pure nonsense, I would say* North by Northwest. *That's sheer fantasy. The point is, though, for audiences, the wilder the story line is, the more realistically it must be told. It's like a nightmare. When you have a nightmare you use the word "vivid." Well that's what the film has to be so that you're glad when you wake up on your way to the guillotine.*

A  REPORTER :   But the films you just mentioned are not your most "vivid" films. To me, *Shadow of a Doubt* is maybe your best film because it's a real town with real people—

A H :   *That's right, that's all part of it.*

A  REPORTER :   —and there's no haunted house up on a hill like in *Psycho*—

A H :   *Well actually the haunted house in* Psycho *is absolutely correct. That's Northern California. There're a hundred of houses like that. We call them California Gingerbread. And they're all over the place.—Although they're gradually being pulled down now. But that was quite authentic. That was intended to be near a place called Redding in Northern California.*

A  REPORTER :   But it does add that Gothic element to it.

A H :   *Well they all do—*

A  REPORTER :   Whereas *Shadow of a Doubt* does not.

A H :   *No, well* Shadow of a Doubt, *you see, was on a residential street. It wasn't isolated. As a matter of fact, when Thornton and I went along to study this town, before anything was written—You know, a lot of things are written, and then they try to find the location afterwards: I prefer to look around and try to find the location, if you've got a rough story line . . . And so first we went and we found the house and Thornton said, "It looks too big to me." I said, "But look at the paint peeling off the doors. Send the assistant in to find out the rent." And the rent was correct for the character. The tragedy was that when we came back in two months for shooting, he was so proud of our using his house that he'd had it painted over. And we had to say, "Do you mind if we put two painters on it to dirty it down a bit." Which we did . . . So they are very typical in that part of the country.*

A  REPORTER :   Can you tell me a little something about your next project?

A H :   *Mmmmmm . . . Well it's too embryonic so far.*

A  REPORTER :   When do you think it will go into production?

A H :   *. . . Whenever we can get a script out.*

A  REPORTER :   What kind of a deal do you have with Universal?

AH: *Picture-to-picture. I get paid by the picture. And then a percentage of the profits.*

A REPORTER: There's no time element involved?

AH: *No, none. Three pictures. No time element.*

A REPORTER: I wanted to ask you about *Frenzy*. That's your first film on which—I think—you made sort of a concession to the—liberalizing—of movies today. You have a close-up of a woman's nipple in a murder scene and the use of a nude double. Am I right in saying you made a concession?

AH: *Well, it may have been a bit "trendy," as they say . . . Well in that particular case, it was true to the facts: the man did tear the woman's dress, he was a maniac.—But at least I did show her try to cover it up, which they don't often do in other films. They let the lung fall out, if you want to call it that. And don't forget, there was nudity in* Psycho. *Oh yes. If you examine the material on that shower sequence. Don't forget, there're seventy-eight pieces of film there. You'll find complete torsos. I used a nude girl, she was a nudist, and—*

A REPORTER: What parts of the anatomy were shown in those brief clips of the shower sequence?

AH: *The whole of the torso, a breast was shown for about two frames. But all the excitement of the killing was done by the cutting.*

A REPORTER: The last time I saw *Psycho* in a theater I noticed that the ratio of the scene changed during the shower sequence. Why was that?

AH: *Well, that was because Janet Leigh didn't want her breast suggested, is all. She was a little puritanical about it. So we had to cover for both proportions. What we call the one eighty-five-to-one proportion and the regular Academy three-by-four.*

A REPORTER: But in the final editing, did you not do something—I don't know the technical situation, but it seemed odd to me that we should see the black borders.

AH: *Well, don't forget, when you're shooting a film, there's a foreign market to be considered. And they have different apertures. So we have to provide for different apertures. After all, in Thailand, they're probably using a 1920 projector.—In fact, they cut the sound off in Thailand. They have a man stand beside the screen and recite the whole story to the people, imitating the sound of the voices on the screen to the people. He gets paid more than they pay for the film.*

A REPORTER: I hope we can take a few shots with your wife and with Mr. Warhol, too. Is that alright?

AH: *Certainly.*

AW: *That was the best play I've ever seen. It's so beautiful to see the background of Central Park and your two profiles in the window. It's great. You shouldn't stop.*
A REPORTER: But it's all words.
AW: That's enough. It's—riveting.

(John Springer introduces everyone to everyone, including AW to AH. Then a few words about the American Film Institute, "Chuck Heston" and "Greg Peck.")

("A Photographer" begins taking the first group of pictures: AH and ARH.)

AH: *(to ARH) Sit on the arm, here.*
AW: That background of the Park is great.
A PHOTOGRAPHER: *Look at me? //// Thank you. Andy?*

(Next group of pictures: AH, ARH & AW)
AW: Nice to meet you.
Wow.
Gee.

(Last group of pictures: AH and AW)

(re-arranging)

AH: *The background of the Park would be out of focus after you get the two figures in the foreground. I don't think there's enough light out there.*
A PHOTOGRAPHER: Why don't you direct something wonderful.
AH: *I'll direct the Park; it's there, we're stuck with it.*

A PHOTOGRAPHER: *// Are you going to interview him, AW? /*
AW: I'm going to have my tape recorder on, but I don't know what to say.
(to AH) It's very hard to talk, isn't it?
AH: *Mmmmmm . . .*
AW: Oh, I know.

A PHOTOGRAPHER: Maybe with you sitting here, and you kneeling like this, AW.

("A Photographer" demonstrates)

AW: Fine. (kneels)

(while they're posed) Did you ever make a movie here in town?

AH: *Only sections. I did a bit in* North by Northwest *here, around the Plaza Hotel.* /

AW: Aren't you ever going to be the whole full star in one of your movies? The big lead?

AH: *It was suggested once years ago.*

AW: Really? You should / do it now. That's what you should do.

AH: *Well maybe I should do one of those Rex Stout things.*

AW: Oh yes! Oh yes!

AH: *In the chair all the time. But they're who-dun-its, you know, and I've never found who-dun-its very satisfying on film, because they're almost like a crossword puzzle, you have to wait until the last page before you find out who did it, you see, and they're non-emotional. Whereas with suspense yarns you provide the audience / with the information ahead of time. You make them a kind of god that oversees all. And then they emote. But there's no emotion on a who-dun-it . . .*
/ . . . . . . /

A PHOTOGRAPHER: AW? Look at me?

AH: *I remember / when they started television, out in Los Angeles, one station was going to run a certain who-dun-it story and the / rival station, trying to screw things, went on the air and said, "At such-and-such a station you're going to see a certain story. But we can tell you now that the butler did it."*

End of Tape #1 Side B (started mid-way)

Tape #2 Side A

A PHOTOGRAPHER: Have you ever met Rex Stout?

AH: *No.*

A PHOTOGRAPHER: He's in wonderful shape. He's eighty-six and he's just as spry—

AW: You mean, Rex Stout is a real person?

Nooooo.

A PHOTOGRAPHER: *Yes. He lives in Brewster, New York.*

AH: *(to the room) Are we going downstairs for some lunch?*

ARH:  Yes.

AH:  *Right. We ought to go. Now, I think, because we have other dates later. (to ARH) Do you want to go downstairs?*

ARH:  No, I thought I'd borrow some money from you and go shopping.

AH:  *Excuse me while I give her some money.*

(AH walks his wife into the corner and does a comedy scene of apportioning her some money.)

AW:  (to "A Photographer") That's a cute picture. You should take it.

A PHOTOGRAPHER:  /

(AH and ARH return from the corner)

AW:  It's all down on film. It's your I.O.U.

(In the background people are discussing whether to go downstairs for lunch or have lunch sent up. AW pulls out his Bigshot.)

AW:  This is my old-fashioned Polaroid. /-* Could I just take one with the hand up here? /-* yes . . . /-*

A PHOTOGRAPHER:  Would you like me to take a picture of you two together with it?

AW:  Would you? How great. . . .

just tell me where to go

closer closer closer closer

three feet

A PHOTOGRAPHER:  Okay, can you put your heads together? Boy, you really have to get close . . .

AH:  *. . . That sounds like a rude remark . . .*

A PHOTOGRAPHER:  Put your heads a little closer? . . . . . . / . . . . . .-*

That looked good, AW. (giggles) I don't know if you can afford it, but it looked awfully good.

A REPORTER:  Thank you very much, Mr. Hitchcock.

AH:  *Delighted.*

A PHOTOGRAPHER:  So are you going to do an interview, AW?

AW:  I'm too nervous, so we'll just do a lunch.

AH:  *We're going to do a tape recording.*

AW:  Yes

(getting ready to leave the room)

A H : *Wait. There's a half of a pen left here. Does anyone have a blue pen? There's a top of a blue pen here.*

A W : (to "A Photographer") Would you like to do the interview for us? I'm getting cold feet. (leaves the room, into the hallway)
Fonda's collapse
Burtons' break-up
(wait for elevator)
still in the hospital
Franco Rossellini
(into the elevator, ride down)
Monte Carlo
Princess Grace
May 15th
(doors open)

A W : The restaurant is on the second floor? . . . Yes?

A PHOTOGRAPHER : (unpeeling the Polaroid) It's too light.
too close
where you told me
tried to focus

A W : Well, it's nice anyway. Do you want to keep your first Bigshot picture?

A PHOTOGRAPHER : No. I want it to appear some day in one of your shows.

A W : Then you have to sign it. Do you know, that scene upstairs was the most beautiful play. You taking photographs and watching, you two—it was beautiful.

A PHOTOGRAPHER : You should have brought your movie camera.

A W : No. Not a movie. A play.

(good-byes to "A Reporter" & "A Photographer")
Are we all separating, or . . . ?

(enter the restaurant, sit at a round table in front of another large window again looking out on the Park and the street)

A H : *We'd better be next to each other, I think.*

A W : Yes.

(seating)


J S : Mr. Hitchcock?

A H : *Nothing to drink for me, thank you.*

J S : AW?

A W : No thanks.

white wine

bloody marys

virtues of the Bigshot


(Restaurant noise, silence for 2 minutes while everyone studies the menu. JS, host, pushes first courses, no one is interested, they go straight to the main.)

A H : *At the Savoy Hotel in London, the whole menu was always in French. Even the plat du jour (?), you see, half a dozen of them. And in red printing underneath would be the English equivalent. What it was. So that the customer who didn't speak French would understand it. And one day I was having lunch there many many years ago and I had L-apostrophe-I-r-i-s-h Stew. "L'Irish Stew." And in red underneath it, "Irish Stew" . . . Have you been to Tokyo at all?*

A W : A long time ago. Twenty years ago. Just a short trip.

A H : *It amazed me at one restaurant where they actually did serve Irish Stews. The Japanese are enterprising. In those days, in the Imperial Hotel, they even had a Pruniers.*

(orders are given in low voices)

A W : You know, I just met the Duchess of Windsor at a dinner the other night. I didn't know what to say to her, so I didn't say anything, and therefore she thought I was an intellectual. Now she wants to see me again and I'm getting really cold feet because I just don't know what to talk to her about. Do you know her at all?

A H : *No. I don't*

A W : I thought maybe you might. I'm looking for a clue. Someone told me to talk about China, so I guess I'll do that. . . .

A H : *Did you ever see the film they made of the Duke and Duchess of Windsor? Richard Chamberlain, Faye Dunaway.*

AW: Yes, it was on tv here. I want to ask you something that I'm sure you've thought about: Can you ever really duplicate characters from history? Can it ever really be the same? An exact replica?

AH: *Not really. I've often said in the case of a small part, "Make him look like McNamara," or some character out of a magazine, but only for a bit part, not for a written character.*

AW: But then do you think that they should always make the person better than what they were—more handsome, more—everything?

AH: *Well, in the very old days when film stars played politicians they were always better-looking. I know Clark Gable once played Parnell. Not with very great success.*

AW: That was just on tv. I'd never even heard of it.

AH: *Oh yes, it was made around 1938 or '39. But I always remember I was working years ago at Gaumont British where they were importing (?) George Arliss. And George Arliss had played Rothschild, Disraeli, Alexander Hamilton, etc., and they were walking up and down wondering what role to get for him. Well actually, they struck up on Stanley and Livingstone, but they couldn't make up their minds which one Arliss should play—Stanley or Livingstone—so I said, "Let him play both parts, so that when the great meeting takes place, he shakes hands with himself and says, "Mr. Arliss, I presume."*

JS: He finally did the Duke of Wellington.

AH: The Iron Duke, *yes.*

JS: George Arliss had the wonderful thing of making everyone in history look exactly the same.

AH: *Of course. Naturally. He had a butler, you know. An English butler. And never mind what the director said or thought, this butler would walk on with a cup of tea, punctually at 4:20, hand it to him and say, "Mr. Arliss. It's time to go home." And that was the end of day's work.*


JS: I talked to two ladies this morning—both of whom were calling about something else, but I mentioned that I was having lunch with you and both of them said they would have given their eye teeth to have made pictures with you. One was Bette Davis and one was Myrna Loy.

AW: You can still use them!

Bette

Myrna

Arthur Hornblow

big actors

small parts

A H : *Well in London you can get a leading man to play a bit in a picture, which in this country is impossible, because the agent gets in the way. . . .*

A W : I like Tippi Hedren.

Grace Kelly

Janet Leigh

Vera Miles

Eva Marie Saint

these cool blondes

A W : I like Tippi Hedren.

A H : *Well the whole theory is that outwardly they're very cool, but the moment they go into action, all hell breaks loose, you see. I think the English women are the worst. You know, they all look like schoolteachers, but in a taxi cab they'll tear you to pieces . . . I was never keen though, on what I call the Marilyn Monroe type of blonde, where I always say their sex hangs around their neck like jewelry.*

Kim Novak

Vertigo

A H : *She had very definite opinions about herself: a) her hair always had to be lavender, b) she would never wear suits under any circumstance. She came to my house, and I'd never met her before, and she brought out these conditions. I said, "Look, Miss Novak, you do your hair whatever color you like, and you wear whatever you like, so long as it conforms to the story requirements." And the story required her to be a brunette and to wear a grey suit. I used to say, "Listen. You do whatever you like: there's always the cutting-room floor." That stumps them. That's the end of that.*

V F : I was wondering where you shot *Shadow of a Doubt*. It's such a great atmosphere with the secure, small town.

A H : *Up until that time, so many of the films were made on the back lot. You know? This was the first time one broke away from all that.*

V F : Was the studio behind you when you did that?

A H : *Well it was such an inexpensive film. I started it in Newark first, and then went to Santa Rosa. It was a pleasure to work with Thornton Wilder on it. He was a very modest man, you know.*

J S : Did you know that Patricia Collinge just died?

A H : *She died???*

JS: Just last week.

AH: *Oh I'm so sorry to hear that. . . .*

JS: She was awfully good in the movie.

AH: *Yes. She used to write for the* New Yorker. *. . .*

Joseph Cotten

AH: *The whole point was, this man is a murderer of rich widows. Well he'd have to be an attractive man. People often make that mistake; they think that because a man is a murderer he's got to look sinister and so forth. Well, unless he were attractive, he'd never get near the victim! You know, there was a man in England known as George Haigh (?). And he murdered his victims by shooting them, and then he had a small garage about thirty miles outside of London. And he bought a carboy. Do you know what a "carboy" is? It's a thing shaped with a narrow neck and a great big base which contains sulfuric acid. And he used to buy these carboys and then put the body in a tub and then pour the sulfuric acid and rotted them away. I think he killed about three or four. And one day he went out with a woman . . . He was staying at a hotel rather like one of those . . . I don't know whether you've been to London. Have you? They're sort of like brownstone houses, about four of them together. They're Georgian in style. And he was living at the Onslow Court Hotel. And that's where he picked up with his last victim, a woman called Mrs. Duran Durrell (?). And he took her out. And the under-manageress of the hotel didn't care for this man very much, and she noticed that he came back that night without her. So she informed the police, the police locked him up, and found he had a record. And eventually they traced the garage and found the bills for sulfuric acid, and some bridgework of Mrs. Duran Durrell that was plastic. And had survived the sulfuric acid attack. You see. Well eventually he was arrested and when arrested he said that he drank his victims' blood. Which was a complete lie, because all he was trying to do was to make himself look insane. Because he said to one of the detectives, "What's it like at Broadmore?" Broadmore was a criminal lunatic asylum.*

VF: It's always the small details like the slips that you put in your movies that are so great.

AH: *In* Rear Window *I put a clue that came out of two cases. One was known as the Patrick Mahon Case and the other was Dr. Crippen (?). Dr. Crippen murdered his wife and was the first murderer known to have been captured by radio. Ship radio. His description went out and he was caught in the St. Lawrence River. Well the point was that he murdered his wife, and the neighbors—especially a Mrs. Martinelli—noticed that Ethel Anibe (?), his secretary, was wearing the wife's jew-*

*elry. And the man never thought about what the neighbors might notice. And that was his undoing. And I put that into the film.*

A W : Since you know all these cases, did you ever figure out why people really murder? It's always bothered me. Why?

A H : *Well I'll tell you. Years ago, it was economic, really. Especially in England. First of all, divorce was very hard to get, and it cost a lot of money.*

A W : But no, what kind of person really murders? I mean, why . . . uh . . . .

A H : *In desperation. They do it in desperation.*

A W : Really? Uh . . . .

A H : *Absolute desperation. They have nowhere to go, there were no motels in those days, and they'd have to go behind the bushes in the park. And in desperation they would murder.*

A W : But what about a mass murderer.

A H : *Well, they're psychotics, you see. They're absolutely psychotic. They're very often impotent. As I showed in* Frenzy. *The man was completely impotent until he murdered. And that's how he got his kicks.*

Covent Gardens

*Frenzy*

colors, marketplace

A H : *But today of course, with the Age of the Revolver, as one might call it, I think there is more use of guns in the home than there is in the streets. You know? And men lose their heads.*

A W : Well I was shot by a gun, and it just seems like a movie. I can't see it as being anything real. The whole thing is still like a movie to me. It happened to me, but it's like watching tv. If you're watching tv, it's the same thing as having it done to yourself.

A H : *Yes. Yes.*

A W : So I always think that people who do it must feel the same way.

A H : *Well a lot of it's done on the spur of the moment. You know. . . .*

A W : Well, if you do it once, then you can do it again, and if you keep doing it, I guess it's just something to do. . . .

A H : *Well it depends whether you've disposed of the first body. That is a slight problem. After you've committed your first murder.*

A W : Yes, so if you do that well, then you're on your way. See, I always thought that butchers could do it very easily. Doctors?

A H : *Pardon?*

A W : I always thought butchers could be the best murderers.

AH: *Butchers. Well they have one. Wasn't there one in Dortmund (?) in Germany years ago? . . . Well you know, with Jack the Ripper, I read a book that gave an extraordinary theory that because of the nature of the use of the knife on the prostitute victims in Whitechapel in what-was-it? 1888? (?) And it was observed at the time that this man, whoever he was, was extremely skillful with the knife. And the theory was . . . You see, at that time, there were a lot of immigrants from Central Europe, Jewish immigrants into London. From Poland, and . . . And they were always treated as second-class citizens. And the theory was that this was committed by the man . . . It isn't the rabbi who does the koshering work, whatever they do, I forget the name, but there's a man under him . . . I forget the name . . . who does the actual butchering work, and it was this man who was really Jack the Ripper, but the group of immigrants was so fearful that this man would be found out, that they killed him themselves, so that he disappeared without a trace. And that's why Jack the Ripper was never discovered. That was a theory.*

JS: Isn't the current theory that he was nobility?

AH: *The son of Edward VII? Oh you get all kinds of wild theories.*

VF: Do you think English people are more prone to be interested in that sort of thing?

AH: *No, I think the English have always been interested in crime as literature. Starting going back to Conan Doyle, going right up to Agatha Christie.*

AW: The Princess Mdvanni lives here at this hotel. She was married to Conan Doyle Jr.

AH: *Oh really?*

AW: Do you know her? Princess Nina Mdvanni?

AH: *I don't know her, no. But the English have always had a great interest in crime. In this country it's second-class literature, and you can name very few well-known crime-writers . . . Dashiell Hammett, Raymond Chandler . . . and even he was educated in London . . . Ross Macdonald . . . But there aren't too many that come to mind.*

AW: It always amazes me how in England, if there's a crime, they broadcast it on television, on radios, the newspaper vendors yell it, the descriptions are sent out all over—"Would you please report any information to the police"—everybody's looking for the criminal, and they find him right away, because people are interested.

AH: *Yes. You'd often read, I remember years ago, if a famous cause célèbre came up, say at the Old Bailey, you'd read in the paper that such-and-such a famous writer was present, that famous actors were present—they all took an interest, you*

*see, and that doesn't happen here. We don't know where the courts are, we know*
*they're down on Foley Square somewhere, but . . . But everybody knows where the*
*Old Bailey is.*

V F :   And Scotland Yard.

A H :   *Yes, another famous thing. To show the increase in crime, the Old Bailey used*
*to have four courts and they've added on and they now have eighteen courts. And*
*they'd had four courts up until last year, since 1907 when the building went up.*
End of Tape #2 Side A

Tape #2 Side B
*Man Who Knew Too Much*

A H :   *Well you say to yourself, "This film is laid in Switzerland. What have they*
*got in Switzerland? They've got Alps, chocolate factories, they've got lakes, and*
*cuckoo clocks," and I'm always a believer in working into a film some of the ele-*
*ments—For instance, in the picture* North by Northwest, *Cary Grant gets trapped*
*in an auction room. How does he get out? By the only way he can, by bidding. So*
*then bidding must be part of your story, because you're in an auction room. It's no*
*good going into an auction room and doing something that doesn't relate. It must*
*relate. Essentially. It's like the climax of that film* The Man Who Knew Too
Much *when the cymbals are going to crash during a concert at the Royal Albert*
*Hall, and that's the signal for the assassin to fire his gun. And the audience waits*
*and waits, and that's using the orchestra, you see.*
*North by Northwest*
cropduster chasing Cary across the corn
*helicopter/copied*
*From Russia With Love*
STATUE OF LIBERTY RADIO CITY
Mount Rushmore

A H :   *Yes, but I was frustrated on Mount Rushmore by the Department of the Inte-*
*rior. It said we mustn't have any of the characters on any of the faces of the Presi-*
*dents. Why not? Because, they said, "It's the Shrine of Democracy." You see, I*
*wanted Cary Grant to slide down Lincoln's nose and hide in the nostril while the*
*other man is looking for him, and while he's in the nostril, Cary Grant gets a*
*sneezing fit. And gives himself away. Wasn't allowed to do it.*
(appreciative one-liners by JS)
*Foreign Correspondent*
*Downhill*

umbrellas

Edmund Gwenn

beautiful little villain

*Saboteur*, kind of an offshoot

*Strangers on a Train*

fantastic moments of madness

kids having the time of their life

merry-go-round

fighting to the death

AH:   *There was a thing in* Strangers on a Train *that I would never do again. I had an old man—an old actor—crawl underneath the real merry-go-round to switch it off. If his head had gone up an inch or two, I would have been in jail. It would have been manslaughter. And I sweat when I even think of it . . . at the time.*

"ALFRED HITCHCOCK INDICTED FOR MURDER"

AW:   Did you ever use your wife in a movie?

AH:   *Never.*

AW:   Not even a walk-on?

AH:   *She wouldn't do it. She's been in movies longer than I have. She was a writer, she was an editor, at nineteen.*

daughter Patricia

AH:   *Yes, she started on Broadway. John Van Druten started her. Came and wanted to borrow her for a play he did on Broadway.*

VF:   And then you used her in *Strangers on a Train*.

AH:   *Yes.*

AW:   I love the way Hollywood is like a store now. With the kids of all the big stars all over. And their kids. Desi Jr., Lucy Arnaz, Liza Minelli and Lorna Luft, Carrie Fisher, Angelica Huston, Tessa Dahl, Tish Sterling, Jeff and Beau Bridges, Geraldine Chaplin, Jeanie Berlin, David Carradine, Tatum . . . Do you like that? The way Hollywood is like a store? Or. . . .

AH:   *Mmmmm.*

AW:   It's a great idea, actually seeing the sons and daughters of the famous stars and the famous marriages.

AH:   *Mmmm.*

AW:   How was it working with Tallulah Bankhead?

AH:   *Great. I got on very well indeed with Tallulah. She was very tough with the other people, though. She kept sitting in that boat looking across at poor Walter Slezak and saying, "You, you goddamn Nazi . . ." One day the unit manager came to me, and you know, I had about three boats made for that* Lifeboat . . . *And so the assistant director came to me and said, "The women are complaining on the set that Miss Bankhead is climbing in and out of the boat with nothing on underneath." And I said, "Well what about it?" And he said, "They want me to talk to her about it." And I said, "I wouldn't if I were you. She'll give you hell." So he said, "What can I do?" and I said "Well, don't ask me because I'm not a 20th Century Fox man; I'm only on loan here. Why don't you go up and see Zanuck? Ask him." So he came back to me and he said, "Zanuck says I'll have to talk to her." I said, "I wouldn't if I were you, she'll absolutely tear you to bits." She was really very vicious. "I don't think it's your department." He said, "Well then, whose department is it?" I said, "It's either Hairdressing or Make-up."*

VF: Did she get along with, say, William Bendix?

AH: *Yes.*

VF: And John Hodiak at all?

AH: *Well, you know, it was right in the middle of a war, so another German became another particular target. You know, Tallulah didn't drink during the whole of the War.*

JS: That's right, she made a vow, didn't she.

AH: *MM hmmm. But when she drank, she drank what they know as French 75s. Do you know what they are? Champagne with gin.*

Canada Lee

John Steinbeck write the original?

*the complete outline but Jo Swerling actual screenplay*

*I know that when we were shooting the storm scene, and we had four dump-tanks, all pointing down, each one held twenty-seven hundred gallons in each. And the screen had to be washed down so that no splashes would show on it. We took it from an actual seascape. And when the first two tanks came down, boy, fifty-four hundred tanks of water and Tallulah took the lot, and the whole crew gave her a round of applause . . . Later on we wanted another effect, which was very amusing. They said, "We've got all four tanks going in all directions. Ten thousand eight hundred gallons." I said, "Let 'em all go." They pressed the button, and I think it was Walter Slezak who was in the scene, and when the water cleared he wasn't there, we couldn't find him. . . .*

AW: . . . . Where was he?

AH: *He'd gone up 'round underneath the boat. The funny thing is, how people take certain scenes for granted. In the film* Foreign Correspondent, *I had a scene where a plane, minus an engine—one of the old clippers, you know, is diving toward*

*the ocean, and without any cuts it goes right down and hits the water, and the
water pours in. Well, nobody asked, "Where was the camera?" or, "What happened to the poor actors?" Nobody ever questioned it. And the way I did it was:
cockpit, glass front
transparency screen
stunt flyer
mechanically controlled
just at the last minute
back projection
had six screens made 12' seamless rice paper
two dump-tankbutton to press, watched the screen
I pressed the button
water through the screen
tore it to shreds
never saw any paper or anything
But nobody ever questioned it. . . .*

AW:   Really?

AH:   *They took it all for granted.*

AW:   Do you think that movies that cost a hundred million dollars will ever
be made again?

AH:   *I hope not.*

AW:   Really? Why?

AH:   *They've had such bad luck with films like* Lost Horizon . . . *It's a strange
thing. The most expensive picture I ever made was* North by Northwest, *which
was four million three (4.3). Well, I don't believe in the theory of trying to top
yourself. I said, "Now I will make a little picture. For eight hundred thousand
dollars."*

AW:   Which was that?

AH:   Psycho. *And it grossed more than* North by Northwest. *It grossed sixteen
million dollars. But I deliberately did that.*

AW:   What made *North by Northwest* cost so much? What parts were the most
expensive?

AH:   *The reproducing of Mount Rushmore in the studio. You see, it was inaccessible
as far as photography is going.*

AW:   It looked so real.

AH:   *It was all done in the studio.*

coffee? coffee? coffee?

AH: *I'm having the ginger ale . . . For me, yes. No, that was all reproduced. The whole of it.*

AW: How great.

VF: *Rear Window had a great set.*

AH: *Well you know, that was made up of photographs taken—I had a man off* Life Magazine *go around all the windows in the back around the city and take a whole variety, and the set was put together from those photos.*

(a Stranger-With-a-French-Accent comes over to the table)

SWFA: *Excuse me. When I am a little boy I like very much your movies. It is possible to give me autograph?*

AH: *Yes. Certainly.*

SWFA: Fank you very much. Please, would you excuse me, on the picture of my child.

(SWFA hands AH a snapshot. AH draws his famous profile)

SWFA: Fanks. Many fanks.

VF: Would I have one of those, too?

SWFA: Ah! Many fanks and excuse me. For me, you are ar-tiz-ist.
(leaves)

AW: Could you sign "AH" on this Polaroid?

AH: *The outline?*

AW: No, just—Yes, that's great. Which one would you like to have? . . . Would you like a picture to get autographed, JS?

JS: I'd love one.

(AW deals Polaroids of AH around the table so everyone can get them autographed)

AH: *I'm afraid these backs have an emulsion on them. Of some kind. It looks like I've done it with dotted lines. . . .*

AW: It looks interesting. Mysterious. When did you first think of your outline?

AH: *1927/28. I remember the first time we used the outline was a Christmas card. It was made up on a square piece of wood, and the wood cut into jigsaw pieces. And put into little linen bags with a label, and sent out. They didn't know what the hell they were putting together until the outline came out.*

tv profile

fitting in

AW: Did you have to work on those tv programs, or were they just done using your name.

AH: *Out of 273 half-hour shows and 90 one-hour, I actually directed 19 myself. In fact I made the picture* Psycho *with a tv crew because they're adjusted to this fast work. Nine minutes a day, you see.*

AW: Have you used a tv crew since then all the time, or . . . ?

AH: *No no. Just on that one picture. But when I came to certain cinematic scenes like the shower, I stopped thinking in tv terms and took seven days to shoot forty-five seconds. When I came to something very cinematic like that, I slowed up. But for ordinary dialogue in other scenes, I just shot with a tv crew.*

AW: Why has the *Trouble With Harry* never been shown on tv?

AH: *Because it was a failure.—Actually, it was shown once. You know it came out ages before the words "black comedy" were introduced. I thought it was very amusing. I think it may have been too sophisticated for ordinary audiences.*

AW: And for a long time *Vertigo* wasn't shown.

private showings

so many not on tv

AH: *In* Young and Innocent—*it was called over here* The Girl Was Young—*and they cut into that over here because it was—It was a young man on the run, and a young girl helping him, and she at one point says, "I've got to go to my aunt's house. I must go." So he agrees to go with her, and the aunt is having a children's party. I wanted to sort of symbolize his whole plight. The aunt becomes blindfolded and she's groping around, and if she catches him, he's for it, because he's going to have to stay for the rest of the party. So the whole epitome of the whole film was expressed in this one scene. They cut it out over here for some reason. Well that's distributors for you. . . .*

Jamaica Inn

Daphne du Maurier

copied the story

DOCTOR SYN

Russell Thorndike

George Arliss

AH: *Yes. DOCTOR SYN was simply the wrecker, the man who used to put a light on the top of the rocks and draw the ships to it and loot them. And at the end of the week he was a parson in the pulpit. So here they take a film with Charles*

*Laughton in the lead, and here he is preaching in the pulpit, and they're searching for the culprit, and it was ridiculous, because any audience would say, "Well it's Laughton, otherwise he wouldn't be the star of the film. In a bit part of the parson." So they started off on completely the wrong foot there . . . Laughton was very peculiar in those days. I was trying to get a close-up of him with Maureen O'Hara, and what he had to do in his close-up was tie her hands, viciously, behind her back. But his close-up said, "I hope I'm not hurting you my dear." Well, we started on this close-up this big, about nine o'clock. And by twelve o'clock we hadn't got it. And he went into a corner and sat and cried. And he looked up at me, and I, you know, patted him on the shoulder and I said, "Listen, Charlie, what are you worried about?" and he looked up at me and he said, "Aren't you and I a couple of babies . . ." And I wanted to say, "Well, include me out, I'm not crying, what have I to do with it?" So I said, "Let's go back and have another go. So after a few more takes we got it, and then he took me aside and he said, "You know how I got it, don't you? It wasn't really different from the other takes, I can tell you." I said, "No, Charles, how." He said, "I thought of myself as a small boy of ten, wetting my knickers." That's Inspiration for you, isn't it?*

AW: Have you ever thought of re-making your movies?

AH: *I re-made one.* The Man Who Knew Too Much.

AW: Really? It's called the same thing? I've only seen Jimmy Stewart and Doris Day. They were both called the same thing?

AH: *Yes. It was first done in London in '35 and it was done here in '55.*

AW: Who starred in 1935?

AH: *It starred Leslie Banks, a London leading man, and Edna Best. Peter Lorre was the heavy. It was Peter Lorre's first English-speaking picture.*

JS: And Nova Pilbeam was in that.

AH: *She was a little girl, yes. I'll never forget, we had a climactic scene at the end, where she was on a roof. It was a reproduction of the famous Sydney Street scene. Do you remember pictures of Churchill hiding in a doorway when they were firing on a group of anarchists? In the east of London? It was about 1910. And I reproduced all this, you see. And the little girl manages to escape and get up on the roof, she'd been kidnapped, you see. And finally one of the anarchists goes after her, and it's the mother who's a good shot and brings down the anarchist after she takes the rifle away from the policeman, who won't shoot because he's afraid he'll hit the little girl. And the father's in the house, and they take the little girl down through the skylight at the top of the stairs. And I said to Nova Pilbeam, I said, "Now look. When they take hold of you, your mother and father, I want you to recoil from*

*them." She said, "Oh I wouldn't do a thing like that, I'd embrace them." I said,*
*"You recoil from them. Or else." She was about eleven years old! They start awful*
*young . . . these actors.*

V F :   Did you get tough and yell at actors?

A H :   *No, I never yell. People say they never see me directing. Well the reason is, I*
*talk it over in the dressing room before-hand. There's no point in going on the stage*
*and behaving like a director. For whose benefit? I've never seen any directors at*
*work. Never. Except once. I was walking around Paramount in 1938 and I saw a*
*director working, and he was directing his people over a public address system, and*
*I thought, "My God, that's an extraordinary way of going on . . ." No, I do all mine*
*off the stage.*

V F :   For each individual actor?

A H :   *Yes. Mm hmm.*

V F :   Did any of them ever get jealous when you spend more time with one
than the other?

A H :   *I don't think so, no. I've had it described to me how directors yell and wave*
*their arms and do "Give it to me!" and all that kind of thing, and I've always*
*referred to that as "all the drama on the set and none on the screen" . . . .*

V F :   How was working with David Selznick?

A H :   *Well he was the Big Producer. You see, in those days all those producers at*
*Metro used to cast the writers, cast the actors, cast the directors, let the film be*
*made, and then they would go into the cutting room and spend weeks. One of the*
*first things that surprised me in* Rebecca *is they said, "There are no re-takes to be*
*done." I said, "Supposing there's a scratch on the film!" "It may not be in the*
*picture." So the editing—It wasn't "editing" in those days, it was "re-making."*
*The producer would re-write and probably, if the film was long, he'd take two*
*sequences and put them in to another section entirely. Producer was king. The most*
*flattering thing Mr. Selznick ever said about me—and it shows you the amount of*
*control—he said I was the "only director" he'd "trust with a film." Another remark*
*he made about a big producer—and this is a strange remark—"He's great with a*
*finished picture." They have to see the picture on the screen before they'd go to work*
*on it. And they'd re-do it. I did three pictures with Selznick. I was on loan out. Seven*
*years. I did* Paradine Case, Spellbound, *and* Rebecca. *For him.*

V F :   *Notorious wasn't Selznick?*

A H :   *It was, right up until the last minute. But because he didn't believe in Ura-*
*nium 235 he sold the whole project to RKO. For fifty percent of the profits. He sold*
*it for $800,000 and it grossed $8,000,000. And he could have had 100%. But he*

*didn't believe in Uranium 235, and he thought the movie was about uranium, and it wasn't! In spy films, in all spy films, we have to have what is called The MacGuffin. The MacGuffin, if you go way back, can be the plans of the fault over-looking the pass if it's in the time of Rudyard Kipling. Or it can be, at the end of 39 Steps, a lot of jumble concerning an airplane secret. It doesn't matter WHAT you put in. It's the MacGuffin, that's why it's nothing. And the word MacGuffin comes from two men in an English railway compartment, and there's a baggage rack overhead, and one of the men looks and says, "Excuse me, sir. What's that strange-looking parcel above your head?" And the man looks and he says, "Oh that's a MacGuffin." "What's a MacGuffin?" "Well, it's an apparatus for trapping lions in the Scottish highlands." So the man says, "Well, there are no lions in the Scottish Highlands." He said, "Then that's no MacGuffin." It doesn't mean anything. And he left the whole thing, he just didn't believe it. I said, "Look David. Make it industrial diamonds. It makes no difference." You know, I went out with Ben Hecht to see Dr. Milliken at Cal Tech. This was 1944, a year before Hiroshima . . . And we walked into his rather impressive office with a bust of Einstein there and so forth, and we said, "Dr. Milliken, how big would an atom bomb be?" And do you know, he spent a whole hour telling us how impossible the whole thing would be. And this was right in the middle of the Manhattan Project. And I understand I was watched by the F.B.I. for three months after that.*

A W :   Really??? Well how did you hear about the atomic bomb? How did you know?

A H :   *Well first of all, I knew Lord Rutherford had split the atom in 1920. I knew the Germans were researching heavy water in Norway, and then a writer in New York, a man called Russell Maloney (?) told me—he did a piece on me once—and he told me where there was a place in New Mexico where men went in and never came out again.*

A W :   Reeally? Wow.

A H :   *And I put this together and thought, "Atom Bomb." It's got to be made from Uranium 235.*

A W :   Wouldn't it have been great to put an atomic bombing in a movie before it ever even came out?

A H :   *Well this was practically it. It was the Germans looking for uranium in South America. That's what it amounted to. And I concealed it in a wine bottle.*

J S :   *Didn't you almost use Garbo in* The Paradine Case?

A H :   *Well, we wanted to, but when Garbo read the book by Robert Hichens (?), she*

*read the description of the principal character, and it was described as a woman*
*who was a barber's assistant in—*

AW: Ooooo.

AH: *Stockholm! Who eventually turned out to be a murderess! She said, "I*
*wouldn't play that part." It was her. He'd based it on her! Because when Selznick*
*proposed to have her in, Gregory Peck was going to be the lead, and at that time the*
*publicity used to be "GARBO SPEAKS" and when they had* Ninotchka *they had*
*"GARBO LAUGHS" and she hadn't made a film for years. So I said to Selznick,*
*"I've got an idea for a slogan for this picture. Why don't we say: GARBO'S BACK*
*. . . and Gregory's scratching it."*

AW: That's great

*press conference yesterday*
*abortion*

AH: *But you know, when you come to talk about abortion and those types of*
*things, they aren't truly cinematic. They're photographs of abortion, which is a very*
*different thing.*

AW: They have abortions on tv now.

AH: *Educational tv?*

AW: No, real tv. They show how it's done, and, you know. . . .

AH: *Why do they do it? So people can buy Home Abortion Sets?*

AW: Well it looked very complicated, what they showed. The girls are
strapped up in a gadget.

AH: *And they tunnel into the vagina? . . . Yes??? . . . Really??? I couldn't be*
*associated with that. I must tell you before we break up, a very funny story. A*
*woman ran out of the Sherry Netherlands stark naked, and jumped into a cab and*
*said, "68 East 100th St." or whatever it is. And the cabbie looks around and sees*
*this nude woman and he says, "You don't have a pocketbook. How're you going to*
*pay me?" She lifted up her right leg and showed him where the money was. He*
*said, "Haven't you got anything smaller?"*

JS: Oh that's funny. Oh that's beautiful.

AW: That's a good scene. Have you gone to see any of the porno movies in
New York ever?

AH: *No, I never have. The only one I've ever seen—this is very strange—I was*
*taken to the press club in Tokyo by an extremely sedate Japanese manager. And he*
*thought he was taking me along there for some kind of an interview. Well, after the*
*steak dinner, we all trooped upstairs into this upper room and there they had a*
*screen that showed these awful films. And—*

AW: Were they Japanese or American?

AH: *American ones. French ones. You know . . . And then they had two live girls sticking a brush between their "legs" and writing on white paper in Japanese characters, and I remember when she was doing this, some man yelled across the room—*

End of Tape #2 Side B

Tape #3 Side A

AW: Well you're making sex sound so fascinating. How come you don't do some?

fireworks/*To Catch a Thief*

last shot/*North by Northwest*

sleeping compartment

*entering a tunnel*

*pick that up*

the train

the screaming

AH: *The screaming woman discovering, and then you cut to the scream of the train. We used to play a lot around with sound in those days. You know, in* Frenzy, *I had to have a short scene at the beginning where a man is there one minute and he's gone the next. And without the audience realizing it, when they look 'round and say, "Oh he's g—" He tells the policeman, "I'd like you to meet my friend." And he turns around, and I cut every bit of sound out of the picture, and portrayed Absence by Silence. Just in the same way, do you remember in the* Frenzy *picture I had the man take the girl up the stairs and you know he's going to murder her, and you pan over to the door, then I turn the camera around, as if to say to the audience, "Don't let's hang around any more, because we know what's going to happen." And I turn the camera right around and brought it down the stairs, and down the hallway right into the street, until we face the facade of the building.*

*suspended camera*

*A hanging turntable*

*And then I got in the studio, and I had a man go by carrying a sack of potatoes or something, and then I went to the real location and had a man do exactly the same thing, and there's a frame cut, and you don't detect it. And that's where we went from the studio to the exterior. And then I pulled back showing the facade where the murder is going to take place, and then I brought the traffic noise up three times volume, so the audience subconsciously would say, "Well, with all this noise, they'll never hear her scream."*

A W :   Maybe you can streak in your next film.

A H :   *Streak. Yes. I'll look pretty streaking.*

J S :   The thing that everybody does is look for your moments, when you appear in the films.

A H :   *You know, I was going to do an appearance once when I'm walking along the street with a girl going (AH uses deaf-mute sign language, as if propositioning the girl) and she slaps my face.*

A W :   Oh do it do it.

A H :   *No, because it was publicized and we got a lot of letters from deaf mutes, "Please don't do this. It will offend many deaf mutes." It would have been a nice gag, though, wouldn't it.*

*Frenzy* by the river

V F :   I loved the scene in *Frenzy* where he's got the body in the sack of potatoes—

A H :   *Oh, and trying to get it out, yes. Do you know, he had to get the body out from among the potatoes, and to avoid the censorship problem, I had a bikini made of potatoes, and I wrapped it 'round the girl, so she had a full bikini of potatoes. The audience was all waiting to see the vagina and the pubic hair, and it never came. . . .*

V F :   With all those camera shots, do you get together with a lot of people—

A H :   *No no, I think them out beforehand.*

V F :   You make them up yourself, though?

A H :   *Oh sure. Sure . . . You see, I had the good fortune to be a technician and art director, long before I became a director.*

A W :   The wonderful thing about watching old movies is that it's not sick. They're not nostalgia, because nostalgia means a re-make or an homage. Old movies are the real thing.

A H :   *Oh yes.*

V F :   I saw another version—a re-make—of *Shadow of a Doubt*.

A W :   Really??? There is such a thing???

A H :   *Universal made it.*

V F :   It was exactly the same story line, but it was very dull. And then I started to wonder if maybe *Shadow of a Doubt* would be dull if I saw it again, but then I did see it right after that again and it was exciting again. No comparison.

A H : *You see, in a re-make, they strip it of all its detail.*

*Strangers on a Train*

on a golf course

Carol Lynley played Robert Walker

A H : *It takes detail to build character and mood and do all those things. It's not just to stick people up there and say a lot of words.*

J S : Well I guess I'd better get you upstairs again to your next interview. You're having a non-stop session.

A H : *Absolutely.*


(getting up, leaving the restaurant)

(AW, VF walk JS & AH to the elevator)

A W : What are they doing on Monday at Lincoln Center? Are they going to show a lot of clips?

A H : *No, I don't think so.*

(chime)

(elevator opens)

(jumbled thank yous and good-byes and see-you-soons)

(elevator doors close)

V F : I have to go to the tailor's.

A W : You do?

(one of the waiters walks, smiling, over to AW & VF)

WAITER : Hi.

A W : H-i.

WAITER : I was with you at dinner the other night. It was really fun.

(AW turns red)


A W : Oh-we're-having-the-screening-on-Monday-at-8:30.

WAITER : 8:30 PM?

A W : Yes-so-tell-your-friend—

WAITER : I'd love to go. I do this three or four days a week. Are you going to call Michael?

A W : Yes-call-him-up.

WAITER : Alright. Good to see you.

AW:  Yes-see-you-bye.

   (in the main lobby)

AW:  Was he somebody's—little brother? I can't remember.

VF:  I wasn't at that dinner.

AW:  Oh. Listen. While we're here I want to call Princess Mdvanni on the house phone. She might not be in, though. She has the chauffeur drive to Nathan's every afternoon.

*End of segment.*

*End of interview.*

(The story ending at the conclusion of Tape #2 Side B is that the young Japanese lady was requested from across the room to "WRITE ALFRED HITCHCOCK!," but she was unable to oblige.)

# INDEX

CONVERSATIONS WITH FILMMAKERS SERIES

PETER BRUNETTE, GENERAL EDITOR

*The collected interviews with notable modern directors, including*

Robert Altman • Theo Angelopolous • Bernardo Bertolucci • Jane Campion • George Cukor • Brian De Palma • Clint Eastwood • John Ford • Jean-Luc Godard • Peter Greenaway • John Huston • Jim Jarmusch • Elia Kazan • Stanley Kubrick • Spike Lee • Mike Leigh • George Lucas • Michael Powell • Martin Ritt • Carlos Saura • John Sayles • Martin Scorsese • Steven Soderbergh • Steven Spielberg • Oliver Stone • Quentin Tarantino • Lars von Trier • Orson Welles • Billy Wilder • Zhang Yimou